C90 11993

Transitional Justice Theories

GW00584937

Bu

Transitional Justice Theories i. . . . . pp... .. the politically sensitive subject of post-conflict or post-authoritarian justice from a theoretical perspective. It combines contributions from distinguished scholars and practitioners as well as from emerging academics from different disciplines, and provides an overview of conceptual approaches to the field. The volume seeks to refine our understanding of transitional justice by exploring often unarticulated assumptions that guide discourse and practice. To this end, it offers a wide selection of approaches from various theoretical traditions ranging from normative theory to critical theory. In their individual chapters, the authors explore the concept of transitional justice itself and its foundations, such as reconciliation, memory and truth, as well as intersections, such as reparations, peace building and norm compliance.

This book will be of particular interest for scholars and students of law, peace and conflict studies, and human rights studies. Even though highly theoretical, the chapters provide an easy read for a wide audience including readers not familiar with theoretical investigations.

Susanne Buckley-Zistel is Professor for Peace and Conflict Studies and Executive Director of the Center for Conflict Studies, Philipps University Marburg.

Teresa Koloma Beck heads a research project on urban violence at the *Centre Marc Bloch*, Berlin.

Christian Braun is a political scientist and currently research fellow at the Center for Conflict Studies, Philipps University Marburg.

Friederike Mieth is a PhD candidate in Social and Cultural Anthropology at the Philipps University Marburg.

Transitional Justice

Series Editor: Kieran McEvoy

Queen's University Belfast

The study of justice in transition has emerged as one of the most diverse and intellectually exciting developments in the social sciences. From its origins in human rights activism and comparative political science, the field is increasingly characterised by its geographic and disciplinary breadth. This series aims to publish the most innovative scholarship from a range of disciplines working on transitional justice-related topics, including law, sociology, criminology, psychology, anthropology, political science, development studies and international relations.

Titles in this series:

Forthcoming titles in the series:

Corporate Accountability in the Context of Transitional Justice
Sabine Michalowski

The Concept of the Civilian
Claire Garbett

Transitional Justice and the Arab Spring
Edited by Kirsten Fisher and Robert Stewart

Truth, Denial and Transition: The Contested Past in Northern Ireland
Cheryl Lawther

The Judiciary and the Politics of Transition: Saviours, Scoundrels, Scapegoats
Marny Requa

The Art of Post-Dictatorship: Ethics and Aesthetics
Vikki Bell

International Trials and Reconciliation
Janine Clark

Transitional Justice Theories

Edited by
Susanne Buckley-Zistel,
Teresa Koloma Beck, Christian Braun
and Friederike Mieth

Routledge
Taylor & Francis Group

LONDON AND NEW YORK

First published 2014
by Routledge
2 Park Square, Milton Park, Abingdon, Oxfordshire OX14 4RN

Simultaneously published in the USA and Canada
by Routledge
711 Third Avenue, New York, NY 10017

First issued in paperback 2015

Routledge is an imprint of the Taylor & Francis Group, an informa business

British Library Cataloguing in Publication
A catalogue record for this book is available from the British Library

Library of Congress Cataloging-in-Publication Data
A catalog record has been requested for this book

ISBN 13: 978-1-138-92445-1 (pbk)
ISBN 13: 978-0-415-82210-7 (hbk)

Typeset in Garamond
by Taylor & Francis Books

Contents

Contributors

Nevin T. Aiken is an Assistant Professor in the Department of Political Science and Global & Area Studies Program at the University of Wyoming. His first book, *Identity, Reconciliation and Transitional Justice: Overcoming Intractability in Divided Societies*, was published in 2013 by Routledge.

Kora Andrieu is a human rights officer and transitional justice focal point at the Office of the United Nations High Commissioner for Human Rights in Tunisia. She is the author of numerous works on transitional justice and political philosophy, including *La justice transitionnelle. De l'Afrique du Sud au Rwanda* (Gallimard, 2012).

Christian Braun is a political scientist and currently research fellow at the Center for Conflict Studies, Philipps University Marburg. His main focus of research lies on the former Yugoslavia, memory studies and transitional justice processes.

Susanne Buckley-Zistel is Professor for Peace and Conflict Studies and Executive Director of the Center for Conflict Studies, Philipps University Marburg. She has published on issues related to peacebuilding, transitional justice, gender and post-structural theory, including a co-edited volume *Gender in Transitional Justice* (Palgrave, 2012) and a forthcoming co-edited volume *Memorials in Times of Transition* (Intersentia 2013).

Hannah Franzki studied politics and law in Marburg, Montevideo and Warwick, and is currently reading for a PhD in law at Birkbeck College, University of London. Her research project is concerned with economic dimensions of state crime and the writing of history in (international) criminal trials.

Thomas Obel Hansen holds a PhD from Aarhus University Law School, Denmark. He currently works as an independent consultant and assistant professor of international law with the United States International University in Nairobi. He has published widely on transitional justice, international criminal law and various human rights issues.

Teresa Koloma Beck heads a research project on urban violence at the *Centre Marc Bloch*, Berlin. Her research focuses on social dynamics of conflict and violence in a globalised world. She has conducted extensive field research in Angola and Mozambique, and published *The Normality of Civil War* (Campus, 2012).

Wendy Lambourne is Deputy Director, Centre for Peace and Conflict Studies, University of Sydney. Recent publications include chapters about transitional Justice in Cambodia, Timor Leste and Rwanda in *Critical Perspectives in Transitional Justice* (Intersentia, 2012), *The Development of Institutions of Human Rights* (Palgrave Macmillan, 2010) and *Julius Stone: A Study in Influence* (Federation Press, 2010).

Lisa J. Laplante is an Associate Professor at New England Law/Boston, where she is also Director of the Center for International Law and Policy. In 2007, she was invited to be a member of the School of Social Science at the Institute for Advanced Study at Princeton (IAS).

Friederike Mieth is a PhD candidate in Social and Cultural Anthropology, Philipps University Marburg, and writes her dissertation about dealing with the past in everyday Life in Sierra Leone. Previously, she worked as a research fellow for the Center for Conflict Studies in Marburg and for the United Nations High Commissioner for Refugees.

Maria Carolina Olarte is reading for a PhD at Birkbeck College, University of London. Her fields of interest include modern constitutionalism, the biopolitics of constitutional design and transitional justice expertise, and the current influence of the field of law and economics.

Jelena Subotić is Associate Professor of Political Science at Georgia State University. She is the author of *Hijacked Justice: Dealing with the Past in the Balkans* (Cornell University Press, 2009), as well as numerous articles about human rights, transitional justice, identity politics and the Western Balkans.

Magdalena Zolkos is a Senior Research Fellow at the School of Humanities and Communication Arts at the University of Western Sydney. She is the author of *Reconciling Community and Subjective Life: Trauma Narrative as Political Theorizing* (Continuum, 2010), and editor of *On Jean Améry: Philosophy of Catastrophe* (Lexington, 2011).

Acknowledgements

The origins of this volume are rooted in a research project on dealing with the past in Sierra Leone, Mozambique, Croatia and Bosnia which we carried out at the Center for Conflict Studies, Philipps University Marburg (2008–12). We are greatly indebted to the German Research Foundation (DFG) for funding the project, which allowed us not only to conduct substantive field research but also to participate in many conferences. In our discussions we became aware of the lack of theoretical engagement with the notion of transitional justice, prompting us to put together this volume.

This would not have been possible without the assistance of a number of people. First, we would like to thank Anne Lang for her copy-editing of bibliographies and references. Next, we would like to thank Colm Campbell and Eilish Rooney for their input and discussant notes at our panel 'Theories of/for Transitional Justice' at the European Consortium for Political Research (ECPR) General Conference in Reykjavik, Iceland (24–27 August 2011). Moreover, we are grateful to the series editor and the reviewers for providing valuable feedback on our book proposal. This appreciation extends to the editorial team at the publishing house that was always available for queries, facilitating a smooth completion process of the manuscript. Lastly, we would like to extend our gratitude to the contributors of this volume who participated in the project even though many were unknown to us at the beginning of the process. Their creative and original ideas stand at the heart of this publication and render it an important contribution to a, so far, still underexposed subject.

List of abbreviations

CAVR	*Commissão de Acolhimento, Verdade e Reconciliação de Timor Leste* (Timorese Commission for Reception, Truth, and Reconciliation)
CEE	Central and Eastern Europe
CRP	Community Reconciliation Process (East Timor)
DC-Cam	Documentation Center for Cambodia
ECCC	Extraordinary Chambers in the Courts of Cambodia
EU	European Union
ICC	International Criminal Court
ICTR	International Criminal Tribunal for Rwanda
ICTY	International Criminal Tribunal for the former Yugoslavia
NATO	North Atlantic Treaty Organization
NGO	Non-governmental organisation
NURC	National Unity and Reconciliation Commission (Rwanda)
PIR	*Plan Integral de Reparaciones* (Peru)
PTRC	Peruvian Truth and Reconciliation Commission
PTSD	Post-traumatic stress disorder
RPF	Rwandan Patriotic Front
TRC	Truth and Reconciliation Commission
UN	United Nations
UNTAET	United Nations Transitional Administration in East Timor

Transitional justice theories: An introduction

Susanne Buckley-Zistel, Teresa Koloma Beck,
Christian Braun and Friederike Mieth

Transitional justice has gained global significance as an umbrella term for approaches to deal with the past in the aftermath of violent conflict or dictatorial regimes. The term was first coined in the early 1990s and has since come to describe an ever expanding range of mechanisms and institutions, including tribunals, truth commissions, memorial projects, reparations and the like to redress past wrongs, vindicate the dignity of victims and provide justice in times of transition.

Despite the range of activities conducted globally and the vibrant academic debate on the topic, there are but a few attempts to conceptualise transitional justice theoretically. In fact, the field can be characterised by a relative lack of theoretical frameworks. Rather, transitional justice discourse and practice are largely based on implicit assumptions about transition and/ or justice that are often commonsensical in Western thinking. These assumptions are strongly influenced and shaped by particular historical experiences, such as the Nuremberg and Tokyo trials after the Second World War, the transitions of South American countries from dictatorship to democracy, international criminal tribunals, such as the tribunals for the former Yugoslavia and Rwanda, or the Truth and Reconciliation Commission (TRC) in South Africa. Thus, the challenge is both to reveal what these underlying assumptions entail and how they influence – or limit – the practice of transitional justice.

Based on a broad understanding of theorising, our volume responds to this challenge by bringing together a range of different theoretical approaches which allow exploring and understanding the dynamics at work in processes commonly associated with the notion of transitional justice. The collection therefore features both normative and critical perspectives from disciplines such as political science, sociology, philosophy or psychology. In doing so, the volume not only reflects the field's interdisciplinarity and the wide range of issues in need to be theoretically captured, but also reveals commonalities as well as tensions between the different perspectives.

The initiative emerged in the context of a research project about dealing with the past in post-civil war societies at the Center for Conflict Studies,

Philipps University Marburg, where our discussions frequently revolved around the question what theories can or should be applied in order to structure our analysis and research of transitional justice.[1] In an open call for papers and a conference panel[2] we invited other scholars to join this debate. We remain impressed about the responses, reflecting the need for clarification as well as the interest and commitment of the academic community in this field. In our view, this highlights once more the importance of promoting theoretical enquiries into topics that derive from practical engagement and of the necessity to reflect – on a conceptual level – about the strengths and weaknesses of these activities.

Transitional justice: an undertheorised field?

Considering the increasing importance of transitional justice one is inclined to ask why, within transitional justice discourse, there have been so few attempts both to theorise the concept transitional justice itself as well as the range of concepts at the core of the debate, such as justice, truth or reconciliation. There are a number of reasons for the relative lack of theoretical enquiries within the field; in the following we will briefly elaborate on four of these reasons, though this list is not exhaustive (see also Clark and Palmer 2012).

First, the field of transitional justice is extremely heterogeneous, which may have prevented a common theoretical language from either emerging or from crossing disciplinary boundaries. By now, scholars and practitioners alike are quick to establish that transitional justice has become a field or discipline of its own, yet the boundaries of the concept have remained elusive and highly negotiable. Not only does the transitional justice community span over disciplines as different as law, political science, sociology, psychology, anthropology or development studies which differ significantly in perspectives and methodology, but the mere range of practices or mechanisms to be discussed makes it difficult to establish what exactly transitional justice is and is not.

Second, transitional justice is a relatively young field driven by practice. In fact, for most of the past two decades academics and practitioners alike sought to understand the phenomenon by discussing which shapes it should or could take and by wondering how it could be improved to better fit the different contexts it was already applied to. As Phil Clark and Nicola Palmer state in their introduction to one of the few volumes dedicated to theorising transitional justice, perhaps the field might have grown too quickly (Clark and Palmer 2012: 1; see also Bell 2009). Similarly, Max Pensky writes that the transitional justice field is oriented so strongly towards practice that it almost seems as if theorists are not needed. Theorists are compelled to think that the field ought to 'slow down' so that it can be investigated if the basic concepts used are really coherent and consistent

(Pensky 2012: 91). Moreover, mainstream transitional justice discourse at times seems to ignore relevant theoretical debates taking place in other disciplines such as law, sociology or philosophy that are often based on a long history of theoretical insight.

Third, the concept of transitional justice appears to be continually in motion. Parallel to the discussions of how transitional justice should or could be understood the concept has continuously been expanded to be applicable in contexts that deviated from those where it was originally applied to, for example in contexts devoid of any form of political transition (see Hansen, Chapter 5 in this volume). Also, the use of the concept of transitional justice was soon expanded beyond its original realm of punitive understandings of justice. A recent debate is, for example, centred around the issue of a socio-economic dimension of justice, which has since sparked a discussion on how transitional justice can be best connected to development (see Mani 2002; de Greiff and Duthie 2009). These calls for an expansion of the transitional justice field further blur the boundaries of the concept, which both leads to important developments and at the same times poses new theoretical challenges.

Lastly, in recent years part of the more critical, analytical engagement has concentrated on how mechanisms of transitional justice – often understood as an international or global set of practices and ideas – are perceived, evaluated, or changed in the localities where they operate. Such research on how transitional justice plays out in different contexts – demonstrated by an increase in publications on the topic, for example a special issue of the *International Journal of Transitional Justice* in 2009, as well as two edited volumes (Hinton 2010; Shaw *et al* 2010) – also reflects a greater interest in exposing the underlying assumptions of transitional justice practices. However, the tenor of many of these important contributions is to call for more inclusion of local knowledge and viewpoints in the design of transitional justice mechanisms rather than for building theories.

Arguably thus, the broadness, negotiability and inclusiveness of both the concept of transitional justice itself and what it seeks to describe – if not prescribe – pose significant theoretical challenges. Yet, why do we need theories of transitional justice?

The driving force behind our desire to collect various theoretical approaches was to better understand what transitional justice is and how it functions. On a more general note, theories improve our ability to explain and understand – and potentially predict – processes and developments. They do so by increasing the level of abstraction, synthesising insights and by conceptualising them in form of models or paradigms, allowing for wider generalisations beyond a particular phenomenon. Moreover, they develop a particular vocabulary which allows communicating about the issues at stake in a precise and accurate manner, leading to a more profound exchange between scholars. This, in turn, can be helpful to practitioners who do not know if the paradigms they are already applying 'have in fact been sufficiently theorized and whether they are as all-encompassing as some proponents of international justice would have us believe' (Okello 2010: 276).

However, to assess critically the assumptions underlying transitional justice practice and discourse, it is also helpful to take a look at the field from an outsider's point of view. As Moses Chrispus Okello (2010) writes, the language used within the field is often limited and may not be sufficient to discuss the various processes and concepts at stake. He thus encourages 'to go outside of the particular view of the world that created them in the first place' (Okello 2010: 277).

Significantly, there is not *one* theory of transitional justice. Rather, approaches to conceptualise the phenomenon can be manifold and highly diverse, and can at times be in tension with each other. The different disciplinary perspectives lead to particular *foci* of research: while for much of the legal and political science research, formal rules and institutional actors tend to be at the centre of interest, anthropological, sociological or psychological research on transitional justice often focuses on the merit and challenges of transitional politics on the group and individual level. Yet, these disciplinary divergences are but one element in explaining the heterogeneity of this field. Of at least equal importance are differences relating to the objectives of the research as well as its epistemological or ethical stance due to different experiences, different interests and different sets of values that are brought into the analysis of processes renegotiating justice in times of transition.

The following outlines which forms transitional justice theories may take – irrespective of a more straightforward order of chapters we have chosen for the book. Rather than continuing the debate along the binaries of peace versus justice, punishment versus reconciliation, retributive versus restorative justice and so forth, as occasionally done in transitional justice literature (Clark and Palmer 2012: 3; see also Roht-Arriaza and Mariezcurrena 2006; Sriram and Pillay 2009), we wish to group current approaches along conceptual lines in order to map the field. Nevertheless, our grouping is by no means exclusive and many of the cited pieces may easily fall into several of the categories established.

Transitional justice theories

A first approach which can be identified is to capture theoretically the notion of transitional justice in and of itself, mainly with the intention to spell out basic assumptions, putting them into context and relating them to each other. This ties in with attempts of providing a better, more adequate theory of transitional justice, often following a highly normative agenda that serves as a basis of how transitional justice *ought* to be. In this sense, David Crocker develops a conceptual notion resting on eight goals of transitional justice, including truth, a public platform for victims, accountability and punishment, the rule of law, compensation to victims, institutional reform, long-term development, reconciliation and public deliberation (Crocker 1999). Similarly, Pablo de Greiff suggests that potential inadequacies of individual transitional justice measures can be overcome by employing them in tandem, i.e. by following a holistic approach (de Greiff 2012). Such normative approaches seek less to explain or understand observed processes but to foster a system of values, to describe why a situation is desirable and how it can be achieved.

Other scholars situate their theoretical investigation into concrete philosophies. For instance, much of our current understanding of the notion of transitional justice is framed by liberal thought. Kora Andrieu's work takes a closer look at John Rawls' liberal theory of justice in order to assess its suitability for redressing past violence (see Hansen, Chapter 5 in this volume), highlighting its strengths and yet also its limitations. In contrast, a more realist perspective is taken by David Dyzenhaus who equates transitional justice with the rule of law (Dyzenhaus 2012). Drawing on Thomas Hobbes, he argues that in the absence of any pre-political forms of justice only a sovereign can determine what counts as just, and what does not. To provide another example, drawing on Edward Said, Nikita Dhawan refers to transitional justice as a travelling norm which can never be filled with one particular meaning but changes over space and time, raising important questions about – and at the same time challenging – the sites of production and reproduction of the notion which she firmly locates in the so-called Western world (Dhawan 2012).

Within this field of seeking to establish a theory of transitional justice, some contributions focus stronger on the notion of justice while others are more concerned with the moment of transition. This distinction is, of course, merely heuristic as all contributions in one way or another deal with both elements. Nevertheless, with regard to transition, questions emerge such as what a transition should lead to, what kind of society is envisaged and how the transition should or could be accomplished. This is for instance central to the work of Catherine O'Rourke who assesses how transitional justice processes contribute to a gendered citizenship at the end of transition (O'Rourke 2013). For Nevin Aiken, the aim of a transition, particularly in divided societies, is the transformation of the antagonistic relationships between the parties to the conflict through transitional justice, i.e. reconciliation. In Chapter 2 of this volume, he develops a social learning model of transitional justice to theoretically reconstruct how such transformation can take place (see also Aiken 2013). Furthermore, the majority of scholars still associate transitional justice with a move towards liberal values and democracy (Teitel 2003; Mihr 2012). Particularly for external actors who fund these processes the promotion of democracy and the rule of law remains an important objective in the transitional processes (Oomen 2005).

In contrast, approaches with a stronger emphasis on the notion of justice are guided by the question what shape justice should take. They outline different understandings of the matter, such as punitive, corrective, restorative, reparative or distributive, and discuss how particular transitional justice mechanisms correspond to these aims. How the form of justice envisaged has profound implications on the measures that are implemented is illustrated by Lisa Laplante in Chapter 3 of this volume, who introduces a theory of reparations. More generally, while there is a strong focus on legal theory in the field, some scholars have argued that it is important to widen the frame of how justice may be defined (Bell *et al* 2007) or how linkages between different dimensions of justice – for example retributive, restorative and distributive – can be analysed (Lambourne, Chapter 1 in this volume; see also Lambourne 2009). This discussion is often highly moral and couched in the tradition of promoting just peace and protecting human rights (Mani 2002; May 2012). Moreover, recent efforts to theorise the notion of justice have focused on the inclusion of economic, social and cultural rights in addition to political and civil rights and are thus seeking to expand the concept (Laplante 2008; Mani 2008; Miller 2008).

Broadening our understanding of justice is also central to the work of Jeremy Webber, who suggests that justice might be both retrospective and prospective. With retrospective, Webber refers to the retributive and/or restorative potential of justice, while prospective describes the improvement of the relationship between the parties to the conflict in the time to come (Webber 2012). Introducing a temporal perspective, Webber thus emphasises that to render justice does not simply entail looking back at the past but also provides resources for a better, non-violent future. This future-oriented perspective is of particular importance as there are sometimes limits to justice in the aftermath of mass violence. Some events might be perceived as being so heinous that any form of justice appears inadequate. Yet, as Gary J. Bass (2012) points out, this limitation is often obscured as the implementation of transitional justice measures frequently carries the promise to redress past wrongs (see also McEvoy 2007).

While all approaches so far seek to establish theories of transitional justice there is a significant body of scholarship which does not seek to develop theories itself but draws on existing theories as a backdrop against which to understand transitional justice. This may be exemplified by Fionnuala Ní Aoláin's and Lilish Rooney's use of the concepts 'underenforcement' and 'intersectionality' to analyse gender aspects in transitional justice (Ní Aoláin and Rooney 2007), the application of discourse analysis by Marlies Glasius and Tim Meijers to assess the Charles Taylor trial (Glasius and Meijers 2012), or theoretical approaches to norm diffusion and compliance to assess the implementation of transitional justice in post-violence countries, such as demonstrated by Jelena Subotić in Chapter 6 of this volume. These examples show that there is a significant body of theories in legal studies, social sciences, gender studies and beyond, which offers valuable frameworks for assessing transitional justice discourses and practice.

Critical approaches to theory, lastly, take issue with the implicit assumptions underlying the discourse and practice of transitional justice, i.e. they challenge its epistemological assumptions and normative orientation. Often, they seek to scrutinise prevailing approaches to the field by situating them into cultural and historical contexts, asking what is excluded from the view. For example, Hannah Franzki and Maria Carolina Olarte, in Chapter 10 of this volume, critically assess transitional justice as a political project. Taking up Robert W. Cox's argument that theory is always for someone and for some purpose, they call for disclosing the unarticulated political and spatio-temporal premises of the concept. This form of theoretical inquiry into transitional justice has been growing in recent years. While only a few years ago Vasuki Nesiah exclaimed that 'the field of transitional justice has been insulated from critical legal studies, post-colonial studies, and other efforts to problematise the emancipatory potential of transitional justice institutions and the monopoly that human rights discourse has claimed over struggles' (Nesiah 2006: 801) there is now a growing body of literature to address this gap.

One rapidly growing critical perspective on transitional justice is offered through the lens of gender and/or feminism (Buckley-Zistel and Stanley 2012). For instance, Christine Bell and Catherine O'Rourke question the current status quo of the field when asking 'where are women, where is gender, and where is feminism in transitional justice' (Bell and O'Rourke 2007: 23). Their critical investigation aims at expanding the remit of transitional justice from a mere 'add women and stir' approach to an emancipatory project which promotes gender justice more generally. Feminist theory further helps to illustrate how transitional justice itself is profoundly gendered (Franke 2006) as well as how it is limited regarding the experience of violence of women (Rubio-Marín 2006), to name but a few of its merits.

More recently, a body of literature is emerging which challenges transitional justice as an emerging global norm (Nagy 2008) and re-assesses it from a local perspective (McEvoy and McGregor 2008; Hinton 2010; Shaw et al 2010). Central to the critical debate is to what extent a norm that has been conceived in the so-called Western world is applicable beyond its contexts of origin. This norm often purports a particular view regarding justice, truth and reconciliation without taking into account that these concepts might mean different things to the people affected by violence in different places of the world. Such a norm becomes visible in how interventions are understood. For example, Vanessa Pupavac argues that trauma work, from the perspective of those who plan interventions in post-violence societies, often takes on an apolitical form of therapeutic governance (Pupavac 2001). This, as Magdalena Zolkos critiques in Chapter 8 in this volume, ignores the important social and political role of trauma.

Yet, the body of critical literature on transitional justice is not limited to debates on a general conceptual level, but some scholars place particular mechanisms under critical scrutiny. As reflected by Susanne Buckley-Zistel in Chapter 7 of this volume, key instruments such as truth commissions are turned into objects of inquiry and their processes as well as their product are revealed as being highly contingent (see also Humphrey 2003). This might be done via narrative theory, as in her chapter, or via other ways of theorising performances and the construction of histories in truth commission, tribunals and beyond (see e.g. Osiel 2000; Wilson 2001). Memory work, for example, as a component of transitional justice can draw on a large body of theoretical investigations conducted under the header of memory studies (Buckley-Zistel and Schäfer 2013). In this context, most approaches theorise explicit memory and the function of memorials, commemorations and memorial-museums (Edkins 2003; Bell 2006). The merit of these queries notwithstanding, Teresa Koloma Beck argues in Chapter 9 in this volume that in times of transition embodied forms of memory have to be considered as well. Experiences of violence affect not only what people think and say, but also have an impact on body structures and patterns of habitual behaviour.

What these approaches share, though, is the application of theoretical concepts to challenge what is often taken for granted and what has become a hegemonic discourse. Together with the theoretical approaches illustrated above they paint a multifaceted picture of an ever growing field to which this volume seeks to contribute. In doing so, we deliberately opted for a transdisciplinary approach. The objective is thus not to define or unify transitional justice research, but to create a platform reflecting the efforts to frame the subject conceptually.

Structure of the volume

We have structured our volume into two distinct yet closely intertwined sections. Part I, Theorising transitional justice, entails contributions which aim to re-form theoretically the field from an internal perspective. Guided by the intention to improve what is perceived to be deficient, the authors engage with the key concepts of justice and transition and conceptually explore the potential of particular transitional justice instruments or mechanisms. The chapters seek to situate transitional justice processes in particular normative frameworks or to deepen the understanding of the social processes involved and thus shed light on a number of familiar debates in the field, for example the dispute over retributive versus restorative justice or justice versus peace.

The contributions in Part II, Exploring the limits of transitional justice, by contrast, take a more critical stance, questioning underlying assumptions of the concept or the concept itself. Drawing either on critical social theories or on theories from outside the field, they challenge transitional justice or its instruments, either by evaluating its practice or by exposing underlying conceptual flaws. The authors deal critically with the expansion of transitional justice as a global norm and its impact on different levels of politics and society, examining power relations and hegemonic discourses in the field.

Part I, Theorising transitional justice

In Chapter 1, drawing on a wide array of case studies, Wendy Lambourne develops the concept of transformative justice to extend the scope of transitional justice in order to pay attention to psychosocial processes, socioeconomic conditions and political contexts. She argues that all of these elements have to be dealt with to enable the implementation of the rule of law, to stimulate the transformation of the antagonistic relationships between the parties to the conflict, and to build sustainable peace. In order to achieve this, she argues, it is vital to include local communities in the design and development of transitional justice mechanisms as the latter are only effective if consistent with local customs, culture and needs. To achieve this, a democratisation of transitional justice processes has to take place including local ownership and capacity building to counter claims of cultural imperialism and to contribute to transformative peacebuilding. Only if scholars and practitioners go beyond Western notions of law and society and open themselves to learning from the communities in which they are engaged in can a locally accepted form of transformative justice emerge and contribute to sustainable peace.

The question of learning and social change is at the centre of Chapter 2 by Nevin T. Aiken, who focuses on divided societies and reconsiders transitional justice through the framework of theories of social learning. Aiken develops a model comprised of three different dimensions: instrumental learning, socioemotional learning and distributive learning. Instrumental learning has the potential to foster reconciliation because it brings together the former parties to the conflict. Based on the ideas of psychosocial contact theory and the concept of transformative dialogue it aims at transforming negative perceptions about the respective other in order to promote trust between former enemies. Socioemotional learning directly targets the legacies of the past by establishing accountability for perpetrators and acknowledgment of the victims. In recovering the truth of what happened during the time of violence the possibility of a shared perception of the past is given and may serve to counter collective memories based on group affiliations, which often keep the conflict alive. Lastly, distributive learning suggests that structural and material inequalities have to be addressed in transitional justice processes as well to prevent the reproduction of conflicting identities based on socioeconomic inequalities or dependence. In developing this ideal concept of transitional justice Aiken criticises the current application of the concept and reveals the potential it may hold for reconciliation processes.

In Chapter 3, Lisa J. Laplante draws attention to the relation between the various possible objectives of transitional justice, on the one hand, and the instruments or means employed to achieve them, on the other. From this perspective, she reconstructs both the notion and the practice of reparations with regard to different dimensions of justice. She argues that in the context of transitional justice, reparations differ strongly from legal conceptions where calculating and compensating the damage inflicted by a defendant to an individual plaintiff is paramount. However, despite these differences, and despite their growing empirical importance, reparations have gained little conceptual attention in transitional justice scholarship. Against this background, Laplante proposes a theory of reparations according to which they are conceived as means to serve the end of justice.

Laplante develops this idea by discussing reparations in a so-called continuum of justice which is divided along a line of four different and increasingly comprehensive conceptualisations of justice. At the narrow end of this continuum she places reparative justice, which strives to compensate a damage or harm through a commensurate material compensation, limiting reparations in transitional justice processes to compensation payments. The second step of her continuum is restorative justice, which does not merely aim to compensate for but to repair a damage by engaging all stakeholders. By emphasising the need to protect and/or restore the dignity of both offenders and offended, the concept of restorative justice draws attention to design and implementation of reparation programmes. The third step in her continuum is civic justice, understood as the opportunity to participate in a society. From this perspective, the aim of reparations is to secure and/or facilitate recognition and inclusion of the people harmed. As a consequence, the range of possible means expands to include not only payments or material goods but also services. Laplante's fourth and broadest conceptualisation of reparations is couched in terms of socioeconomic justice, which aims to remedy historic socioeconomic inequalities, turning socioeconomic (re-)distribution into a substantial part of reparation processes. Through this reflection on the theoretical foundations of reparations Laplante seeks to elevate the attention the concept and its application have received so far in order to secure its role as one of the central components of any transitional justice process.

In Chapter 4, Kora Andrieu draws of John Rawl's theory of justice to investigate the normative foundations of transitional justice in political liberalism, and thus continues the critique of the prevailing understandings of justice from a different angle. The empirical background of these considerations is the discursive and practical intimacy between transitional justice processes, on the one hand, and the promotion of liberal democracies, on the other. She argues that – despite this strong empirical connection – transitional justice processes in their aims as well as in their implementation conflict with a number of fundamental aspects of liberal political thought.

Andrieu explores John Rawl's theory of justice to situate transitional justice practice and thinking within the liberal project. In a first move, she confronts transitional justice with core principles of political liberalism, disclosing disconnects and contradictions. Based on this analysis, she then proposes not to reform transitional justice in line with liberal ideas, but to re-think the liberal project of justice itself. She identifies three main contradictions between transitional justice and liberal ideas about politics and society: first, in its retributive version, the strong moral dimension of transitional justices clashes with the procedural, legalistic impulse underlying liberal thought. Second, in its restorative sense, transitional justice's understanding of the individual as a socially embedded and narrated self is in conflict with the vision of a monadic, disembodied self which underlies Rawl's thinking. Lastly, in its broad socioeconomic vision, transitional justice challenges liberal ideas about the distribution of primary goods as well as the liberal primacy of individual over collective rights. Based on this analysis, Andrieu argues for enriching liberal theories of justice to make them responsive to the particularities of periods of transition. She proposes to introduce a Habermasian deliberative perspective for processes of producing justice, and Amartya Sen's capability approach for considering the content of justice itself.

Moving to a different level of analysis, Thomas Obel Hansen in Chapter 5 explores the evolution of transitional justice to critically discuss the implications of this process for the value of transitional justice as an analytical concept. He starts from the observation that transitional justice has lost its status of being an extraordinary measure but has turned into the normal way of dealing with past violence. This has rendered the field more complex, bringing in new actors and contexts and leading to some uncertainty regarding the main goals of the concept. The author introduces the distinction between vertical and horizontal expansions of transitional justice to analyse and explain these processes. Vertical expansion refers to the actors involved in transitional justice processes which used to be mainly governments. More recently, though, in a number of cases local and international non-governmental organisations (NGOs) as well as United Nations (UN) agencies have become actively involved in promoting and implementing transitional justice mechanisms. Today, institutions such as the International Criminal Court (ICC) have powers that reach beyond the control of governments and can even turn against them, for example when acting heads of states are indicted. Further to this vertical expansion in terms of actors, transitional justice has also been broadened to be applicable to new contexts, a dynamic to which Hansen refers to as horizontal expansion. While the concept of transitional justice used to be referred to in transitions to peace and democracy it is increasingly used in environments where no such transitions seem to take place. Broadening the concept in these ways, Hansen warns, runs the risk of undermining its analytical strength and reducing its value for both academia and practice.

Part II, Exploring the limits of transitional justice

The second part of this volume begins with Chapter 6 by Jelena Subotić, who draws attention to the role of domestic politics during the implementation of transitional justice measures. Focusing on countries that have adopted mechanisms due to external pressure she reveals that the global norm of transitional justice is less strong when it comes to its implementation on the ground. Local elites are bound to comply with this norm, yet they may use it for their own benefit to achieve political goals such as discrediting political opponents, obtaining financial assistance from international donors or gaining membership in prestigious international organisations. Thus, Subotić argues, in some cases transitional justice mechanisms are merely implemented to appease the international community. Domestically, however, the fear that their results might destabilise the new regime is so high that mechanisms are often framed differently to render them more acceptable to the population, which decreases the overall impact of transitional justice. She reveals that although being a global norm, transitional justice continues to be dependent on local elites. Subotić, hence, warns against relying too heavily on transitional justice because instead of facilitating peace and reconciliation in a post-conflict society, it may turn into a threat to democracy.

While Subotić focuses on power relations in states of transition, Susanne Buckley-Zistel in Chapter 7 theoretically deconstructs power relations underlying the production of 'truth' in truth commissions. The starting point of her analysis is the observation that truth commissions generate knowledge about the past in the form of testimonies and oral accounts, for example, as stories about the past. Against this backdrop, narrative theory is employed to analyse this process of knowledge production, simultaneously emphasising the importance of narratives in the (re-)production of identity. In transitional contexts, especially in so-called divided societies, such processes are of particular importance since representations of the Self and the Other influence the chances for reconciliation. Buckley-Zistel argues that through the way witnesses testify in front of a commission, truth commissions institutionally condition the form of the narratives presented in their framework. In other words, their settings and the spirit of their hearings as well as the preconceptions guiding the questions of the commissioners inform the content of the accounts elicited in the process. As a consequence, truth commissions tend to produce hegemonic narratives of the past. They can therefore be understood as being part of particular 'regimes of truth' (Foucault), which, in a transitional situation, re-define what can be said and how, establishing the discursive framework for transitional and post-transitional politics.

In Chapter 8, Magdalena Zolkos engages with memory as a component of transitional justice processes, exploring the relationship between the redress of traumatic memory, transitional justice and reconciliation. She challenges the common assumption that the instruments necessary to achieve each of these goals converge, an approach which she characterises as the logic of 'all good things together'. Engaging critically with ideals of therapeutic governance and the associated confessional engagement of State or non-State institutions with the inner lives of individuals and communities, Zolkos argues that traumatic memories clearly mark the limitation of combining the pursuit of historical justice with the one to attend to individual suffering. Discussing attempts to incorporate traumatic memory into normative approaches of transitional justice, she traces the ambiguous relation between therapeutically framed post-atrocity politics and individual trauma recovery. Depending on the particular case, the impact of transitional justice processes such as truth commissions and trials might range from re-traumatisation to repair. Yet, Zolkos argues, such therapeutic modes of transitional politics can be criticised not only for their questionable empirical successes but also for the conceptualisation of trauma implicit in such approaches: therapeutic forms of post-conflict governance propose a medicalisation and de-politicisation of traumatic memories in post-conflict settings. Mobilising critical theories of trauma and traumatisation, Zolkos develops a counter-perspective which emphasises the social and political character of trauma in post-atrocity contexts. From this perspective, trauma no longer appears as a psychological disorder of essentially private character, but as a condition marking the breakdown of meaning and the social narratability of experiences in the aftermath of collective violence.

In Chapter 9, Teresa Koloma Beck continues this discussion of memory, exploring the role of body memory in transitional justice processes. She argues that transitional justice discourse and practice suffer from a limited conception of memory that reduces memory to the sphere of the mind and neglects its attachment to bodily aspects of human existence. Accordingly, classical transitional justice institutions such as trials and commissions revolve around the verbal articulation of individual memories. Yet, the violence of armed conflict or State repression produce not only such explicit, representational memories. Drawing on theories of memory from phenomenology, Koloma Beck shows that, as people learn to live with violence and fear, this situation comes to be inscribed into the structures of the living body and (re-)shapes the patterns of habitual everyday actions: on the one hand, combatants incorporate the readiness for and resilience to violence, and, on the other hand, non-combatants reorganise everyday life to secure the continuation of subsistence activities in the face of an existential threat. The problem in transitional situations is that such embodied memories of violent rule cannot easily be shed off or left behind. The persistence of patterns of habitual behaviour which have been acquired during the violent period then becomes a major challenge to reconciliation. Taking such body memory into account, therefore, shifts attention from performative transitional justice institutions, which are designed to uncover facts in speech, to such transitional justice measures which act upon the dimension of everyday life. Of particular importance in this regard are policies striving for socioeconomic or civic justice in transitional situation.

In Chapter 10, the critique articulated by Hannah Franzki and Maria Carolina Olarte goes beyond the analysis of specific aspects of transitional justice to challenge the concept in and of itself. The authors argue that transitional justice does not simply denote a particular set of phenomena, but rather fosters a particular perspective on these phenomena. Drawing on the history of the concept, they show how transitional justice serves to frame the moment of political transitions as an endeavour of fostering liberal democracy. Criticising the core principles of transitional justice scholarship, Franzki and Olarte argue that instead of being politically neutral it is a highly political project, which aims to strengthen the global norm of liberal democracy, including market economy. This bias towards neo-liberal ideals makes it difficult to comply with principles of social equality. In other words, the kind of justice that is put forward by transitional justice is unlikely to include social justice because the economic system it purports enables socioeconomic inequalities. In order to counter this liberal bias in transitional justice discourse and practice, the authors call for a more critical perspective on possible normative choices in processes of political change. Instead of taking transitional justice for granted one should be open to seek alternative options, which go beyond the perspective of liberal democracy and may be more suitable to the conditions of particular societies in times of transition.

Notes

1 The project 'The Politics of Building Peace: Transitional Justice, Reconciliation Initiatives and Unification Policies in War-torn Societies' (2009–12) was funded by the German Research Foundation and compared peacebuilding mechanisms in Bosnia, Croatia, Mozambique and Sierra Leone.
2 The Panel 'Theories of/for Transitional Justice' was held at the European Consortium for Political Research general conference in Reykjavik, Iceland (24–27 August 2011).

Bibliography

Aiken, N.T. (2013) *Identity, Reconciliation and Transitional Justice: Overcoming Intractability in Divided Societies*, New York, NY: Routledge.

Bass, G.J. (2012) 'Reparations as a Noble Lie', in Williams, M.S., Nagy, R. and Elster, J. (eds) *Transitional Justice*, New York, NY: New York University Press.

Bell, C. (2009) 'Transitional Justice, Interdisciplinarity and the State of the "Field" or "Non-Field"', *International Journal of Transitional Justice*, 3: 5–27.

Bell, C., Campbell, C. and Ní Aoláin, F. (2007) 'Transitional Justice: (Re)conceptualising the Field', *International Journal of Law in Context*, 2 (3): 81–88.

Bell, C. and O'Rourke, C. (2007) 'Does Feminism Need a Theory of Transitional Justice? An Introductory Essay', *International Journal of Transitional Justice*, 1 (1): 23–44.

Bell, D. (ed.) (2006) *Memory, Trauma and World Politics*, Basingstoke: Palgrave.

Buckley-Zistel, S. and Schäfer, S. (eds) (2013) *Memorials in Times of Transition*, Antwerp: Intersentia.

Buckley-Zistel, S. and Stanley, R. (eds) (2012) *Gender in Transitional Justice*, Basingstoke: Palgrave.

Clark, P. and Palmer, N. (2012) 'Challenging Transitional Justice', in Palmer, N., Clark, P. and Granville, D. (eds) *Critical Perspectives in Transitional Justice*, Antwerp: Intersentia.

Crocker, D.A. (1999) 'Reckoning with Past Wrongs: A Normative Framework', *Ethics & International Affairs*, (13): 43–64.

de Greiff, P. (2012) 'Theorizing Transitional Justice', in Williams, M.S., Nagy, R. and Elster, J. (eds) *Transitional Justice*, New York, NY: New York University Press.

de Greiff, P. and Duthie, R. (eds) (2009) *Transitional Justice and Development: Making Connections*, New York, NY: Social Science Research Council.

Dhawan, N. (2012) 'Transitions to Justice', in Buckley-Zistel, S. and Stanley, R. (eds) *Gender in Transitional Justice*, Basingstoke: Palgrave.

Dyzenhaus, D. (2012) '*Leviathan* as a Theory of Transitional Justice', in Williams, M.S., Nagy, R. and Elster, J. (eds) *Transitional Justice*, New York, NY: New York University Press.

Edkins, J. (2003) *Trauma and the Memory of Politics*, Cambridge: Cambridge University Press.

Franke, K.M. (2006) 'Gendered Subjects of Transitional Justice', *Columbia Journal of Gender and Law*, 3 (15): 813–28.

Glasius, M. and Meijers, T. (2012) 'Constructions of Legitimacy: The Charles Taylor Trial', *International Journal of Transitional Justice*, 2 (6): 229–52.

Hinton, A.L. (ed.) (2010) *Transitional Justice. Global Mechanisms and Local Realities after Genocide and Mass Violence*, New Brunswick, NJ: Rutgers University Press.

Humphrey, M. (2003) 'From Victim to Victimhood: Truth Commissions and Trials as Rituals of Political Transition and Individual Healing', *Australian Journal of Anthropology*, 2 (14): 171–87.

Lambourne, W. (2009) 'Transitional Justice and Peacebuilding after Mass Violence', *International Journal of Transitional Justice*, 3 (1): 28–48.

Laplante, L.J. (2008) 'Transitional Justice and Peace Building: Diagnosing and Addressing the Socioeconomic Roots of Violence through a Human Rights Framework', *International Journal of Transitional Justice*, 3 (2): 331–55.

McEvoy, K. (2007) 'Beyond Legalism: Towards a Thicker Understanding of Transitional Justice', *Journal of Law and Society*, 34 (4): 411–40.

McEvoy, K. and McGregor, L. (eds) (2008) *Transitional Justice From Below. Grassroots Activism and Struggle for Change*, Oxford: Hart Publishing.

Mani, R. (2002) *Beyond Retribution. Seeking Justice in the Shadows of War*, Cambridge: Polity Press.

——(2008) 'Dilemmas of Expanding Transitional Justice, or Forging the Nexus between Transitional Justice and Development', *International Journal of Transitional Justice*, 3 (2): 253–65.

May, L. (2012) 'Transitional Justice and the Just War Tradition', in Palmer, N., Clark, P. and Granville, D. (eds) *Critical Perspectives in Transitional Justice*, Antwerp: Intersentia.

Mihr, A. (ed.) (2012) *Transitional Justice. Between Criminal Justice, Atonement and Democracy*, Utrecht, SIM Special Issue No. 37.

Miller, Z. (2008) 'Effects of Invisibility: In Search of the "Economic" in Transitional Justice', *International Journal of Transitional Justice*, 3 (2): 266–91.

Nagy, R. (2008) 'Transitional Justice as Global Project: Critical Reflections', *Third World Quarterly*, 2 (29): 275–89.

Nesiah, V. (2006) 'Discussion Lines on Gender and Transitional Justice', *Columbia Journal of Gender and Law*, (15): 799–812.

Ní Aoláin, F. and Rooney, E. (2007) 'Underenforcement and Intersectionality: Gendered Aspects of Transition for Women', *International Journal of Transitional Justice*, 3 (1): 338–54.

Okello, M.C. (2010) 'Afterword: Elevating Transitional Local Justice or Crystallizing Global Governance?' in Shaw, R., Waldorf, L. and Hazan, P. (eds) *Localizing Transitional Justice. Interventions and Priorities After Mass Violence*, Stanford, CA: Stanford University Press.

Oomen, B. (2005) 'Donor-Driven Justice and its Discontent: The Case of Rwanda', *Development and Change*, 5 (36): 887–910.

O'Rourke, C. (2013) *Gender Politics in Transitional Justice*, Abingdon: Routledge.

Osiel, M. (2000) *Mass Atrocities, Collective Memory and the Law*, New Brunswick, NJ: Transaction.

Pensky, M. (2012) 'Commentary on Critiquing Core Transitional Justice Concepts', in Palmer, N., Clark, P. and Granville, D. (eds) *Critical Perspectives in Transitional Justice*, Antwerp: Intersentia.

Pupavac, V. (2001) 'Therapeutic Governance. Psycho-social Intervention and Trauma Risk Management', *Disaster*, 4 (25): 358–72.

Roht-Arriaza, N. and Mariezcurrena, J. (eds) (2006) *Transitional Justice in the Twenty-First Century: Beyond Truth versus Justice*, Cambridge: Cambridge University Press.

Rubio-Marín, R. (2006) 'The Gender of Reparations: Setting the Agenda', in Rubio-Marin, R. (ed.) *What Happened to the Women? Gender and Reparations for Human Rights Violations*, New York, NY: Social Science Research Council.

Shaw, R., Waldorf, L. and Hazan, P. (eds) (2010) *Localizing Transitional Justice. Interventions and Priorities After Mass Violence*, Stanford, CA: Stanford University Press.

Sriram, C.L. and Pillay, S. (eds) (2009) *Peace versus Justice? The Dilemma of Transitional Justice in Africa*, Scottsville: University of KwaZulu Natal Press.

Teitel, R.G. (2003) Transitional Justice Genealogy, *Harvard Human Rights Journal*, (16): 69–94.

Webber, J. (2012) 'Forms of Transitional Justice', in Williams, M.S., Nagy, R. and Elster, J. (eds) *Transitional Justice*, New York, NY: New York University Press.

Wilson, R. (2001) *The Politics of Truth and Reconciliation in South Africa: Legitimizing the Post-Apartheid State*, Cambridge: Cambridge University Press.

Part I

Theorising transitional justice

Chapter I

Transformative justice, reconciliation and peacebuilding[1]

Wendy Lambourne

Introduction

What is the purpose of transitional justice? The answer to this question has too often been assumed rather than explicitly articulated in the theory and practice of transitional justice. From the perspective of those recovering from mass violence and gross human rights violations, justice may be sought as redress for crimes, but it may also be sought as a way of coming to terms with the past and building a peaceful future. Justice, reconciliation and peace are seen as inextricably intertwined (Lambourne 2002). And yet, relatively few transitional justice scholars consider the goals of peace and reconciliation, instead continuing to focus primarily on the promotion of human rights, democracy and the rule of law without situating their research in a peacebuilding context.[2]

I argue that analysing and evaluating transitional justice in terms of its contribution to peacebuilding enables a more holistic perspective that takes into account the expectations of affected communities as well as the links between dealing with the past and building peace and reconciliation for the future. In determining the specific path to take in any particular transitional justice context, it is therefore critical to take into account the needs, expectations and experiences of the perpetrators, victims, survivors and other members of society directly affected by the violence and who are intimately involved in reconciliation and peacebuilding.

My research has focused on understanding how local affected communities view transitional justice in the context of peacebuilding after mass violence. Drawing on these research findings and theories of conflict transformation, reconciliation and peacebuilding, I have developed a model of transformative justice that requires rethinking our focus on 'transition' as an interim process that links the past and the future, to 'transformation' that implies long-term, sustainable processes embedded in society. It involves recognising and addressing the multiple justice needs of the local population in a way that draws on the various cultural approaches that co-exist with the dominant Western worldview and practice. In addition to transitional legal justice mechanisms, transformative justice requires a transformation in social, economic and political structures and relationships. By proposing a syncretic or integrated approach to restorative and retributive justice,[3] it seeks to avoid compromise whilst also acknowledging that the process is inevitably messy and inadequate to deal with the enormity of the psychological and physical pain and destruction of war and other mass violence.

Reconciling retributive and restorative justice: a syncretic approach

The Western, liberal tradition of accountability for crimes promotes an adversarial, prosecutorial, retributive model of formal legal justice (Findlay and Henham 2005). Based on this model, in the context of transitional justice, the international community has pursued prosecutions through ad hoc international criminal tribunals, hybrid domestic/international courts and the permanent ICC (Cassese 2003; Romano et al 2004; Schiff 2008). Meanwhile, proponents of restorative justice promote the use of truth and reconciliation commissions or informal customary mechanisms where the focus is on rebuilding or restoring relationships and community (Tutu 1999; Hayner 2010; Isser 2011).[4] More recently, the international community has recognised that Western legal trials and a truth commission, perhaps incorporating traditional, indigenous rituals, may be seen as complementary strategies to support both retributive and restorative justice in transitional societies such as in East Timor and Sierra Leone (Roht-Arriaza and Mariezcurrena 2006). But this pluralistic solution is also inadequate because it fails to break out of the dominant Western worldview of justice and to question the 'standardization of transitional justice goals and methods' driven by external interventions (Lutz 2006: 333).[5]

Advocates of an alternative restorative justice model for modern Western societies, building on the traditional, informal, restorative model of communitarian justice practised by indigenous peoples, often simplify and generalise the benefits of this approach to crime (Zehr 1990; Braithwaite 2003). I argue that the distinction between retributive justice in the Western formal legal system and restorative justice in indigenous, informal justice mechanisms is oversimplified and serves to mask rather than illuminate the multiple, complex human needs, expectations and experiences in relation to justice and reconciliation.[6] Not only do the traditions of different societies vary in the relative weight placed on restorative and retributive components of justice, in many cases these distinctions may in fact be merged or conceived in very different terms (Dinnen 2003; Sriram and Pillay 2009).[7] Traditional informal justice mechanisms and indigenous reconciliation rituals can thus provide examples of approaches that treat restorative and retributive justice as interdependent rather than mutually exclusive processes.[8] For example, the traditional *gacaca* community justice in Rwanda required the offender to 'appreciate the gravity of the damage s/he had caused' and the agreed outcome was construed as a form of punishment albeit not one so severe that it would interfere with the primary goal of reconciliation (Molenaar 2005: 14).[9] Thus *gacaca* could be experienced as both retributive and restorative at the same time.[10] As argued by Joanna Quinn, 'while the more formalized Western models often allow for only one form of justice – retributive, restorative, or reparative – these traditional institutions seek to combine various of these and other elements in keeping with the values of the community' (Quinn 2005: 10).

Thus the idea that informal customary law practices might be more appropriate as a transitional justice model for genocide and other serious crimes against humanity is misleading and may be seen as imposing an unfair burden on survivors to accept restorative justice as sufficient when retributive justice would otherwise be expected.[11] And vice versa, imposing primarily retributive legal justice mechanisms may also be seen as inadequate by failing to take into account local community needs for restorative justice and reconciliation. Instead, we should look at creative and locally relevant ways to incorporate principles of both restorative and retributive justice in accountability mechanisms, as well as structures and relationships to support future respect for human rights and the rule of law.[12] Rather than following the pluralist approach of separate institutions, I propose that a more successful approach might be to take a lead from indigenous traditional customary practices in order to design a more syncretic transitional justice mechanism that combines retributive and restorative elements.[13]

My research and that of others who study traditional justice in different cultural contexts suggests that such a hybrid approach is possible. The pervasive influence of colonisation and globalisation is evident in the apparent synthesis of Christian and animist rituals and beliefs in the reconciliation ceremonies of Bougainville and East Timor, for example (Tombot 2003; Babo-Soares 2005). This syncretic approach to justice after mass violence is incorporated in the model of transformative justice which I develop in this chapter, placing transitional justice in the context of conflict transformation, peacebuilding and reconciliation.

Transitional justice and peacebuilding

As defined by the UN, peacebuilding encompasses a wide range of political, developmental, humanitarian and human rights programmes and mechanisms designed to prevent the outbreak, recurrence or continuation of armed conflict (United Nations Security Council 2001). Peacebuilding has short-term as well as long-term objectives aimed at ensuring sustainability in the security, political, economic and justice spheres. These include the promotion of democracy and accountable governance, as well as eradication of poverty and sustainable development, and respect for human rights and the rule of law (United Nations Security Council 2001; Jeong 2005). Justice as part of peacebuilding must therefore be seen as more than transitional: it must set up structures, institutions and relationships to promote sustainability.

Sustainable peace requires pursuing the twin objectives of preserving 'negative peace' (absence of physical violence) and building 'positive peace' (presence of social justice), and alleviating if not eliminating the underlying causes of conflict (Galtung 1969). This holistic perspective suggests that peacebuilding and transitional justice involve promoting socioeconomic and political justice, as well as legal justice that combats a culture of impunity and sets up structures to ensure ongoing respect for human rights and the rule of law.

This holistic and comprehensive approach to peacebuilding implies a commitment to establishing the security, legal, political, economic, structural, cultural and psychosocial conditions necessary to promote a culture of peace in place of a culture of violence. As argued by John Paul Lederach (2000), peacebuilding requires a transformation in relationships between people as well as the ending of violence and construction of the conditions for peace. Rama Mani similarly proposes that peacebuilding is a dynamic process that is essentially a political task, but also a 'social and associative process that rebuilds fractured relationships between people' (Mani 2002: 15). It is this theory of peacebuilding as transformative that I have applied to the justice and reconciliation sector of peacebuilding, hence leading to a proposed reconceptualisation of transitional justice as transformative justice incorporating political, economic and psychosocial as well as legal dimensions.

I propose the term 'psychosocial justice' to encapsulate the dimensions of justice that address the need for truth in terms of both knowledge and acknowledgement of the violation and its human and relational impact: knowledge of who was responsible, how it happened, where the bodies or remains are located, and acknowledgement of the loss, pain, hurt and suffering caused. Both knowledge and acknowledgment can contribute to a psychological process of healing and building of inner peace. Combining this inner transformation with relational transformation provides the foundation for reconciliation and a sense of psychosocial justice. Reconciliation is thus seen as a process of relationship-building as part of conflict transformation, as well as an outcome that is part of the experience of sustainable peace (Lederach 1997).

To be sustainable, this transformative process must be based on recognition of the particular cultural and conflict context and the effective participation of civil society. Or as Lederach (2000: 55) puts it: a realistic peace process requires 'the tools of contextualization and empowerment'. Stover and Weinstein (2004) also stress the importance of social reconstruction being contextualised and adapted to each unique post-war setting and being informed by the opinions, attitudes and needs of the local population. Peacebuilding and transitional justice thus become transformative when they emphasise the principles of local participation and empowerment. Furthermore, I suggest that transformation requires a transdisciplinary mindset that incorporates insights and lessons from many disciplinary perspectives and experiences in order to create new ways of thinking about peacebuilding and transitional justice theory and practice. As argued by Luc Reychler (2006), the narrow disciplinary mindset of peacebuilding theory is a conceptual impediment to developing a comprehensive understanding of sustainable peacebuilding architecture.

From this analysis emerges a transdisciplinary model of transformative peacebuilding that involves a transformation of relationships as well as structures and institutions: what Reychler (2006) refers to as the 'software' and 'hardware' of sustainable peacebuilding architecture. The sustainability of this transformative process requires attention to the needs and expectations of local affected populations, as well as a co-ordinated focus on the multidimensional or multidisciplinary aspects of peacebuilding incorporating attention to all the dimensions of human security. It requires attention to psychosocial as well as political, economic and law and order aspects of peace and justice. In the next section, I will explore further how this model of transformative peacebuilding can be applied to the transitional justice sector.

Towards a theory of transformative justice

I developed this model of transformative justice based on field research conducted in Cambodia in 1999, Rwanda in 1998 and 2005, East Timor in 2004 and Sierra Leone in 2006.[14] All of these countries experienced mass violence that was ended some years before my interviews were conducted,[15] and genocide, crimes against humanity and/or war crimes were committed. The approaches taken to peacebuilding and transitional justice by the international community and national governments in each case varied markedly.

In Cambodia, a government policy of 'national reconciliation' and amnesties was accompanied by a lack of accountability for the crimes of the Khmer Rouge at the international level. Thirty years after the genocide of 1975–79,[16] the culture of impunity was ended with the establishment of a hybrid UN-Cambodian tribunal, the Extraordinary Chambers in the Courts of Cambodia (ECCC), which began trials of key surviving Khmer Rouge leaders in 2009. By contrast, the UN established the International Criminal Tribunal for Rwanda (ICTR) and the Rwandan government instituted domestic trials almost immediately after the 1994 genocide. The Rwandan government subsequently created a National Unity and Reconciliation Commission (NURC) and adapted traditional *gacaca* community justice to deal with the large numbers of accused and promote both justice and reconciliation. Truth commissions, in addition to legal trials, were established following the 1991–2002 civil war in Sierra Leone and the mass violence that took place in Timor Leste between 1975 and 1999. The Serious

Crimes Unit in Timor Leste and the Special Court for Sierra Leone, like the ECCC, have been described as hybrid UN-national transitional justice mechanisms. The Timorese Commission for Reception, Truth, and Reconciliation (known as CAVR from its Portuguese acronym) conducted community reconciliation processes based on traditional *nahe biti* throughout the country,[17] while the Sierra Leone TRC incorporated some traditional practices in its public hearings.

In each country, I interviewed a cross-section of the population in urban and rural areas, except for Cambodia where I was only able to conduct interviews in the capital, Phnom Penh.[18] My interviewees included victims and survivors, perpetrators and accused, and representatives of transitional justice bodies, international and government institutions, NGOs and civil society more generally. These comments should not be taken as representative of the views of the whole population in each case, but should be seen as indicating the views of some people in each country who can provide an insight into transitional justice processes and how they are being experienced by different sectors of the general population and the non-government sector.[19]

Based on my field research in these countries, and building on existing theories and models of transitional justice and the principles of transformative peacebuilding outlined in the previous section, the model of transformative justice I have developed proposes four key elements or aspects of justice: accountability, or legal justice; psychosocial justice, including truth and healing; socioeconomic justice; and political justice.

Four elements or aspects of transformative justice

Accountability or legal justice

My research in Cambodia, Rwanda and East Timor suggested that accountability and/or legal justice were important components of transitional justice. In Cambodia, interviewees supported the idea of a tribunal to provide justice and accountability for the former Khmer Rouge. For example, a female survivor of the genocide who heads a Cambodian human rights NGO, maintained that 'almost the whole Cambodian population would like a tribunal'. Another female genocide survivor said that 'if they [former Khmer Rouge] are still detained and there is no tribunal, then all Cambodian people will be unhappy because they want the UN to find the justice for Cambodian victims.' There are also a number of surveys and other evidence of Cambodian support for a tribunal, including the petition signed by 84,195 Cambodians presented by the Cambodian Human Rights Action Committee to the United Nations Secretary General on 20 January 1999 that read:

> We, the people of Cambodia, whose signatures and thumbprints are attached, request the United Nations to establish an international

tribunal to try the Khmer Rouge leaders for the mass killings and crimes against humanity committed during their rule from 1975 to 1979.[20]

Similarly, survivors in East Timor and Rwanda called for accountability and punishment for perpetrators. Interviewees in both countries expressed dissatisfaction with the limited retributive justice being meted out to the leaders of the mass violence and perpetrators of serious crimes. According to a Rwandan genocide survivor interviewed in Arusha in July 1998: 'No-one in Rwanda is ready to confess. It is not enough. There has to be some kind of punishment. It is not the same situation as in South Africa.' Many saw the ICTR as remote and irrelevant, and the lack of death penalty and maximum sentences awarded as insufficient punishment or retribution for the genocide leaders.

In East Timor, interviewees expressed dissatisfaction and a sense of 'unfinished business' because the main perpetrators of the violence had not been tried and held accountable. I found that Timorese wanted justice for the militia who committed serious crimes; an international tribunal and justice for the Indonesian generals and the international community who were complicit; and traditional reconciliation with militia and with Indonesian leaders, but only after they faced justice. For example, a Timorese victim interviewed in Suai said she wanted the militia to get justice: 'the militia who killed my brother have to go to prison.' She also said, however, that she wanted to 'make reconciliation with the militia'. Another Timorese victim interviewed in Suai in July 2004 said he agreed with President Xanana Gusmao's reconciliation with Indonesian General Wiranto, but that Wiranto should still go to trial in Timor for ordering the deaths of people: 'Timorese are angry about Wiranto – what he did to people ... Justice has to keep happening in Timor. Militia still must go to prison.'

Comments from interviewees and my observations in East Timor, Rwanda and Cambodia support the assertion that both retributive and restorative elements should be part of accountability and legal justice. A truth commission that fails to pursue promised prosecutions, as in East Timor, can promote restorative justice but does not deal with survivors' needs for retributive justice. It therefore may fail to reinforce respect for the rule of law and enable the conditions necessary for peace and security to prevail. Contrariwise, a focus on accountability and prosecutions for war crimes and other past human rights abuses that does not rebuild relationships through some kind of restorative process is unlikely to overcome the societal divisions that undermine peace and security. For example, the Rwandan government introduced the NURC and the *gacaca* trials with the explicit aim of promoting reconciliation along with justice. In Sierra Leone, the international community established the TRC and later the Special Court with the intention to promote both restorative and retributive justice, but lack of coordination undermined the promotion of either form of justice (Schabas and Darcy 2004).

Truth: knowledge and acknowledgment

I argue that 'truth', whether expressed as truth-seeking, truth-telling or truth recovery, is an inadequate concept to encapsulate the full meaning of truth, knowledge and acknowledgement to the various conflict participants in a transitional justice context, including both victims and perpetrators. The word 'truth' is also misleading, as it is often interpreted as the finding of a single truth of what happened, who was responsible and why. I draw on the distinction between four different types of truth made by the South African TRC and outlined by Stephan Parmentier (2003) in his model of transitional justice: forensic or factual truth; personal or narrative truth; social or dialogical truth; and healing or restorative truth (Boraine and Valentine 2006). All four of these dimensions of truth are important to understanding what different people need from a transitional justice process, and these needs may vary at different times and in different circumstances.

The transformative justice model presented here also draws on Williams and Sharf's focus on 'historical record' as one aspect of truth that is important (Williams and Sharf 2002). This entails establishing some kind of agreed record of the conflict, the human rights violations that occurred and who was responsible. This type of truth I have termed 'knowledge'. It might include various 'truths' or interpretations held by the various conflict participants. In other words, it comprises both factual or forensic truth, and narrative or personal truth.

From my field research in 1999, I concluded that Cambodians needed to know what happened during the Pol Pot era and why, and they needed acknowledgement from the former Khmer Rouge that what they did was wrong. For example, a genocide survivor I interviewed in Phnom Penh in October 1999 said he had a great interest to know the 'real truth – why they did what they did, their rationale'. He went on to say that: 'Truth can be more important than justice. Justice needs to be objective, not vindictive. Without truth, [you] don't really have justice. Truth can help with justice.' The Documentation Center for Cambodia (DC-Cam) has gathered evidence (factual/forensic truth) as well as stories from survivors (personal/narrative truth) about the genocide, thereby providing knowledge and some sense of acknowledgement of people's sufferings during the Pol Pot era. As argued by a 40-year-old journalist and genocide survivor I interviewed in Phnom Penh in October 1999, DC-Cam is 'good for Cambodia' because the 'new generation especially can understand what happened before – some don't believe – good to open to all people to understand and know'. Subsequently, the creation of the ECCC, with associated victim participation and extensive

NGO outreach, has greatly increased the potential for factual and personal truth to be revealed, but opportunities for pursuing social/dialogue and healing/restorative truth are still limited (Lambourne 2012).

In East Timor and Rwanda, survivors also wanted to know what happened to their loved ones and to experience some acknowledgement from perpetrators. In relation to perpetrators of less serious crimes, the CAVR's Community Reconciliation Process (CRP) brought deponents (perpetrators) and victims together. The sharing of knowledge and expressions of acknowledgement were a critical step in the reconciliation process which enabled peacebuilding in the community. The CRP incorporated a combination of a factual/forensic truth, as well as personal/narrative truth, social/dialogical truth and the potential for healing/restorative truth, the last being an integral component of the traditional *nahe biti* process.

In relation to the perpetrators of serious crimes in East Timor, victims I interviewed were dissatisfied because they most likely would not find out the factual truth of what happened to their loved ones, as the perpetrators were either not prosecuted or the trials were held in Dili and they were unable to attend. For example, a Timorese victim in Suai was not satisfied because his daughter had been killed by militia and 'I don't know where her remains are ... I want to know who exactly killed my daughter.' Even if former members of the militia were prosecuted, and the victims were able to attend the court hearings in Dili, the perpetrators were unlikely to acknowledge their crimes in the adversarial legal court system. This means that the retributive justice achieved was insufficient to effect transformative justice. In relation to the former militia leaders and Indonesian leaders, interviewees expressed an even stronger desire for acknowledgement of the crimes that were committed and the human rights violations that were perpetrated from the time of the invasion in 1975, during the Indonesian occupation and the post-referendum violence in 1999.

In the case of Rwanda, the remote location of the ICTR in Arusha in Tanzania ensured that most victims and survivors had no personal experience of 'truth'. They were unable to learn what happened to their loved ones, to tell their stories or to hear any acknowledgment of the crimes of the genocide leaders even if this did occur (as, e.g. in the case of former Prime Minister Kambanda). In 1998, however, it was not clear that Rwandans wanted this type of opportunity to publicly explore the 'truth' of what happened. A female genocide survivor I interviewed in Kigali said: 'It is a long process to get to the truth. People are not ready or willing to look at history because it will get them in trouble somewhere, especially if they are named and are now in government. It is a long process ... We are not ready for a truth commission.' And yet the need for knowledge and acknowledgement was expressed by a number of interviewees. For example, a genocide survivor I interviewed in Kigali in July 1998 said he thought Kambanda's confession was 'a good thing. It will help justice, but it is not enough. It would be more helpful if Bagasora confessed. It would also be better if he told everything he knows.'

Attitudes towards truth and reconciliation began to change in Rwanda soon after my visit in 1998 as the government set up the NURC and began to actively promote national reconciliation. This included *gacaca* trials which provided an opportunity for the accused to acknowledge their crimes and for survivors to tell their stories (narrative/personal truth). However, as I observed during my field research in July 2005, not all the forensic or factual truth was being told, and the survivors were again unable to find out all that had happened to their loved ones. There was a lack of any real dialogue or engagement in gaining a sense of 'social truth', although the Rwandan government was seeking to impose this through its policy of national unity and reconciliation. Furthermore, by reducing the restorative justice and reconciliation aspect of the traditional *gacaca* process, the modernised *gacaca* was failing to provide a sense of healing or restorative truth (Lambourne 2010a).

In Sierra Leone, people seemed less concerned about the role of truth in providing a sense of justice or peace. There was a generally low level of participation in the TRC which was perceived by many as a foreign intervention. Unlike in East Timor and Cambodia, the population apparently had less need for previously denied atrocities to be acknowledged by perpetrators. As in Rwanda, what happened was publicly well-known. Whilst interviewees did seem to appreciate that the TRC hearings had contributed to peacebuilding, they were more concerned with the immediate needs of socioeconomic and political justice as a means of promoting peacebuilding in the country. This suggests that legal accountability and truth, including knowledge and acknowledgement, are not the only ingredients necessary for transformative justice.

The model I have proposed emphasises the importance to victims and survivors, and arguably perpetrators, of acknowledgement as part of the 'truth' aspect of transitional justice. Even if the knowledge of what happened is obtained and recorded, having perpetrators acknowledge what they have done and its impact on victims can also be critical for justice, reconciliation and peacebuilding. Despite the criminal trials and truth commissions that establish a historical record and/or details of the crimes committed, the continuing denial of culpability and defence of their actions by those accused of mass human rights violations has led Cambodians, Rwandans and East Timorese alike to express the need for acknowledgement as an important part of transitional justice and psychosocial healing necessary for peacebuilding.

Socioeconomic justice

I use the term 'socioeconomic justice' to incorporate the various elements of justice that relate to financial or other material compensation, restitution or reparation for past violations or crimes (historical justice) and distributive or socioeconomic justice in the future (prospective justice) (Lambourne 2004). The idea is both to establish a feeling of justice about what occurred in the past and to ensure that structural violence in the future is minimised in order to promote a sustainable peace. This element of justice was highlighted in the interviews I conducted in all four countries. However, while most models of transitional justice include the idea of reparation, they tend to focus on historical reparations rather than the need for future socioeconomic justice as a conflict preventive measure. My concept of socioeconomic justice as decisive in transitional justice draws on Rama Mani's model that includes distributive justice as one of three critical dimensions of reparative justice (Mani 2002). Based on my field research and consideration of conflict theory, I concur with Mani's argument that alleviating impact and targeting causes through distributive justice are important for transitional justice to contribute to peacebuilding.

Interviewees in all four countries described their inability to meet basic needs as a significant impediment to peace and reconciliation. Victims in Cambodia, Rwanda and East Timor indicated that they thought it was unjust that they were living in poverty while perpetrators of mass violence and human rights violations were living in comparative luxury. In Cambodia, former Khmer Rouge leaders were seen as living well and as being treated as honoured guests by Prime Minister Hun Sen when they visited the capital, Phnom Penh. For example, one Cambodian refugee returnee interviewed in Phnom Penh in October 1999 said that inviting Khieu Samphan to Phnom Penh and giving him 'VIP treatment' was a 'mockery', whilst a genocide survivor asked 'Why should the former Khmer Rouge live so freely and be received by Hun Sen in a five star hotel? This makes a lot of people angry.'

In Rwanda, interviewees saw the genocide leaders being tried by the ICTR as living in 'comfortable Western jails' while at the same time the Tribunal was seen as not responding to the material needs of victims and witnesses (providing no compensation or restitution, healthcare or other financial assistance). For example, a genocide survivor working for the ICTR said that 'women in Rwanda want compensation. They don't understand that the ICTR is not a social institution so they are not fulfilled; their expectations are not being met.' Another genocide survivor interviewed in July 1998 observed that 'Rwandans don't see the ICTR addressing the issue [of justice] – as if suspects are being well looked after – too well-treated.' A genocide survivor working with the ICTR in Arusha talked about the importance of restitutive justice in fostering peace and reconciliation:

> In practice it is very difficult compared with theory. People still need material things to reconstruct houses and replace stolen or burnt things. Therefore they can't forget and live peacefully together with others.

They need some compensation. If their material needs are met, they are more able to reconcile.

This view was echoed by another genocide survivor, interviewed in Kigali seven years later, who said that 'the government is asking us to forget – but how? ... The government should try to reduce poverty, especially for the survivors, because it is hard to forget when living in such conditions.' A Rwandan refugee returnee and lawyer, interviewed in Kigali in July 1998, argued for a more victim-oriented justice that would foster reconciliation by addressing social and economic justice as well as legal justice. She maintained that the current 'lack of rehabilitation [of prisoners] and reparations and communication can't help in the process of national reconciliation'.

East Timorese interviewees noted that accused Indonesian generals still had their jobs, that former militia leaders were living in West Timor, and that both groups were seen as doing well compared with the poverty in Timor Leste. Interviewees in Sierra Leone, meanwhile, perceived ex-combatants as being in a better position to earn a living than the amputees, who in many cases did not have shelter, let alone jobs and a means of satisfying their basic needs. For example, a young amputee interviewed in November 2006 in Kenema indicated that she and other female amputees were forced to sleep in the market because they had not benefited from housing projects and had nowhere else to go. A young male amputee interviewed in Freetown in December 2006 said that amputees living in resettlement camps 'still think justice has left them behind', adding that they were rejected by families and friends and many were reduced to begging on the streets. He noted that they were pressuring for a reparations trust fund but things were 'moving too slowly'.

In Rwanda, the national compensation fund linked to *gacaca* was not yet in operation at the time of my field research in July 2005, and survivors and released prisoners alike mentioned their need for money for food, roofing materials, more help with school fees for children, healthcare and assistance in meeting other material needs. My interviews and observations during that trip suggested that whether Tutsi or Hutu,[21] returnee or survivor, the common perception was that government policies favoured the other group. For example, two recently released prisoners in Kanombe both complained about their situation, including lack of funding to pay for roof repairs and that they were ineligible to receive assistance that survivors received. My Hutu taxi driver echoed their sentiments, claiming that Tutsi were receiving all of the economic benefits after the genocide. On the other side, Tutsi survivors felt disadvantaged because they were required to actively seek out benefits from the survivors' fund, while ex-combatants automatically received aid packages after attending *Ingando* solidarity camps. Jealousy and resentment of the other ethnic group based on perceived socioeconomic injustice appeared to be undermining reconciliation and peacebuilding in Rwanda.

Only a minority of Cambodians interviewed in October 1999 mentioned the concept of social or economic justice. One of these, a genocide survivor and human rights advocate, said that justice is 'not only punishment of a criminal or somebody who has done something bad for people or society; it is also equity of distribution of resources and wealth of the nation'. By contrast, a majority of the East Timorese I interviewed in July 2004, when asked about justice, spoke about their need for jobs, healthcare, safe water, assistance with school fees, help to start a new business and so on. For example, a community leader in Liquica mentioned the need for access to safe drinking water, while a victim interviewed in Suai reported that his sight was impaired by a militia attack which meant he could no longer work as a school teacher. For him, justice meant financial support that would enable him to buy a pair of glasses.

Interviewees in Sierra Leone in November/December 2006 also mentioned high levels of poverty and lack of development as significant contributors to their feelings of injustice. A Freetown resident said that 'justice is only there for rich people in Sierra Leone' and that he did not feel peaceful because he had 'not had enough food to eat'. One ex-combatant in Bo mentioned the need for government support to return to his previous work as a tailor, while another argued that the government needed to do more to combat illiteracy as the low standard of education contributed to war. Amputees with children and former child soldiers were particularly concerned about the need for support in paying school fees.

In both East Timor and Rwanda, some interviewees said that perpetrators should provide recompense directly (e.g. replace a cow that was stolen or rebuild a house), though they acknowledged that perpetrators were often also poor so this was probably unrealistic. So instead they said they saw it as the responsibility of the government, and sometimes the international community, to provide these services and reduce poverty as a contribution to justice, reconciliation and peacebuilding.

Political justice

When asked about their experiences of justice, interviewees in Sierra Leone emphasised dissatisfaction with the government's ability to provide basic services, the corruption and the lack of commitment to good governance and responsible leadership. For example, an ex-combatant in Freetown said 'The government is not committed to doing what is necessary to produce a "just peace"', while another said Sierra Leoneans needed to 'pray for a very good, strong political leader who is not biased, who talks straight and that will be justice'.

Political injustice was mentioned less often in East Timor during my interviews in 2004, although it has become apparent since the riots in 2006 that unresolved political divisions and perceived socioeconomic discrimination have disrupted the peace. In Cambodia, it seems that the inclusion of some former Khmer Rouge in the government and a lack of democratisation had contributed to an absence of respect for the rule of law, continuing abuses of human rights and a culture of impunity that undermined experiences of justice. As one genocide survivor interviewed in Phnom Penh in October 1999 noted: 'We have to punish [the former Khmer Rouge] ... a matter of national responsibility ... biggest case of impunity in the world and the mother of other smaller impunities in Cambodia.' Even though this 'biggest impunity' is being addressed, perceptions of political injustice continue, and threaten to undermine the potential impact of the ECCC as the government is seen to exercise undue influence over the judicial process (Lambourne 2012).

In Rwanda, a lack of democratisation and a perception of victor's justice were causing discontent amongst the Hutu majority, while the government was perceived as dominated by the Tutsi minority. One genocide survivor interviewed in July 1998 commented that Rwanda 'needs good leaders. They can help or not help reconciliation by what they say', while another survivor maintained that the mistakes of the previous government in excluding part of the population must not be repeated. Unfortunately, it appears that the government's policy of exclusion has been repeated (in reverse), although not as systematically as in the Hutu-dominated government prior to 1994. A perception of victor's justice that reinforces experiences of political injustice has been reinforced by the official designation that only Tutsi can be survivors in post-genocide Rwanda and that only Hutus can be perpetrators (Mamdani 2001: 266–67).

In all four cases, we can see how a lack of political justice is undermining peacebuilding. Political justice is necessary to ensure the successful implementation of transitional justice measures including institutional reform, rule of law and respect for human rights, addressing socioeconomic needs, and avoiding the appearance of victor's justice or a culture of impunity. As argued by Mahmood Mamdani (2001), political justice requires a delinking of political identity from cultural identity and a move towards democracy that involves institutional reform, and separates and makes accountable the powers of the executive, legislature, judiciary and administration. In other words, political justice involves transforming both institutions and relationships to eliminate corruption and promote a sense of fair representation and participation for the general population. Without political justice, transformative justice is therefore incomplete and peace unsustainable.

Six principles of transformative justice

Transformative peacebuilding thus requires a commitment to political and socioeconomic justice as well as psychosocial justice through restoration of relationships and legal justice or accountability that includes retribution. In

Table 1.1

Elements or aspects of transformative justice	Principles of transformative justice
1 accountability, or legal justice, that reconciles retributive and restorative justice (rectificatory justice, restores public order and rule of law, removes culture of impunity) 2 'truth' and healing, or psychosocial justice: knowledge and acknowledgement (factual/ forensic truth, personal/narrative truth, social/dialogical truth, healing/restorative truth) 3 socioeconomic justice (reparation, restitution, compensation, distributive justice) 4 political justice (political reform, governance, democratisation)	1 symbolic and ritual, as well as substantive, aspects of justice 2 prospective (future oriented, long term) as well as present (including procedural) and historical justice (dealing with the past) 3 local ownership and capacity-building 4 structural transformation and institutional reform 5 relationship transformation and reconciliation 6 holistic, integrated and comprehensive

addition to these four aspects or elements, this model of transformative justice incorporates six principles that apply to all of the four elements or aspects (see Table 1.1).

Two of the principles emphasise the significance of transformation – of both structures and relationships – to promoting transitional justice that supports transformative peacebuilding; hence the proposal to reframe transitional justice as transformative justice. Transformative justice not only deals with the past, but also establishes conditions and structures to ensure justice in the present and the future, creating a longer term vision and commitment than suggested by the term 'transitional justice'. This applies to legal justice that promotes accountability for past violations and 'truth' that creates a historical record, as well as structures and relationships to ensure procedural justice in the present, and future respect for human rights and the rule of law. It also suggests the necessity of considering not only reparative or restitutive justice for past inequities, but also distributive or socioeconomic justice for the future. Factual or forensic truth dealing with the past may be needed as well as healing or restorative truth that creates the conditions for transformation of relationships necessary for sustainable peace.

Transformative justice recognises the significance of symbolic and ritual processes to ensuring the local and personal relevance of transitional justice mechanisms that are consistent with the worldviews of the people involved (Sutherland 2005). In East Timor, for example, local community reconciliation processes were experienced as personally meaningful because of the inclusion of the traditional *nahe biti* rituals. Political structures and accountability processes need to be designed for local conditions and with local ownership, and to incorporate culturally relevant symbolism and rituals, in order to support capacity-building and meaningful personal and societal transformation. Lastly, transformative justice implies a holistic and comprehensive approach to all aspects of justice, including legal, psychosocial, socioeconomic and political justice, thereby overcoming the narrow association of transitional justice with formal legal justice only.

The model aims to maximise the inclusiveness of the language used in an attempt to produce a potentially universally applicable model that leaves room for cultural interpretation and application.[22] For this reason, references to elements and aspects of 'truth' and 'justice' are qualified through the provision of alternative terms and concepts. Although inevitably limited by challenges of translation, the research has been informed by observations regarding the terms and concepts used in other languages in the countries where field research was conducted. It is critical to analyse how language and culture affect the interpretations and expectations of local populations and governments in the negotiation and implementation of transitional justice mechanisms. Earlier in this chapter, I explored an example of this phenomenon in relation to the diverse cultural understandings of retributive and restorative justice and the relationship between them, with particular reference to the concept of traditional *gacaca* community justice in Rwanda, suggesting that this could point the way forward to a more holistic and effective approach to transitional justice in different cultural settings.

Conclusion

I have argued that transitional justice requires attention to more than just legal justice if it is to contribute to sustainable peace. In addition to accountability or legal justice, attention needs to be paid to the psychosocial processes, socioeconomic conditions and political context in order for transitional justice to support peacebuilding. In a stable society, these conditions need to be present in order to enable the implementation of the rule of law. Where a society is endeavouring to rebuild (or build for the first time) after mass violence, these elements cannot be taken for granted.

Transitional justice mechanisms that do not seek to reconcile the retributive and restorative aspects of justice and to promote some form of acknowledgement or truth and healing, in addition to transforming political institutions and socioeconomic distribution, will most likely not create the required transformation in relationships necessary to support sustainable peace. A concept of transformative justice that links the past and the future through locally relevant mechanisms and processes that provide accountability, acknowledgment, political and socioeconomic justice should be the basis for an integrated and comprehensive peacebuilding process.

This chapter has highlighted the importance of involving local communities in the development of transitional justice mechanisms that are consistent with local customs, culture and needs. Transformative justice requires that conflict participants become subjects and not just objects in the design and implementation of transitional justice mechanisms in order to counter claims of cultural imperialism, as well as to ensure that the needs of survivors and perpetrators are being met (Lambourne 2006).[23] Democratisation of the transitional justice process, which results in local ownership and capacity-building, is more likely to contribute to transformative justice and peacebuilding (Lambourne 2012).

What is needed is a revolution in thinking that challenges the dominance of Western legal discourse and creatively and inclusively develops new ways of conceiving of accountability mechanisms that provide a more comprehensive and holistic experience of justice. As Lederach (2005) advocates, we need to nurture our moral imagination in order to overcome dualism and embrace paradox. Rather than seeing issues in dualistic terms – peace versus human rights, reconciliation versus justice, retributive versus restorative justice – we need to be able to simultaneously hold multiple and apparently contradictory perspectives and to transcend the dominant, Western worldview of justice which often serves more to divide and separate than to unite and reconcile. The insights and languages of multiple cultural traditions could provide the key for developing new syncretic approaches to transitional justice that are transformative and supportive of sustainable peace and reconciliation.

Notes

1 This chapter is based on an article in the *International Journal of Transitional Justice*, 2009, 3: 28–48, reprinted with permission from Oxford University Press. I wish to express my appreciation to colleagues, students and interviewees in a number of countries who contributed ideas and experiences to enrich this research, and to the University of Sydney which provided research and travel grants to make empirical data collection possible. My special thanks go to the Centre for Peace and Conflict Studies, and to Professor Luc Reychler at the Centre for Peace Research and Strategic Studies, Katholieke Universiteit Leuven, Belgium, who hosted my visit and seminar in 2006 where the ideas for the original article were first presented and developed.

2 The term 'transitional justice' was first used in the context of societies transitioning from undemocratic regimes rather than in the context of peacebuilding after armed conflict (Kritz 1995; Teitel 2000). It was later defined by United Nations Secretary General, Kofi Annan, in relation to the goals of reconciliation and peacebuilding (United Nations Security Council 2004). Scholars who have analysed aspects of transitional justice in a peacebuilding context include Borer (2006), Mani (2002) and van Zyl (2005).

3 Retributive justice may be defined as justice that involves punishment of the wrongdoer and is generally associated with legal trials in the Western legal justice system. Restorative justice, by contrast, means justice that restores community or relationships and is regarded as an alternative form of justice outside the formal judicial court system, at least according to Western legal practice.

4 However, see also Rama Mani (2007) who has pointed out that the divisive role of truth commissions in their identification of victims and perpetrators may mitigate against reconciliation and restoration of relationships.

5 By contrast, Lars Waldorf (2006: 87) concludes his review of local justice for mass atrocities by arguing for a legally pluralistic solution for transitional justice.

6 Kathleen Daly also argues that 'we should stop comparing "retributive justice" and "restorative justice" in oppositional terms' as 'such a strong, oppositional contrast cannot be sustained empirically' (Daly 2000: 3).

7 Not all traditional indigenous processes are restorative and communitarian; many are indeed autocratic, power based and focused on retribution. For example, punishments may be quite severe, including banishment or revenge in the case of serious or 'blood' crimes.

8 Finca (2006) also argues that restorative and retributive justice should be seen as complementary rather than contradictory.

9 Furthermore, Daly (2000) argues that we cannot presume to judge whether restorative justice processes are also perceived as punishment by the participants. The more useful distinction is whether a particular mechanism encourages rehabilitation, reintegration and reconciliation, as well as retribution in the form of acknowledgment and censure of wrongdoing, as in the Rwandan *gacaca* example.

10 However, some argue that in its modern form, *gacaca* became a branch of the formal retributive legal system and all but completely lost its restorative justice character (Waldorf 2006: 53; Lambourne 2010a). By contrast, Clark (2010), while acknowledging the challenges of *gacaca*'s hybridity, suggests that it has been relatively successful in navigating the balance between reconciliation and retribution.

11 Waldorf (2006: 19) argues further that such local justice may do more to further modern political interests than promote community harmony.

12 Local preferences in relation to transitional justice will be affected by globalisation, modernisation and international expectations, as Quinn (2005) has reported from her research in Uganda.

13 Findlay and Henham (2005: xiv) have also made the radical argument for the 'harmonization of restorative and retributive justice' within international criminal justice.

14 In October 1999 I interviewed 22 survivors and descendants of survivors of the Cambodian genocide living in the capital, Phnom Penh, as well as seven NGO and UN workers. In June–July 1998 I interviewed eight Rwandan genocide survivors and five refugee returnees, as well as NGO workers and 10 officials of the ICTR, in the capital, Kigali, and in Arusha, Tanzania. I subsequently interviewed 11 Rwanda refugees living in the UK, US and Canada. When I returned to Rwanda in July 2005 I conducted a total of 48 interviews in four regions: Kigali-Ville, Butare in the south, Byumba in the north and Kibuye in the west. Interviewees included 17 *gacaca* judges, 12 genocide survivors, nine accused/prisoners or their relatives, and ten others including NGO representatives and officials of the NURC and *Inkiko Gacaca*. In July 2004 I interviewed 20 East Timorese including 14 victims and three perpetrators in the capital, Dili, and the regional towns of Liquica and Suai, as well as NGOs and officials of the CAVR. In Sierra Leone in November–December 2006, I interviewed 30 victims and 30 ex-combatants in the capital, Freetown, in the West; Bo in the South; Kenema in the East; and Makeni in the North. I also spoke with representatives of 15 local NGOs and civil society groups; public affairs and outreach staff at the Special Court; and former officials of the TRC.

15 Cambodia: 20 years; Rwanda: 4 and 11 years; East Timor: 5 years; Sierra Leone: almost 5 years.

16 See Lambourne (2002) for a full explanation and justification for classifying the Khmer Rouge violence as genocide for the purposes of analysis of peacebuilding, justice and reconciliation.

17 *Nahe biti* refers to the symbolic rolling out of a mat as a venue to discuss and settle an issue among interested parties through consensus (Babo-Soares 2005). The process involved voluntary acceptance of culpability and agreement on reconciliation acts such as reparation, community service or public apology, and was usually finalised with a symbolic exchange of 'betel nut' ceremony to show sincerity and commitment (Lambourne 2010b).

18 I subsequently returned to Cambodia in 2009 and conducted interviews in Phnom Penh and six rural locations: Kompong Thom, Battambang, Prey Veng, Anlong Veng, Kampot

and Kompong Speu. I interviewed NGOs in Phnom Penh, attended NGO-organised outreach sessions in rural areas, and the first day of Duch's trial at the ECCC.

19 Further details about these research projects, their methodologies, limitations and findings can be found in Lambourne (2002, 2008, 2010a, 2010b, 2012).

20 See Lambourne (2002: 297–307) for an overview of this evidence.

21 The population of Rwanda comprises approximately 85 per cent Hutu, 14 per cent Tutsi and 1 per cent Twa ethnic groups.

22 Whilst this model risks trying to include too much and thus becoming analytically overstretched and impractical, I believe it is important nonetheless to develop a theory that encourages practitioners to be inclusive and mindful of the complexity of human needs and responses in order to avoid the tendency to oversimplify and impose limited or one-size-fits-all solutions.

23 See also David Crocker (2000: 109–18), who analyses the potential role and dangers of involving civil society both domestically and internationally in the establishment and implementation of transitional justice.

Bibliography

Babo-Soares, D. (2005) 'Nahe biti: Grassroots Reconciliation in East Timor' in Skaar, E., Gloppen, S. and Suhrke, A. (eds) Roads to Reconciliation, Lanham, MD: Lexington Books.

Boraine, A. and Valentine, S. (eds) (2006) Transitional Justice and Human Security, Cape Town: International Center for Transitional Justice.

Borer, T.A. (ed.) (2006) Telling the Truths: Truth Telling and Peace Building in Post-Conflict Societies, South Ben, IN: University of Notre Dame Press.

Braithwaite, J. (2003) 'Restorative Justice and a Better Future' in McLaughlin, E. et al (eds) Restorative Justice: Critical Issues, London: Sage Publications.

Cassese, A. (2003) 'The Establishment of International Criminal Tribunals' in Cassese, A., International Criminal Law, Oxford: Oxford University Press.

Clark, P. (2010) The Gacaca Courts, Post-Genocide Justice and Reconciliation in Rwanda: Justice without Lawyers, Cambridge: Cambridge University Press.

Crocker, D.A. (2000) 'Truth Commissions, Transitional Justice, and Civil Society' in Rotberg, R.I. and Thompson, D. (eds) Truth v. Justice: The Morality of Truth Commissions, Princeton, NJ: Princeton University Press.

Daly, K. (2000) 'Revisiting the Relationship between Retributive and Restorative Justice' in Strang, H. and Braithwaite, J. (eds) Restorative Justice: Philosophy to Practice, Aldershot: Ashgate Publishing.

Dinnen, S. (ed.) (2003) A Kind of Mending: Restorative Justice in the Pacific Islands, Canberra: ANU/Pandanus Press.

Finca, B. (2006) 'They treat the wounds of my people cheaply' in Boraine, A. and Valentine, S. (eds) Transitional Justice and Human Security, Cape Town: International Center for Transitional Justice.

Findlay, M. and Henham, R. (2005) Transforming International Criminal Justice: Retributive and Restorative Justice in the Trial Process, Uffculme: Willan Publishing.

Galtung, J. (1969) 'Violence, Peace and Peace Research', Journal of Peace Research, 6 (3): 166–92.

Hayner, P.B. (2010) Unspeakable Truths: Transitional Justice and the Challenge of Truth Commissions, 2nd edn, New York, NY: Routledge.

Isser, D. (ed.) (2011) Customary Justice and the Rule of Law in War-Torn Societies, Washington, DC: United States Institute of Peace Press.

Jeong, H.W. (2005) *Peacebuilding in Postconflict Societies: Strategy and Process*, London and Boulder, CO: Lynne Rienner.

Kritz, N.J. (ed.) (1995) *Transitional Justice: How Emerging Democracies Reckon with Former Regimes*, Vols I–III, Washington, DC: United States Institute of Peace Press.

Lambourne, W. (2002) 'Justice and Reconciliation: Post-Conflict Peacebuilding in Cambodia and Rwanda', unpublished thesis, University of Sydney.

——(2004) 'Post-Conflict Peacebuilding: Meeting Human Needs for Justice and Reconciliation', *Peace, Conflict and Development*, 4. Available at: <http://www.bradford.ac.uk/ssis/peace-conflict-and-development/issue-4> (accessed 8 May 2013).

——(2006) 'Justice in the Aftermath of Mass Crimes: International Law and Peacebuilding', in Dolgopol, U. and Gardam, J. (eds) *The Challenge of Conflict: International Law Responds*, Leiden: Martinus Nijhoff.

——(2008) 'Towards Sustainable Peace and Development in Sierra Leone: Civil Society and the Peacebuilding Commission', *Journal of Peacebuilding and Development*, 4: 47–59.

——(2010a) 'Transitional Justice After Mass Violence: Reconciling Retributive and Restorative Justice', in Irving, H., Mowbray J. and Walton, K. (eds) *Julius Stone: A Study in Influence*, Sydney: Federation Press.

——(2010b) 'Unfinished Business: The Commission for Reception, Truth and Reconciliation and Justice and Reconciliation in East Timor' in Barra, L.A. and Roper, S.D. (eds) *Development of Institutions of Human Rights*, London: Palgrave Macmillan.

——(2012) 'Outreach, Inreach and Civil Society Participation in Transitional Justice' in Palmer, N., Clark, P. and Granville, D. (eds) *Critical Perspectives in Transitional Justice*, Cambridge: Intersentia.

Lederach, J.P. (1997) *Building Peace: Sustainable Reconciliation in Divided Societies*, Washington, DC: United States Institute of Peace Press.

——(2000) 'Journey from Resolution to Transformative Peacebuilding' in Sampson, C. and Lederach, J.P. (eds) *From the Ground Up: Mennonite Contributions to International Peacebuilding*, Oxford: Oxford University Press.

——(2005) *The Moral Imagination: The Art and Soul of Building Peace*, Oxford: Oxford University Press.

Lutz, E. (2006) 'Transitional Justice: Lessons Learned and the Road Ahead' in Roht-Arriaza, N. and Mariezcurrena, J. (eds) *Transitional Justice in the Twenty-First Century: Beyond Truth versus Justice*, Cambridge: Cambridge University Press.

Mamdani, M. (2001) *When Victims Become Killers: Colonialism, Nativism, and the Genocide in Rwanda*, Princeton, NJ: Princeton University Press.

Mani, R. (2002) *Beyond Retribution: Seeking Justice in the Shadows of War*, Cambridge: Polity Press.

——(2007) 'Does Power Trump Morality? Reconciliation or Transitional Justice' in Hughes, E., Schabas, W.A. and Thakur, R. (eds) *Atrocities and International Accountability: Beyond Transitional Justice*, Tokyo/New York, NY: United Nations University Press.

Molenaar, A. (2005) *Gacaca: Grassroots Justice After Genocide: The Key to Reconciliation in Rwanda?* African Studies Centre Research Report No. 77, Leiden: African Studies Centre.

Parmentier, S. (2003) 'Global Justice in the Aftermath of Mass Violence. The Role of the International Criminal Court in Dealing with Political Crimes', *International Annals of Criminology*, 41: 203–24.

Quinn, J.R. (2005) 'The Role of Informal Mechanisms in Transitional Justice', paper presented at Canadian Political Science Association Annual Meeting, June 2005. Available at: <http://cpas-acsp.ca/papers-2005/Quinn.pdf> (accessed 21 January 2013).

Reychler, L. (2006) 'Challenges of Peace Research', *International Journal of Peace Studies*, 11: 1–16.

Roht-Arriaza, N. and Mariezcurrena, J. (eds) (2006) *Transitional Justice in the Twenty-First Century: Beyond Truth versus Justice*, Cambridge: Cambridge University Press.

Romano, C.P.R., Nollkaemper, A. and Kleffner, J.K. (eds) (2004) *Internationalized Criminal Courts: Sierra Leone, East Timor, Kosovo, and Cambodia*, Oxford: Oxford University Press.

Schabas, W.A. and Darcy, S. (eds) (2004) *Truth Commissions and Courts: The Tension Between Criminal Justice and the Search for Truth*, Dordrecht: Kluwer Law Publishers.

Schiff, B.N. (2008) *Building the International Criminal Court*, Cambridge: Cambridge University Press.

Sriram, S.L. and Pillay, S. (eds) (2009) *Peace versus Justice? The Dilemma of Transitional Justice in Africa*, Scottsville: University of Kwa-Zulu Natal Press.

Stover, E. and Weinstein, H.M. (eds) (2004) *My Neighbor, My Enemy: Justice and Community in the Aftermath of Mass Atrocity*, Cambridge: Cambridge University Press.

Sutherland, J. (2005) *Worldview Skills: Transforming Conflict from the Inside Out*, Canada: Worldview Strategies.

Teitel, R.G. (2000) *Transitional Justice*, Oxford and New York, NY: Oxford University Press.

Tombot, J. (2003) 'A Marriage of Custom and Introduced Skills, Restorative Justice Bougainville Style' in Dinnen, S. (ed.) *A Kind of Mending: Restorative Justice in the Pacific Islands*, Canberra: ANU/Pandanus Press.

Tutu, D. (1999) *No Future Without Forgiveness*, London: Rider.

United Nations Security Council (2001) 'Statement by the President of the Security Council', UN Doc. S/PRST/2001/5, 20 February 2001.

——(2004) 'The Rule of Law and Transitional Justice in Conflict and Post-Conflict Societies', Report of the Secretary General, UN Doc. S/2004/616, 24 August 2004.

van Zyl, P. (2005) 'Promoting Transitional Justice in Post-Conflict Societies' in Bryden, A. and Hänggi, H. (eds) *Security Governance in Post-Conflict Peacebuilding*, Münster: LIT Verlag.

Waldorf, L. (2006) 'Mass Justice for Mass Atrocity: Rethinking Local Justice as Transitional Justice', *Temple Law Review*, 79: 1.

Williams, P.R. and Sharf, M.P. (2002) *Peace with Justice? War Crimes and Accountability in the Former Yugoslavia*, London: Rowman & Littlefield.

Zehr, H. (1990) *Changing Lenses: A New Focus for Crime and Justice*, Scottdale, PA: Herald Press.

Chapter 2

Rethinking reconciliation in divided societies

A social learning theory of transitional justice[1]

Nevin T. Aiken

Alongside their primary role in providing accountability for gross human rights violations, transitional justice interventions have gained growing recognition in recent years as key components of broader peacebuilding and reconciliation efforts in societies recovering from legacies of gross human rights violations.[2] In particular, an increasing number of studies suggest that some form of transitional justice intervention may in fact be a necessary, if not sufficient, component of reconciliation processes in those societies that have been 'deeply divided' by past histories of internal violence committed between ethnic, national, political or religious identity groups (Fletcher and Weinstein 2002; Long and Brecke 2003; Gibson 2004; Stover and Weinstein 2004; Drumbl 2007; Aiken 2009; Lambourne 2009; Aiken 2010, 2013; Arthur 2010). However, existing understandings of the causal mechanisms that link transitional justice interventions to reconciliation in deeply divided societies continue to remain largely underspecified and under-theorised.[3]

As a way to begin theorising the relationship between transitional justice and reconciliation, I contend that greater attention must first be paid to exploring how these justice interventions interact with the politics of identity underlying intergroup violence. Indeed, recent insights from the growing body of 'conflict transformation' scholarship drawn from the related areas of research such as peace studies, conflict resolution, and political science have highlighted the central role that antagonistic perceptions of collective identity necessarily play in the commission and perpetuation of mass violence and gross human rights violations in divided societies. As a result, this literature has underscored the necessity of altering the antagonistic nature of these identities and the hostile system of relationships and belief systems associated with them to achieve lasting societal reconciliation and sustainable peace (Lederach 1997; Kelman 1999, 2001, 2004; Bar-Tal 2000; Bar-Siman-Tov 2004).

By opening a new line of dialogue between the conflict transformation literature and the field of transitional justice, I theorise that transitional justice interventions will contribute to reconciliation to the degree that they are able to serve as crucial catalysts for social and psychological processes of 'social learning' between former enemies in the post-conflict environment of divided societies. In essence, I contend that it is these learning processes through which former enemies can be brought to challenge – and potentially transform – the collective animosities and antagonistic identifications underpinning past abuses and thereby serve as the crucial 'linchpins' in the causal path linking transitional justice and reconciliation in divided societies. More specifically, it is argued that those transitional justice interventions that will be most successful in advancing reconciliation will be those that are able to work to promote interrelated processes of instrumental, socio-emotional, and distributive forms of 'social learning' among former antagonists – all of which have been identified in the conflict transformation literature as being necessary, if not sufficient, conditions for reconciliation in deeply divided societies (Nadler *et al* 2008).

Transitional justice and reconciliation in divided societies

Divided societies such as Rwanda, the former Yugoslavia, Northern Ireland or South Africa are characterised by the presence of deep societal cleavages centred on perceived divisions of collective ethnic, national, religious or political identity. In deeply divided societies, these collective or group identifications can take on a 'monolithic quality' and come to permeate all facets of social, economic, and political life (Lederach 1997; Bar-Tal 2000; Coleman 2002; Gibson 2004; Kriesberg 2004; Oberschall 2007; Arthur 2010). Furthermore, interactions between identity groups are often characterised by the presence of negative stereotypes and prejudice as well as relationships marked by distrust, fear, animosity and an underlying devaluation of the Other (Ryan 1995, 2007; Lederach 1997; Oberschall 2007). The human rights violations to which transitional justice interventions are called to respond in divided societies are, by their very nature, therefore often committed as part of broader 'community identity conflicts' motivated by these collective antagonisms (Azar 1990; Kriesberg 1998; Gibson 2004; Stover and Weinstein 2004; Drumbl 2007; Eriksen 2001; Aiken 2010, 2013). Indeed, what distinguishes acts of 'intergroup mass violence' in divided societies (such as mass repression, genocide, 'ethnic cleansing' and other gross human rights violations) is that they are inherently carried out by 'individuals who injure, kill and murder' not because of the individual characteristics of their victims but rather because of their perceived membership in a denigrated identity group (Staub and Bar-Tal 2003: 710).

The onset of overt physical violence can itself increase polarisation and deepen existing antagonisms between identity groups in divided societies, resulting in the creation of protracted and seemingly intractable communal identity conflicts (Northrup 1989; Kriesberg 1998; Bar-Tal 2000; Aiken 2008). Violence has been shown to break down meaningful contact and communication between identity groups, thereby destroying essential networks of trust and reciprocity that enable more cooperative intergroup interactions (Colletta and Cullen 2000: 4; Shirlow 2001; Oberschall 2007). This distancing, in turn, limits the potential for groups to challenge their existing negative perceptions of one another by fostering mutual ignorance, suspicion, prejudice, and negative stereotypes (Gross-Stein 2002: 294; Tausch et al 2007). The experience of violence has also been linked to a reduction in the ability for members of divided groups to empathise with one another and, in extreme cases, can contribute to a 'dehumanisation' of the Other that lifts moral restraints against the future commission of violence (Duster 1971; Staub 1989, 2001, 2006; Fein 1999; Staub and Bar-Tal 2003). Further, over the course of identity-based violence, groups can develop antagonistic myths, collective memories or biased communal beliefs regarding responsibility for past violence that can further polarise and ossify communal relationships (Bar-Tal 2003; Cairns and Roe 2003; Devine-Wright 2003).

However, while these factors can contribute to making identity-based conflicts in deeply divided societies notoriously difficult to resolve, research has shown this does not mean that these animosities are inevitable or that they cannot ultimately be reconciled and replaced by more peaceable relations.[4] Reconciliation can be defined as 'transforming the relations between rival sides from hostility and resentment to friendly and harmonious relations', a long-term endeavour that requires former antagonists to 'form new relations of peaceful coexistence based on mutual trust and acceptance, cooperation, and consideration of each other's needs' (Bar-Siman-Tov 2004: 72). Understood in this way, reconciliation is a fundamentally transformative process, one that ultimately requires 'changing the motivations, goals, beliefs, attitudes, and emotions of the great majority of society members regarding the conflict, the nature of the relationship between the parties, and the parties themselves' (Bar-Tal and Bennink 2004: 12).

This conception underpins a growing body of recent conflict transformation scholarship which contends that reconciliation after periods of mass group-based violence in divided societies must therefore necessarily include a degree of positive 'social learning' between former antagonists; namely, 'an active process of redefinition or reinterpretation of reality – what people consider real, possible, and desirable – on the basis of new causal and normative knowledge' (Adler and Barnett 1998: 43; Bar-Siman-Tov 2004; Aiken 2010, 2013). In essence, such reconciliatory social learning involves social and psychological processes that engage former enemies in challenging and redefining the antagonistic identities and belief systems that motivated past violence and which can replace these with more positive relationships and understandings (Lederach 1997; Kelman 1999, 2001, 2004; Miall et al 2000; Coleman 2002; Bar-Siman-Tov 2004; Bar-Tal and Bennink 2004). Indeed, as Herbert Kelman argues, given that collective identity is a prime contributor to violent conflicts in divided societies, so too will it necessarily have to be transformed through the processes of social learning processes ultimately required for reconciliation. As he contends, 'identities have to change, at least tacitly, if protracted identity conflicts are to be settled and, certainly, if they are to be resolved in a way that transforms the relationship and opens the way to reconciliation' (Kelman 2001: 194).

A social learning theory of transitional justice

It has been recognised that the post-conflict period brings with it a unique 'transformative moment' for reconciliation in divided societies, as the end of widespread conflict can offer an initial opportunity, however difficult, for former enemies to begin to redefine their antagonistic identifications and relationships (Vayryen 1999; Coleman 2002; Eder *et al* 2002; Jeong 2005). I theorise that transitional justice interventions may be uniquely situated to serve as sites of social learning in such transformative moments as they often provide the first, and sometimes only, societal venue in which former antagonists are brought together in the post-conflict environment to confront the legacies of past violence and to reconsider the nature of their relations with the Other (Aiken 2009, 2010, 2013). In this way, I contend that it may be these crucial processes of social learning that ultimately serve as the central causal links mediating the relationship between transitional justice and reconciliation in divided societies.

To be clear, this is not to make the overly ambitious claim that transitional justice interventions represent a 'magic bullet', that they will in and of themselves be able to foster lasting intergroup reconciliation in divided societies. Rather, it is argued that these interventions have the potential to serve as catalysts for the social and psychological processes through which former enemies can come to alter their perceptions and the nature of their relations with one another, and through this social learning, begin to create the conditions necessary to reconciliation and sustainable peace in divided societies.[5] However, this still leaves a number of questions as to what particular forms of social learning may be needed for reconciliation in divided societies and, more specifically, what role transitional justice interventions might play in advancing these processes. A recent 'state of the art' collection of conflict transformation work on intergroup relations suggests that reconciliation in deeply divided societies may ultimately require transitional justice interventions that are capable of promoting a combination of three distinct forms of social learning (Nadler *et al* 2008; Aiken 2010, 2013).

The first of these social learning processes, *instrumental learning*, refers to the use of interventions designed to engage former antagonists in sustained cooperative interaction in the post-conflict period, through which they can begin to transform their relationships with one another and 'gradually learn to replace enmity with trust and negative with positive perceptions of the

Other' (Nadler *et al* 2008: 138). *Socioemotional learning*, by way of contrast, involves interventions designed to directly confront the emotional and perceptual legacies of past violence as a means of breaking down obstacles to reconciliation caused by existing feelings of victimisation, guilt, distrust, and fear between divided groups (Nadler *et al* 2008: 5). As Arie Nadler and Nurit Shnabel illustrate:

> socioemotional reconciliation is focused on the past of the conflict and asserts that the key to a reconciled future lies in a constructive confrontation with the painful past [whereas] efforts of instrumental reconciliation are focused on the present and are based on the premise that ongoing cooperation between the adversaries in the present will result in a reconciled future
>
> (Nadler and Shnabel 2008: 44)

Lastly, reconciliatory social learning in deeply divided societies will also ultimately require elements of what might be termed *distributive learning* – interventions designed to ameliorate existing structural and material inequalities between divided groups that might otherwise continue to sustain intergroup antagonisms even in the absence of overt physical violence. In essence, it is recognised that alongside instrumental and socioemotional learning, ultimately 'the move to peaceful intergroup relations hinges on ensuring that the adversarial groups perceive equality of opportunities to procure material and social resources' (Nadler *et al* 2008: 10).[6]

  That said, while the distinction between instrumental, socioemotional, and distributive learning processes offers a useful entry point for beginning to theorise the link between transitional justice and reconciliation, it still falls short of operationalising the specific means by which these broader categories of social learning might be advanced in practice to promote intergroup reconciliation. This operationalisation remains crucial to considering how the particular design of transitional justice interventions and the strategies they employ might serve to impede or impel processes of social learning and, in so doing, either detract from or contribute to advancing the potential for reconciliation in divided societies. Drawing on a synthesis of insights derived from recent work in the fields of conflict transformation and transitional justice, five 'subcategories' of interventions are identified as being necessary, if not sufficient, mechanisms through which transitional justice interventions might engender the kinds of instrumental, socioemotional, and distributive learning ultimately required to advance reconciliation in divided societies.

Instrumental learning

The first category of social learning, 'instrumental learning', refers to interventions that focus on rebuilding relationships and interactions that can foster less antagonistic perceptions between formerly divided groups. In particular, a renewal of positive contact and communication between former antagonists that extends across group boundaries are often identified as being among the most crucial interventions required to advance reconciliation in the post-conflict environment of divided societies. However, a review of the conflict transformation literature indicates that an increase in the quantity of positive intergroup interactions, while important, does not itself prove a potent enough challenge to polarised identifications and entrenched animosities formed through past violence. What matters most for social learning, these scholars suggest, is the nature and quality of the interactions and communication that take place and the societal context in which they occur.

Positive intergroup contact

The argument that increased contact can lead to better relations among groups in conflict is the central assertion underlying the longstanding 'contact hypothesis' in social psychology. In its most basic incarnation, this theory holds that an increase in intergroup contact, if undertaken under certain conditions and in specific contexts, will lead to an improvement in intergroup relations by reducing misperceptions and negative stereotypes of the Other (Hewstone and Brown 1986; Pettigrew 1998). More specifically, to be 'positive' and to have a beneficial impact on group relations, contact must be of a non-adversarial quality, must take place between groups afforded equal status in society, must ideally be conducted over an extended period of time, and must be undertaken in the pursuit of cooperative or superordinate goals which actively aim to transform group divides (Brewer and Gaertner 2001; Stephan and Stephan 2001). Additionally, to be of greatest effect, such contact must take place in a context marked by supportive institutional structures, the agreement of relevant authorities, and a broader social and normative climate conducive to improved intergroup relations (Hewstone and Brown 1986). Even outside of these optimal conditions, however, scholars have indicated the potential benefits of developing personal friendships and initiating even 'superficial' or 'indirect' positive contact across group boundaries, suggesting that these efforts might have 'ripple effects' that can spread throughout a group (Hewstone et al 2005: 19).

Indeed, a substantial body of experimental and empirical research undertaken by social psychologists indicates that positive contact can have an independent effect on improving intergroup relations, as it directly reduces prejudice, challenges misperceptions, and breaks down rigidified perceptions of the Other as a monolithic and inherently hostile group (Kenworthy et al 2005; Hewstone et al 2005; Tausch et al 2007). Further, this kind of positive contact has been directly linked within the social psychological literature to the formation of more inclusive collective identities – a process that greatly reduces discriminatory bias and prejudice. Indeed, the work of Samuel

Gaertner and his colleagues on the 'Common Ingroup Identity Model' shows that the experience of positive contact can help to "transform members' cognitive representations of their memberships from separate groups to one more inclusive group ... [essentially] from 'us' and 'them' to a more inclusive 'we'" in which positive feelings, equal moral standards, and cooperative behaviour are more likely to prevail (Gaertner et al 1994: 22; Gaertner and Dovidio 2000).

Beyond its own independent role as a means of overcoming prejudice and hostility, the restoration of contact is also widely theorised as a primary process upon which other factors integral to social learning and reconciliation rely (Staub 2006). For instance, the opportunity for meaningful intergroup dialogue and communication is intrinsically dependent on renewed interaction between divided groups. Similarly, a renewal of positive contact seems an essential starting point for the development of mutual trust between former enemies following the end of violence. Indeed, the formation of lasting trust requires a history of positive reciprocal interaction that allows actors to develop reasonable expectations of the Other's future behaviour – patterns that themselves depend on the initial renewal of contact and the extension of more constructive relations beyond group boundaries (Ryan 1995, 2007; Kelman 2004). Other authors have cited the renewal of positive 'encounters' as the primary way in which former enemies can come to understand one another's perspectives and develop the shared sense of empathy necessary to restoring an equitable moral community in the wake of mass violence (Staub and Bar-Tal 2003). In effect, such encounters become the vital first step in processes of 'rehumanisation' means by which enemies begin to see members of the 'Other' as people entitled to the same rights and protections as the 'Self', and to challenge the 'reversal of morality' that legitimised the use of intergroup violence in the past and could threaten to do so again if left unaddressed (Staub 2001: 162).

This review suggests that it may therefore be of key importance that transitional justice interventions in divided societies incorporate mechanisms of positive contact into their strategies in order to promote the kind of instrumental learning required for reconciliation. In particular, the strategies employed by these institutions may need to allow for periods of direct or indirect encounter between former enemies during which as many of the conditional and contextual conditions of positive contact as possible can be met. It may be equally imperative that these strategies create a relatively supportive or at least neutral environment in which such encounters can take place, as studies show that contact which is adversarial, threatening or initiated under conditions of high anxiety is extremely unlikely to reduce prejudice and negative stereotypes and may in fact even serve to reinforce such biases (Kenworthy et al 2005; Tausch et al 2007). Additionally, if the interactions these strategies produce among former enemies are predominantly adversarial instead of cooperative, it is doubtful whether this contact will be of the type conducive to building mutual trust, rehumanising the Other, and patterning the kind of relations on which more positive social learning can be based.

Transformative dialogue

As important as renewed interaction might be for providing a basis on which new identities and more cooperative relationships can be built, it is clear that simple contact, while significant, is only a first step towards meaningful social learning in divided societies. What is of equal importance is the *content* of such interaction and, in particular, whether it can ultimately provide the basis for a second stage of meaningful dialogue and communication extending across group boundaries (Stephan and Stephan 2001; Ellis 2006). The breakdown of meaningful intergroup communication over the course of conflict limits opportunities for dialogue and understanding and provides an environment in which biases, misconceptions, and cognitive distortions about Self and Other can flourish (Abu-Nimer *et al* 2001; Maoz 2004). Accordingly, a renewal of this kind of 'bridging' communication among former enemies in the post-conflict environment has been cited as a key mechanism underlying the potential for future reconciliation (Rothman 1997; Fisher 2001; Ropers 2004; Ellis 2006).

Indeed, a number of scholars working within the conflict transformation field have argued for the importance of intergroup dialogue in challenging the antagonistic perceptions of the Other developed over the course of past violence in divided societies. Jay Rothman, for instance, notes the particular need for engaging former enemies in processes of 'reflexive dialogue' in order to allow prior combatants to reframe their understandings of their own and each other's identities, suggesting that this can foster empathy and a sense of similarity between Self and Other in terms of basic values and needs (Rothman 1997: 234). Similarly, Donald Ellis has argued in favour of 'transformative communication' in the wake of intergroup violence to 'widen the circle of identity inclusion', reduce entrenched biases and prejudice, and promote the kind of 'moral growth' in which practices of dehumanisation are replaced by feelings of empathy and a mutual recognition of the Other's humanity (Ellis 2006: 129). Lastly, other scholars such as Tamar Hermann have argued that a precondition for reconciliation is 'the need to open channels, or space, for direct and candid communication between the protagonists', to create a 'dialogical space' in which former enemies are brought together to critically reassess the images they hold of one another and the nature of their shared relationship (Hermann 2004: 58).

Ultimately, what all of these authors share is a recognition of the crucial importance of this kind of transformative dialogue to the processes of 'identity negotiation' needed for reconciliatory social learning in the aftermath of protracted identity conflicts (Kelman 2001). In effect, alongside positive contact, intergroup dialogue is held to be the necessary mechanism through which groups can begin to 'unfreeze' the rigidified perceptions about the Other that informed past conflict, and the means by which former enemies might come to transform these understandings and construct more inclusive and more peaceable conceptions of their identities (Northrup 1989; Kelman 1999, 2001, 2004; Abu-Nimer *et al* 2001). Empirically, these assertions have been largely borne out by authors testing the impact of 'interactive conflict resolution' strategies, 'dialogue groups', and 'problem-solving work-shops', all programmes that have achieved some success in bringing together former enemies to engage in processes of critical communication (Rothman 1997; Kelman 1999; Fisher 2001; Ropers 2004). However, to date, these insights have not explicitly been considered in the design of transitional justice interventions.

Much like provisions for positive contact, there are, however, conditions and contexts in which this kind of reflexive dialogue is more likely to be effective in transforming entrenched perceptions. These factors are of parti-cular importance in considering how the benefits of communication could be incorporated into transitional justice strategies. In particular, the quality of the interaction is especially significant, because if the communication facili-tated by the transitional justice process is of an antagonistic or adversarial nature, it will likely not work to positively transform existing identities and expectations. This suggests the importance of supportive inbuilt forums in institutional structures for encouraging reconciliatory forms of communica-tion. Indeed, dialogue processes between recent enemies should be carefully mediated and monitored – what Ellis refers to as 'controlled commu-nication' – and it is therefore critical to design justice strategies around providing opportunities for these appropriately facilitated encounters (Ellis 2006: 143). In addition, the recognition that communication must occur over a longer period of time suggests that provisions be included to secure ongoing intergroup dialogue after the often-limited 'one-off' timeframes of formal justice interventions themselves are complete. As Norbert Ropers has argued, while it may be necessary to begin by anchoring such processes in an institutional structure, to ensure the stability of future peace it may be of equal importance to also establish enduring and self-sustaining processes of intergroup communication (Ropers 2004: 186).

However, it is clear that these processes cannot be limited to the small number of individuals who have the chance to interact directly with formal transitional justice institutions if they are to have a sustainable impact on reconciliation at wider group or societal levels. Accordingly, transitional interventions may therefore need to consider how they might establish mul-tiple opportunities for transformative dialogue throughout the target society as part of their work, including in local communities, between elites, and at a broader societal level (Lederach 1997; Stover and Weinstein 2004). Indeed, a particularly important aspect of transitional justice interventions capable of fostering instrumental learning may be their ability to engage the local populations in which they work by ensuring that their institutions, processes and findings remain open, accessible and disseminated to the wider public. This can provide a crucial opportunity for transitional justice interventions to foster a wider 'societal dialogue' about past abuses that allow former enemies living in divided societies to hear one another's perspectives and stories, often for the first time – a process that may be essential to altering antagonistic identifications and restoring the sense of empathy ultimately needed to rehumanise the Other (Minow 1999; Gibson 2004; Rushton 2006). In part, this may be why the public nature of transitional justice interventions seems of particular importance to their ability to advance reconciliation, as it can provide the means for such transformative dialogue to be extended in order to engage the broader society in crucial processes of social learning about both past and future Self/Other relations (Aiken 2010, 2013).

Socioemotional learning

While contact and communication may be required to help build more inclusive intergroup relations among former enemies, reconciliation in deeply divided societies is likely to remain elusive if there is not also some attempt to come to terms with the history of past violence. Indeed, the ways in which transitional authorities choose to acknowledge and provide accountability for past abuses may be crucial to processes of social learning as such issues, if left unaddressed, can serve to maintain hostile relations and antagonistic identifications even in the absence of overt violence. In particular, there is an emerging consensus among scholars working within the fields of both conflict transformation and transitional justice that reconciliation and in the aftermath of violence may require an element of 'justice' that formally recognises responsibilities wrongs committed during past violence and seeks in some way to acknowledge and repair the injustices done to the principal victims. Further, there is a parallel recognition among many scholars within both of these fields regarding the importance of providing an accounting of the 'truth' about what took place between former antagonists in order to limit the potential that the past might be appropriated to serve as the basis for the kind of myth, propaganda or discriminatory history that might spark future returns to violence. The next section discusses each of these mechanisms in turn and considers their relation to social learning and reconciliation in order to draw implications for the design of transitional justice interventions in deeply divided societies.

Justice: accountability and acknowledgement

The provision of justice has been widely recognised by scholars working within the fields of both conflict transformation and transitional justice as a necessary, if not sufficient, condition for intergroup reconciliation in societies divided by past histories of intergroup violence (Lederach 1997; Minow 1999; Lerche 2000; Biggar 2001; Kriesberg 2001, 2004; Fletcher and Weinstein 2002; Gibson 2004; Goldstone 2004; Stover and Weinstein 2004). Indeed, a number of prominent authors in these fields have argued that justice is inextricably linked with the potential for sustainable peace in the post-conflict environment, noting that in the long journey towards reconciliation between former enemies 'the passage from negative to positive peace runs through justice' (Miall *et al* 2000: 208). In particular, many of these authors have warned against the inherent dangers of adopting strategies of 'oblivion' or 'impunity' in post-conflict societies, as victims have shown little inclination to simply 'forgive and forget' experiences of past violence and such grievances can provide fertile ground for future returns to conflict (Staub 1989; Minow 1999; Bar-Tal and Bennink 2004).

While great division exists within these literatures as to which 'type' of justice is most effective in addressing past abuses and as to what specific form justice interventions should take, there is nonetheless widespread agreement about the need for transitional authorities to act in some way to reduce the sense of injustice felt by victims in order to reduce communal antagonisms in the post-conflict environment of divided societies (Rigby 2001; Fletcher and Weinstein 2002; Gibson 2002, 2004; Goldstone 2004; Ross 2004; Stover and Weinstein 2004). As Nigel Biggar has argued, any sense of injustice has the tendency to fester among victims if left unaddressed, and this 'help[s] to infect future generations with an indiscriminate hatred of the perpetrators and their descendants – and also with an endemic mistrust of the state that, having failed in its duty to vindicate victims past, seems ready to tolerate the injury of victims future' (Biggar 2001: 8). By the same token, scholars also recognise that the kind of justice employed in transitional societies must necessarily be 'partial' if it is to contribute to reconciliation. In essence, this requires forgoing the total retribution of unrestrained revenge in favour of more tempered accountability that will not simply become another component in the cycle of injury and counter-injury between former antagonists that could further retrench existing societal divisions (Lederach 1997; Minow 1999; Long and Brecke 2003: 30).

There are several ways in which scholars working within the fields of conflict transformation and transitional justice suggest that the provision of justice could have an independent effect on promoting the kind of socio-emotional learning needed to advance reconciliation in divided societies. First, acknowledging injustices done to victims and holding perpetrators accountable can be processes of critical importance in symbolising a shift in the normative ethos of post-conflict societies and in delegitimizing violence against the Other (Teitel 2002; Ross 2004; Chinapen and Vernon 2006). In this capacity, justice can serve as a 'bridge' between a society's divisive past and its more inclusive future, signalling an expansion of the boundaries of moral and political community and an extension of equal rights and protections across previous communal divides (Lerche 2000; Mani 2001, 2002; Teitel 2002). Second, by indicating that the use of violence will no longer be permitted as a means of resolving conflict between groups, justice also provides expectations of more cooperative intergroup relations in the future, thereby providing the minimal basis on which mutual trust might develop between former antagonists (Jeong 2005; Santa-Barbara 2007). Third, by directly acknowledging the injustice of past violence, the experience of justice can also begin to reduce feelings of victimisation and animosity linked to collective identities that, if left unaddressed, could threaten to reignite conflict (Minow 1999; Mani 2001). Lastly, several scholars have noted that the recognition of dignity and basic moral worth afforded by processes of justice may be vital to victims' healing and therefore a key determinant of their future willingness to engage in reconciliation with the Other (Zehr 1990; Lederach 1997; Minow 1999; Staub and Bar-Tal 2003; Bar-Tal and Bennink 2004; Jeong 2005).

Truth recovery

Aside from justice, a number of scholars have posited that coming to terms with the past also requires an attempt to establish the 'truth' between former antagonists about past events in order for post-conflict societies to achieve reconciliation and sustainable peace (Hayner 1994, 2002; Lederach 1997; Minow 1999; Kiss 2000; Lerche 2000; Miall *et al* 2000; Gibson 2002, 2004, 2006; Imbleau 2004; Kriesberg 2004; Llewellyn 2006; Rushton 2006; Brahm 2007; Kelman 2008) Indeed, as Tristan Anne Borer has noted, within the transitional justice literature there now exists a 'near unanimity among most scholars, as well as practitioners, that societies coming out of periods of violence must in some way examine, acknowledge, and account for violence committed by various groups in order to move forward' (Borer 2006: 4). However, for the most part, these authors tend to discount the simplistic argument that uncovering a factual record of the past can itself bring about more peaceful relations (the assumption that 'revealing is healing') and suggest instead that truth recovery processes are only one required element of broader transitional justice processes needed for reconciliation (Adam and Moodley 2005; Brahm 2007). Further, there is acknowledgement that the truth uncovered by such mechanisms in the wake of mass violence will never be factually complete or all-encompassing, and at best will amount to a highly selective or 'representative truth' of the causes and scope of past atrocity and the roles played by former antagonists (Hayner 2002; Imbleau 2004; Rushton 2006; Chapman and Ball 2008). Nonetheless, throughout much of the transitional justice literature there is a recognition that truth recovery may represent an element vital to reconciliation as it can help to 'narrow the range of permissible lies' that could otherwise potentially be appropriated in the future to reignite conflict or sustain communal antagonisms (Ignatieff 1998).

However, despite the importance placed on recovering the truth, the exact causal connection thought to exist between truth and reconciliation remains largely underexplored by transitional justice scholars. While a strong correlation between the two has been proposed, explanations of this connection have been critiqued for being largely based on anecdotal evidence with very few sustained theoretical or empirical studies as support (Hamber 2001; Rushton 2006; Brahm 2007).[7] In particular, little attention has been given as to how truth recovery is able to make a positive contribution to the social and psychological components of identity negotiation and social learning highlighted as being essential to reconciliation by conflict transformation scholars – an oversight which is likely due, in large part, to the limited dialogue which has existed to date between these two areas of scholarship.

By synthesising insights from these fields, I contend that the establishment of 'truth' may contribute to social learning primarily by helping to overcome antagonistic belief systems formed through the experience of past violence in divided societies. Indeed, in the aftermath of violence in deeply divided societies former enemies are therefore likely to have widely divergent views about the 'truth' of past events, as each group bases its interpretations upon its own inevitably biased and exclusionary beliefs about the past (Cairns and Roe 2003; Devine-Wright 2003). These beliefs can work to maintain an oversimplified understanding of in-group/out-group relations, casting all members of the Other as responsible for the evils of past abuses and therefore as intractable enemies and legitimate targets for future intergroup violence (Staub 1989, 2000, 2001, 2006; Azar 1990; Cairns and Roe 2003; Devine-Wright 2003; Staub and Bar-Tal 2003). Noted social psychologist Daniel Bar-Tal has written extensively about the dynamics surrounding the formation of such belief systems in divided societies, suggesting that:

> [o]ver the years, groups involved in conflict selectively form collective memories about the conflict. One the one hand, they focus mainly on the other side's responsibility for the outbreak and continuation of the conflict and its misdeeds, violence and atrocities; on the other hand, they concentrate on their own self-justification, self-righteousness, glorification, and victimization.
>
> (Bar-Tal 2003: 78)

Once formed, these 'collective memories', in turn, are actively institutionalised and maintained by groups over the course of conflict and become socialised through cultural and political channels and transmitted to future generations, eventually coming to colour all aspects of intergroup relations and forming a central component of antagonistic group identities (Bar-Tal

2003: 78). Psychologist John Mack has dubbed such processes the 'egoism of victimization', illustrating how the perpetuation of these hostile communal narratives can effectively ensure that fear, threat, and negative stereotypes continue to divide groups long after the initial cessation of violence (Mack 1990: 124). As Mack notes, if left unchallenged these biased beliefs can continue to preclude any chance for intergroup reconciliation by limiting the potential for the kind of social learning needed to develop new understanding, trust, and empathy between former antagonists – in essence, 'stand [ing] rigidly in the way of new information that might provide a correcting view to the prevailing group dichotomization' (Mack 1990: 124).

Accordingly, I propose that perhaps the most important aspects of establishing a truthful accounting of the past for social learning may be the ability of these new narratives to facilitate a critical re-examination of the biased collective memories preventing the development of more positive identifications among former enemies. Indeed, as William Long and Peter Brecke have noted, truth recovery processes can provide the space for the dissemination of new information needed by former enemies to transcend existing antagonisms and their own preoccupations with victimisation and 'begin a process of redefinition of identity of the [O]ther from enemy to potential partner in a negotiated settlement and common new future' (Long and Brecke 2003: 149). In this way, while truth recovery may not in and of itself be enough to achieve social learning, it nonetheless 'plays a critical, perhaps indispensible role in the process of national reconciliation and contributes directly and indirectly to the redefinition of identity' which is itself essential to attaining this goal (Long and Brecke 2003: 69).[8] Truth recovery, understood as a process of social learning, therefore becomes an integral component of the ongoing 'negotiation of identity' needed for reconciliation in the post-conflict transformative moment, as it both helps to 'unfreeze' antagonistic perceptions of identity and to transform hostile relationships between former enemies rigidified by the memories of past violence (Bar-Tal 2000; Kelman 2001; Gibson 2002, 2004, 2006; Stanley 2002; Staub and Bar-Tal 2003; Bar-Tal and Bennink 2004; Imbleau 2004; Rushton 2006).

Transitional justice institutions can be essential to this process, as they often serve as the initial forums for post-conflict truth recovery in divided societies, providing the mechanism with which a new official shared understanding of the past can be built (Minow 1999; Kiss 2000; Gibson 2004; Borer 2006). Indeed, the mandate of most truth commission processes employed to date has been one of discovering, clarifying, and formally composing an official historical record of periods of past violence (Hayner 1994, 2002). However, it is likely that for this new understanding of the past to be widely accepted and to thereby contribute to intergroup reconciliation, these institutions and the truth they produce must be viewed as legitimate by all parties involved in past conflict. It is, therefore, essential to include all groups in the process of gathering the truth and shaping the historical record to avoid the perception that the new narrative simply represents the biased viewpoint of the victors – a perception which would only further entrench division and feelings of victimisation (Imbleau 2004). Indeed, there is evidence to suggest that it is not truth per se, but the 'moderating truth' that comes from mutual acknowledgement of complicity in past conflict that may be the essential ingredient in dismantling understandings of the Other as an essentially evil and intractable foe (Gibson 2002, 2004, 2006).[9]

Distributive learning

It is, however, increasingly evident that the kind of social learning required for reconciliation cannot simply be limited to changes in existing social interactions, cognitive perceptions, or understandings of the past. Indeed, a strong recognition has emerged among both conflict transformation scholars that such efforts must also be matched by concrete material and structural changes in the day-to-day lives of individuals in divided societies (Azar 1990; Lederach 1997; Miall *et al* 2000; Staub and Bar-Tal 2003; Bar-Siman-Tov 2004; Bar-Tal and Bennink 2004; Kriesberg 2004; Jeong 2005). Severe challenges to basic human needs, the experience of living under difficult conditions, and, in particular, acute inequalities in the distribution of economic wealth, social status, or access to political power have all been cited as significant contributing factors around which protracted and intractable identity conflicts can coalesce (Staub 1989; Azar 1990; Staub and Bar-Tal 2003; Amstutz 2005). These deeper forms of 'structural violence' associated with inequality may continue to preclude more cooperative relations and significant changes to the politics of identity between divided groups even when active violence comes to a close with the signing of a formal peace agreement. As Johan Galtung has argued, fostering reconciliation and a lasting, sustainable peace among former enemies in divided societies may require not only the end of physical violence, but the creation of a more 'positive peace' addressing the deeper structural violence underlying such conflicts (Galtung 1969: 183).

Amelioration of structural and material inequalities

To be sure, growing evidence now exists within the conflict transformation literature to suggest that the amelioration of material inequalities may play a central role in the processes of social learning required to alter antagonistic identifications and advance reconciliation in divided societies (Ryan 1995, 2007; Gibson 2004; Aiken 2008, 2009, 2010, 2013). For instance, in their study of the conflict in Northern Ireland, Joseph Ruane and Jennifer Todd note that structural and economic inequalities can themselves be constitutive of divided identities, and that they have helped to create a self-reinforcing system of conflict by encouraging greater levels of both ingroup solidarity and outgroup differentiation (Ruane and Todd 1996: 5–6, 12–13). In addition, Ruane and Todd's study illustrate how the continued presence of inequality can limit the potential for perceptual and ideological changes regarding the Other even when myths and biased understandings of the past are directly challenged by new information (Ruane and Todd 1996: 207).

Furthermore, the transformative potential for the key instrumental learning mechanisms of contact and communication can be greatly limited when these interactions take place in conditions of material inequality. In the most basic sense, the opportunities for such encounters may themselves be limited in a society divided by severe structural differences, as the places in which different groups members live, work, and socialise may be directly mediated by socioeconomic status. Moreover, where interactions do occur, these structural and material disparities may be so wide that the contact between members of different groups remains cursory and superficial, resulting in relationships that can be 'contiguous yet utterly remote' (Foster and Finchilescu 1986: 125; Durrheim and Dixon 2005; Foster 2005). Indeed, in a series of recent social psychological studies carried out by Nicole Tausch and her colleagues in Northern Ireland, perceptions of inequalities in relative group status were found to be both a strong predictor and mediator of intergroup contact. In effect, those with perceptions of lower status were far less likely to seek to engage in meaningful contact and, when contact did occur, it often led to feelings of increased anxiety and threat. As a result, these interactions were shown to have little positive effect for altering intergroup hostilities through social learning by breaking down existing stereotype, reducing established prejudice, increasing empathy, or improving trust (Tausch et al 2007).

The insights of these and other related studies within the conflict transformation literature suggest that in order to advance social learning and reconciliation in divided societies, attention must be paid to ameliorating the structural systems of dominance, dependence, and inequality that serve to reinforce and reproduce antagonistic intergroup identifications (Azar 1990; Ryan 1995, 2007; Cairns and Darby 1998; Lerche 2000; Jeong 2005). Indeed, the work of the prominent social psychologists Ervin Staub and Daniel Bar-Tal, for example, has stressed the importance of combining psychological transformations with real changes in the socioeconomic conditions of groups to advance reconciliation, noting, 'when conflict is already entrenched and groups have inflicted violence on each other, psychological changes are required for overcoming hostility. But without structural changes, psychological changes may not be possible to bring about or maintain' (Staub and Bar-Tal 2003: 731). Notably, in recent years these findings have also been reflected within the field of transitional justice itself, in which an increasing number of scholars has shown recognition that distributive reforms may be essential components of any broader justice package aimed at advancing post-conflict peacebuilding efforts (Mani 2001, 2008; Rigby

2001; Aiken 2008, 2010, 2013; Miller 2008; Lambourne 2009; Muvingi 2009).

Taken together, these studies suggests that active efforts to address and reduce structural and material inequalities may need to be incorporated into transitional justice interventions if they are to contribute to social learning and reconciliation in divided societies. That said, it is highly unrealistic to expect that transitional justice interventions will, in and of themselves, be able to affect this kind of societal change – it is a task simply beyond the limited budgets, mandates and timelines accorded these interventions. However, as potentially crucial catalysts of social learning in the transformative post-conflict moment, it nonetheless remains important that these justice interventions, at a minimum, at least signal a commitment to a general improvement in the material conditions experienced by former antagonists.

There are two particular ways in which transitional justice interventions might practically seek to incorporate attempts to address structural and material inequalities and thereby contribute to distributive learning in divided societies. The first is to include provisions for some form of reparations programme for those worst impacted by past violence or for those who experienced severe socioeconomic and socio-political disadvantage under previous systems of repression. While the sheer scale of mass violence may realistically mean that such reparations can only ever be emblematic, reparations nevertheless remain an important way in which transitional authorities can acknowledge the injustice of past disparities and indicate their commitment to establishing more equitable future relations (Rigby 2001; Villa-Vicencio 2001, 2006; Stanley 2002; de Greiff 2006; Sharpe 2007). As Brandon Hamber and Richard Wilson argue, while the limited material gain of reparations may certainly be of immediate help to the most disadvantaged, their real importance may be found in their symbolic ability to mark a clear break with the inequalities of the past (Hamber and Wilson 2003: 4). They note, however, that such endeavours can be fraught with difficulty, as determining which groups or individuals might be eligible recipients of compensation is always a challenge, and they also argue that reparations will need to be part of a broader series of justice initiatives and reforms to avoid being stigmatised as a 'payoff' offered in lieu of real social change (Hamber and Wilson 2003: 14).

Second, transitional justice institutions might be designed to work in tandem with or alongside broader structural and material reforms as part of a package of initiatives undertaken by transitional authorities to address legacies of past abuses. Similarly, justice strategies might make recommendations or suggest binding reforms for transitional societies to carry out after the formal justice mechanisms themselves have completed their work (Minow 1999; Hayner 2002; Stanley 2002). In either case, such an approach can help signal to former antagonists that alongside the instrumental and socioemotional initiatives associated with transitional justice, more forward-looking and longer term efforts are also being undertaken to correct existing structural and material imbalances. However, as Elizabeth Stanley warns, if these distributional or developmental policies are not actually carried out, they run a high risk of making all transitional justice efforts appear 'toothless' and illegitimate, greatly damaging their ability to contribute to broader processes of social learning and reconciliation (Stanley 2002: 11).

Conclusion: rethinking reconciliation in divided societies

Building on insights from the field of conflict resolution, this chapter offers a new framework for theorising the causal relationship between institutions of transitional justice and intergroup reconciliation in divided societies. The central contention of the social learning theory developed in this essay is that the link between transitional justice and reconciliation remains – at least in divided societies – heavily mediated by the politics of identity. In essence, it is argued that transitional justice interventions will be successful in promoting reconciliation to the extent that they are able to facilitate positive forms of social learning between former antagonists that, in turn, help to fundamentally challenge and transform the antagonistic identities and hostile systems of relations between former enemies that underpin acts of mass intergroup violence in divided societies. More specifically, the reconciliatory potential of transitional justice interventions in such societies is held to be dependent on their ability to promote five key mechanisms of positive social learning between former antagonists, mechanisms that include contact, dialogue, the promotion of truth and justice, and the amelioration of material inequalities. It is these mechanisms, in turn, that advance the respective aspects of each of the broader processes of instrumental, socioemotional, and distributive social learning ultimately required to facilitate intergroup reconciliation and sustainable peace in divided societies. Having outlined this framework, what implications might it suggest for the broader field of transitional justice?

First, this social learning theory may offer a new way to assess the reconciliatory potential of transitional justice strategies and provide new insight as to why different interventions have been more or less successful in advancing reconciliation and sustainable peace in deeply divided societies. In particular, insights derived from this framework suggest the need to move beyond previous comparative debates within the field about the primacy of any single 'type' of justice intervention for advancing the goal of reconciliation.[10] Instead, the social learning theory presented here underscores that such debates about which kind of intervention is intrinsically 'better' than another seems less important than asking whether the processes and mechanisms employed by each approach serves to catalyze those critical elements of social learning ultimately required to advance intergroup reconciliation in deeply divided societies. Accordingly, by refocusing our attention from structure to process and concentrating on what these institutions *do* rather than what they *are*, the social learning theory introduced here offers a potential new avenue for assessing transitional justice interventions based on their relative ability to foster instrumental, socioemotional, and distributive forms of social learning – be they restorative or retributive, trial, truth commission or incorporate traditional practices. This framework, therefore, reflects the need for 'context-dependent' theories of transitional justice, leaving open the possibility that these processes of social learning might be promoted across a range of different justice interventions.

Furthermore, it remains likely that the particular requirements of each divided society that employs a transitional justice intervention will be different in their relative need for each of the three instrumental, socioemotional and distributive learning processes. In this way, it may be more useful to think of each of the social learning processes presented here as a continuum, and to acknowledge that each may need to be promoted by different justice interventions to a greater or lesser degree in different cases. Indeed, the highly individuated nature of context, culture and each society's unique requirements for justice and reconciliation in the post-conflict environment means that no one 'best' intervention is ever likely to be beneficial or even practicable across all societies. Instead, what this social learning theory seeks to offer is a set of common guidelines against which the needs of any particular society can be assessed on a case-by-case basis, providing the information necessary to tailor an appropriate transitional justice intervention to meet the contours and contexts of each country's unique needs for reconciliation.

Second, and perhaps most importantly, this new theoretical framework offers new considerations that could be used to help to inform 'best practices' in the design of future transitional justice interventions in deeply divided societies. As this social learning theory suggests, transitional justice interventions capable of promoting reconciliation in divided societies may ultimately need to foster a combination of distributive, instrumental and socioemotional reconciliation. However, to date, studies in transitional justice have tended to focus almost exclusively on how these interventions might contribute to post-conflict peacebuilding and reconciliation through their capacity to promote what has here been referred to as socioemotional learning; in other words, by fostering aspects of 'truth' and 'justice'. While these efforts too remain vitally important, insights from the conflict transformation literature suggest that such initiatives will necessarily need to work alongside longer term interventions designed to promote contact, dialogue and distributive equality if they are ultimately going to be successful in building reconciliation and providing the foundation for sustainable peace.

Accordingly, in beginning to unpack the complex relationship between transitional justice and reconciliation in divided societies, this social learning theory suggests that what might ultimately be needed is a broader consideration of transitional justice itself, one which pays attention to how instrumental and distributive aims might be incorporated alongside – or indeed within – the institutions and mechanisms designed to provide accountability for the past. In essence, such a reinterpretation suggests that the relative success of any transitional justice intervention in contributing to intergroup reconciliation will ultimately depend on its ability to promote instrumental and distributive processes of social learning alongside truth and justice or, at the very least, be designed so as to work in tandem with other ongoing societal efforts to rebuild relations and establish more equitable relationships between former enemies in divided societies.

Notes

1 This chapter is based on arguments that are taken up in much greater detail in Nevin T. Aiken, *Identity, Reconciliation and Transitional Justice* (New York, NY: Routledge, 2013). Elements of this larger work appear here with permission of Routledge Press.

2 A recent survey of the transitional justice literature suggests that the perceived contribution of transitional justice interventions to post-conflict reconciliation processes is one of the primary reasons they have been increasingly employed in recent decades (Oduro 2007: 3).

3 In a recent reflection on the existing state of the transitional justice literature, Audrey Chapman notes that 'systematic research on reconciliation is just beginning ... we do not yet have clear procedures for how to achieve reconciliation, or even for measuring and evaluating the success of efforts to that end' (Chapman 2009: 143).

4 As many scholars working within the field of conflict transformation have evidenced, since collective identities are constructions that are constantly created and recreated by social practices, the 'space for innovation' for their transformation is never fully closed (Lederach 1997; Kelman 1999; Vayryen 1999).

5 This argument builds on earlier studies which have explored the ability of transitional justice institutions as being able to act as catalysts for reconciliation between former antagonists in transitional societies emerging from legacies of mass violence. See Fletcher and Weinstein 2002; Gibson 2002, 2004, 2006; Stover and Weinstein 2004; Rushton 2006; Lambourne 2009.

6 It is important to note that all three of these aspects of social learning are recognised as being highly interdependent in their ability to advance reconciliation. For example, the trust and cooperation built through instrumental learning might provide the basis for a successful engagement with the past, while acts of socioemotional learning help societies to overcome the emotional and psychological barriers to interaction which otherwise militate against the development of more positive – and peaceful – contemporary intergroup interactions (Nadler and Shnabel 2008; Nadler et al 2008; Aiken 2010, 2013).

7 A notable exception here is the work of James L. Gibson, who has attempted to both theoretically and empirically explore the causal path between truth and reconciliation in his study of South Africa (Gibson 2002, 2004, 2006).

8 This sentiment is echoed by the work of psychologist Herbert Kelman, who has extensively the dynamics of reconciliation in divided societies and concludes that 'confronting

history and coming to terms with the truth [through the] re-examination of historical narratives and the re-evaluation of national myths – on both sides of the conflict – [are] essential components of any reconciliation effort' (Kelman 2004: 123).

9 As James L. Gibson notes, 'accepting the viewpoint that both sides did terrible things is perhaps the first tentative step towards reconciliation' (Gibson 2004: 329).

10 These have centred on debates over whether it is better to employ 'restorative' or 'retributive' approaches to justice, the relative utility of truth commissions versus trials, whether these interventions should be located at local, national, or international levels, and whether formal Western legal approaches to justice are more or less productive than culturally specific 'traditional' or 'indigenous' local responses (Roht-Arriaza 2006).

Bibliography

Abu-Nimer, M., Abdul, A.S. and Lakshitha. S.P. (2001) 'The Long Road to Reconciliation', in Abu-Nimer, M. (ed.) *Reconciliation, Justice, and Coexistence: Theory and Practice*, New York, NY: Lexington Books.

Adam, H. and Moodley, K. (2005) *Seeking Mandela: Peacemaking between Israelis and Palestinians*, Philadelphia, PA: Temple University Press.

Adler, E. and Barnett, M. (1998) 'A Framework for the Study of Security Communities', in Adler, E. and Barnett, M. (eds) *Security Communities*, Cambridge: Cambridge University Press.

Aiken, N.T. (2008) 'Post-Conflict Peacebuilding and the Politics of Identity: Insights for Restoration and Reconciliation in Transitional Justice', *Peace Research*, 40 (2): 9–38.

——(2009) 'The (Re)Construction of a Culture of Human Rights: Transitional Justice and Human Security', *Human Security Journal*, 8: 10–18.

——(2010) 'Learning to Live Together: Transitional Justice and Intergroup Reconciliation in Northern Ireland', *International Journal of Transitional Justice*, 4 (2): 166–88

——(2013) *Identity, Reconciliation and Transitional Justice*, New York, NY: Routledge.

Amstutz, M.R. (2005) *The Healing of Nations: The Promise and Limits of Political Forgiveness*, Lanham, MD: Rowman & Littlefield.

Arthur, P. (ed.) (2010) *Identities in Transition: Challenges for Transitional Justice in Divided Societies*, Cambridge: Cambridge University Press.

Azar, E. (1990) *The Management of Protracted Social Conflict: Theory and Cases*, Aldershot: Dartmouth.

Bar-Siman-Tov, Y. (2004) 'Dialectics between Stable Peace and Reconciliation', in Bar-Siman-Tov, Y. (ed.) *From Conflict Resolution to Reconciliation*, Oxford: Oxford University Press.

Bar-Tal, D. (2000) 'From Intractable Conflict through Conflict Resolution to Reconciliation: Psychological Analysis', *Political Psychology*, 21 (1): 351–65.

——(2003) 'Collective Memory of Physical Violence: Its Contribution to the Culture of Violence', in Einar, B., Boas, M. and Saether, G. (eds) *Ethnicity Kills? The Politics of War, Peace and Ethnicity in Subsaharan Africa*, New York, NY: St. Martin's Press.

Bar-Tal, D. and Bennink, G.H. (2004) 'The Nature of Reconciliation as an Outcome and as a Process,' in Bar-Siman-Tov, Y. (ed.) *From Conflict Resolution to Reconciliation*, Oxford: Oxford University Press.

Biggar, N. (ed.) (2001) *Burying the Past: Making Peace and Doing Justice after Civil Conflict*, Washington, DC: Georgetown University Press.

Borer, T.A. (2006) 'Truth Telling as a Peace-Building Activity: A Theoretical Overview', in Borer, T.A. (ed.) *Telling the Truths: Truth Telling and Peace Building in Post-Conflict Societes*, South Bend, IN: University of Notre Dame Press.

Brahm, E. (2007) 'Uncovering the Truth: Examining Truth Commission Success and Impact', *International Studies Perspectives*, 8 (1): 16–35.

Brewer, M.B. and Gaertner, S.L. (2001) 'Toward Reduction of Prejudice: Intergroup Contact and Social Categorization', in Brown, R. and Gaertner, S.L. (eds) *Blackwell Handbook of Social Psychology: Intergroup Processes*, Oxford: Blackwell.

Cairns, E. and Darby, J. (1998) 'The Conflict in Northern Ireland: Cause, Consequences, and Controls', *American Psychologist*, 53 (7): 754–60.

Cairns, E. and Roe, M.D. (2003) 'Why Memories in Conflict', in Cairns, E. and Roe, M.D. (eds) *The Role of Memory in Ethnic Conflict*, New York, NY: Palgrave.

Chapman, A.R. (2009) 'Approaches to Studying Reconciliation', in van der Merwe, H., Baxter, V. and Chapman, A.R. (eds) *Assessing the Impact of Transitional Justice: Challenges for Empirical Research*, Washington, DC: United States Institute of Peace Press.

Chapman, A.R. and Ball, P. (2008) 'Levels of Truth: Macro-Truth and the TRC', in Chapman, A.R. and van der Merwe, H. (eds) *Truth and Reconciliation in South Africa: Did the TRC Deliver?*, Philadelphia, PA: University of Pennsylvania Press.

Chinapen, R. and Vernon, R. (2006) 'Justice in Transition', *Canadian Journal of Political Science*, 39 (1): 117–34.

Coleman, P.T. (2002)*Polarized Collective Identities: A Review and Synthesis of the Literature*, New York, NY: Columbia University.

Colletta, N.J. and Cullen, M.L. (2000) *Violent Conflict and The Transformation of Social Capital*, Washington, DC: World Bank.

de Greiff, P. (ed.) (2006) *The Handbook of Reparations*, Oxford: Oxford University Press, 2006.

Devine-Wright, P. (2003) 'A Theoretical Overview of Memory and Conflict', in Cairns, E. and Roe, M.D. (eds) *The Role of Memory in Ethnic Conflict*, New York, NY: Palgrave.

Drumbl, M. (2007) *Atrocity, Punishment, and International Law*, Cambridge: Cambridge University Press.

Durrheim, K. and Dixon, J. (2005) *Racial Encounter: The Social Psychology of Contact and Desegregation*, New York, NY: Routledge.

Duster, T. (1971) 'Conditions for Guilt-Free Massacre', in Sanford N. and Comstock C. (eds) *Sanctions for Evil*, San Francisco, CA: Jossey-Bass.

Eder, K., Gisen, B., Schmidtke, O. and Tambini, D. (2002) *Collective Identities in Action: A Sciological Approach to Ethnicity*, Aldershot: Ashgate Publishing.

Ellis, D.G. (2006) *Transforming Conflict: Communication and Ethnopolitical Conflict*, New York, NY: Rowman & Littlefield.

Eriksen, T.H. (2001) 'Ethnic Identity, National Identity, and Intergroup Conflict', in Ashmore, R.D., Jussim, L. and Wilder, D. (eds) *Social Identity, Intergroup Conflict, and Conflict Reduction*, Oxford: Oxford University Press.

Fein, H. (1999) 'Testing Theories Brutally: Armenia (1915), Bosnia (1992) and Rwanda (1994)', in Chorbajjan, L. and Shirinian, G. (eds) *Studies in Comparative Genocide*, New York, NY: St. Martin's Press.

Fisher, R.J. (2001) 'Social-Psychological Processes in Interactive Conflict Analysis and Reconciliation', in Abu-Nimer, M. (ed.) *Reconciliation, Justice, and Coexistence: Theory and Practice*, New York, NY: Lexington Books.

Fletcher, L.E. and Weinstein, H.M. (2002). 'Violence and Social Repair: Rethinking the Contributions of Justice to Reconciliation', *Human Rights Quarterly*, 24 (3): 573–639.

Foster, D. (2005) 'Racial Relations and the Microecology of Contact', *South African Journal of Psychology*, 35 (1): 494–504.

Foster, D. and Finchilescu, G. (1986) 'Contact in a "Non-Contact" Society: The Case of South Africa', in Hewstone, M. and Brown, R. (eds) *Contact and Conflict in Intergroup Encounters*, Oxford: Blackwell.

Gaertner, S.L. and Dovidio, J.F. (2000). *Reducing Intergroup Bias: The Common Ingroup Identity Model*, Philadelphia, PA: Psychology Press.

Gaertner, S.L., Rust, M., Dovidio, J.F., Bachman, B.A. and Anastasio, P. (1994) 'The Contact Hypothesis: The Role of a Common Ingroup Identity on Reducing Intergroup Bias', *Small Group Research*, 25 (2): 224–49.

Galtung, J. (1969) 'Violence, Peace, and Peace Research', *Journal of Peace Research*, 6 (3): 167–91.

Gibson, J.L. (2002) 'Truth, Justice, and Reconciliation', *American Journal of Political Science*, 46 (3): 540–56.

——(2004) *Overcoming Apartheid*, New York, NY: Russell Sage.

——(2006) 'The Contributions of Truth to Reconciliation: Lessons from South Africa', *Journal of Conflict Resolution*, 50 (1): 409–32.

Goldstone, R.J. (2004) 'Justice and Reconciliation in Fragmented Societies', in Wimmer, A. et al (eds) *Facing Ethnic Conflicts: Toward a New Realism*, New York, NY: Rowman & Littlefield.

Gross-Stein, J. (2002) 'Psychological Explanations of International Conflict', in Carlsaes, W., Risse, T. and Simmons, B.A. (eds) *The Handbook of International Relations*, Thousand Oaks, CA: Sage.

Hamber, B. (2001) 'Does The Truth Heal? A Psychological Perspective on Political Strategies for Dealing with the Legacy of Political Violence', in Biggar, N. (ed.) *Burying the Past: Making Peace and Doing Justice after Civil Conflict*, Washington, DC: Georgetown University Press.

Hamber, B. and Wilson, R.A. (2003) 'Symbolic Closure through Memory, Reparation and Revenge in Post-Conflict Societies', in Cairns, E. and Roe, M.D. (eds) *The Role of Memory in Ethnic Conflict*, New York, NY: Palgrave.

Hayner, P. (1994) 'Fifteen Truth Commissions – 1974 to 1994: A Comparative Study', *Human Rights Quarterly*, 16 (4): 597–655.

——(2002) *Unspeakable Truths: Facing the Challenges of Truth Commissions*, London: Routledge.

Hermann, T. (2004) 'Reconciliation: Reflections on the Theoretical and Practical Utility of the Term', in Bar-Siman-Tov, Y. (ed.) *From Conflict Resolution to Reconciliation*, Oxford: Oxford University Press.

Hewstone, M. and Brown, R. (eds) (1986) *Contact and Conflict in Intergroup Encounters*, Oxford: Oxford University Press.

Hewstone, M., Cairns, E., Voci, A., Paolini, S., McLernon, F., Crisp, R.J. and Niens, U. (2005) 'Intergroup Contact in a Divided Society: Challenging Segregation in Northern Ireland', in Abrams, D., Hogg, M.A. and Marques, J.M. (eds) *The Social Psychology of Incusion and Exclusion*, Philadelphia, PA: Psychology Press.

Ignatieff, M. (1998) *The Warrior's Honor: Ethnic War and the Modern Conscience*, New York, NY: Henry Holt.

Imbleau, M. (2004) 'Initial Truth Establishment by Transitional Bodies and the Fight against Denial', in Schabas, W.A. and Darcy, S. (eds) *Truth Commissions and Courts: The Tension between Criminal Justice and the Search for Truth*, Dordrecht: Kluwer.

Jeong, H.W. (2005) *Peacebuilding in Postconflict Societies: Strategy and Process*, London and Boulder, CO: Lynne-Rienner.

Kelman, H.C. (1999) 'Transforming the Relationship between Former Enemies: A Social-Psychological Analysis', in Rothstein, R.L. (ed.) *After the Peace: Resistance and Reconciliation*, Boulder, CO: Lynne-Rienner.

——(2001) 'The Role of National Identity in Conflict Resolution', in Ashmore, R.D., Jussim, L. and Wilder, D. (eds) *Social Identity, Intergroup Conflict, and Conflict Reduction*, Oxford: Oxford University Press.

——(2004) 'Reconciliation as Identity Change: A Social-Psychological Perspective', in Bar-Siman-Tov, Y. (ed.) *From Conflict Resolution to Reconciliation*, Oxford: Oxford University Press.

——(2008) 'Reconciliation from a Social-Psychological Perspective', in Nadler, A., Malloy, T. E. and Fisher, J.D. (eds) *The Social Psychology of Intergroup Reconciliation*, Oxford: Oxford University Press.

Kenworthy, J.B., Turner, R.N., Hewstone, M. and Voci, A. (2005) 'Intergroup Contact: When Does It Work and Why?' in Dovidio, J.F., Glick, P. and Rudman, L.A. (eds) *On The Nature of Prejudice: Fifty Years after Allport*, Oxford: Blackwell.

Kiss, E. (2000) 'Moral Ambition Within and Beyond Political Constraints: Reflections on Restorative Justice', in Rotberg, R.I. and Thompson, D. (eds) *Truth v. Justice: The Morality of Truth Commissions*, Princeton, NJ: Princeton University Press.

Kriesberg, L. (1998) 'Intractable Conflicts', in Weiner E. (ed.) *The Handbook of Interethnic Coexistence*, New York, NY: Continuum Publishing.

——(2001) 'Changing Forms of Coexistence', in Abu-Nimer, M. (ed.) *Reconciliation, Justice, and Coexistence: Theory and Practice*, New York, NY: Lexington Books.

——(2004) 'Comparing Reconciliation Actions within and between Countries', in Bar-Siman-Tov, Y. (ed.) *From Conflict Resolution to Reconciliation*, Oxford: Oxford University Press.

Lambourne, W. (2009) 'Transitional Justice and Peacebuilding after Mass Violence', *International Journal of Transitional Justice*, 3 (1): 28–48.

Lederach, J.P. (1997) *Building Peace: Sustainable Reconciliation in Divided Societies*, Washington, DC: United States Institute of Peace Press.

Lerche, C. (2000) 'Peace Building through Reconciliation', *Peace Studies*, 5: 1–10.

Llewellyn, J. (2006) 'Restorative Justice in Transitions and Beyond: The Justice Potential of Truth-Telling Mechanisms for Post-Accord Societies', in Borer, T.A. (ed.) *Telling the Truths: Truth Telling and Peace Building in Post-Conflict Societies*, South Bend, IN: University of Notre Dame Press.

Long, W.J. and Brecke, P. (2003) *War and Reconciliation: Reason and Emotion in Conflict Resolution*, London: MIT Press.

Mack, J.E. (1990) 'The Psychodynamics of Victimization among National Groups in Conflict', in Volkan, V.D., Montville, J.V. and Demetrios, J.A. (eds) *The Psychodynamics of International Relationships*, Toronto: Lexington.

Mani, R. (2001) 'Rebuilding an Inclusive Political Community after War', *Security Dialogue*, 36 (4): 511–26.

——(2002) *Beyond Retribution: Seeking Justice in the Shadows of War*, Cambridge: Polity Press.

——(2008) 'Dilemmas of Expanding Transitional Justice, or Forging the Nexus between Transitional Justice and Development', *International Journal of Transitional Justice*, 2 (3): 253–65.

Maoz, I. (2004) 'Social-Cognitive Mechanisms in Reconciliation', in Bar-Siman-Tov, Y. (ed.) *From Conflict Resolution to Reconciliation*, Oxford: Oxford University Press.

Miall, H., Ramsbotham, O. and Woodhouse, T. (2000) *Contemporary Conflict Resolution: The Prevention, Management and Transformation of Deadly Conflicts*, Cambridge: Polity Press.

Miller, Z. (2008) 'Effects of Invisibility: In Search of the "Economic" in Transitional Justice', *International Journal of Transitional Justice*, 2 (3): 266–91.

Minow, M. (1999) *Between Vengeance and Forgiveness. Facing History after Genocide and Mass Violence*, Boston, MA: Beacon Hill Press.

Muvingi, I. (2009) 'Sitting on Powder Kegs: Socioeconomic Rights in Transitional Societies', *International Journal of Transitional Justice*, 3: 163–82.

Nadler, A., Malloy, T.E. and Fisher, J.D. (2008) 'Intergroup Reconciliation: Dimensions and Themes', in Nadler, A., Malloy, T.E. and Fisher, J.D. (eds) *The Social Psychology of Intergroup Reconciliation*, Oxford: Oxford University Press.

Nadler, A. and Shnabel, N. (2008) 'Instrumental and Socioemotional Paths to Intergroup Reconciliation', in Nadler, A., Malloy, T.E. and Fisher, J.D. (eds) *The Social Psychology of Intergroup Reconciliation*, Oxford: Oxford University Press.

Northrup, T.A. (1989) 'The Dynamic of Identity in Personal and Social Conflict', in Kriesberg, L., Northrup, T.A. and Thorson, S.J. (eds) *Intractable Conflict and Their Transformation*, Syracuse, NY: Syracuse University Press.

Oberschall, A. (2007) *Conflict and Peace Building in Divided Societies: Responses to Ethnic Violence*, New York, NY: Routledge.

Oduro, F. (2007) *What Do We Understand by 'Reconciliation?' Emerging Definitions of Reconciliation in the Context of Transitional Justice*, Ottawa: International Development Research Centre, March 2007.

Pettigrew, T. (1998) 'Intergroup Contact Theory', *Annual Review of Psychology*, 49: 65–85.

Rigby, A. (2001) *Justice and Reconciliation: After the Violence*, London: Lynne-Rienner.

Roht-Arriaza, N. (2006) 'The New Landscape of Transitional Justice', in Roht-Arriaza, N. and Mariezcurrena, J. (eds) *Transitional Justice in the Twenty-First Century: Beyond Truth versus Justice*, Cambridge: Cambridge University Press.

Ropers, N. (2004) 'From Resolution to Transformation: Assessing the Role and Impact of Dialogue Projects', in Wimmer, A. *et al* (eds) *Facing Ethnic Conflicts: Toward a New Realism*, New York, NY: Rowman & Littlefield.

Ross, M.H. (2004) 'Ritual and the Politics of Reconciliation', in Bar-Siman-Tov, Y. (ed.) *From Conflict Resolution to Reconciliation*, Oxford: Oxford University Press.

Rothman, J. (1997) *Resolving Identity-Based Conflict in Nations, Organizations, and Communities*, San Francisco, CA: Jossey-Bass.

Ruane, J. and Todd, J. (1996) *The Dynamics of Conflict in Northern Ireland: Power, Conflcit, and Emancipation*, Cambridge: Cambridge University Press.

Rushton, B. (2006) 'Truth and Reconciliation: The Experience of Truth Commissions', *Australian Journal of International Affairs*, 60 (1): 125–41.

Ryan, S. (1995) *Ethnic Conflict and International Relations*, Aldershot: Dartmouth.

——(2007) *The Transformation of Violent Intercommunal Conflict*, Aldershot: Ashgate Publishing.

Santa-Barbara, J. (2007) 'Reconciliation', in Webel, C. and Galtung, J. (eds) *The Handbook of Peace and Conflict Studies*, New York, NY: Routledge.

Sharpe, S. (2007) 'The Idea of Reparation', in Johnstone, G. and Van Ness, D. (eds) *Handbook of Restorative Justice*, Portland, OR: Willan Publishing.

Shirlow, P. (2001) 'Fear and Ethnic Division', *Peace Review*, 13 (1): 67–74.

Stanley, E. (2002) 'What Next? The Aftermath of Organized Truth Telling', *Race & Class*, 44 (1): 1–15.

Staub, E. (1989) *The Roots of Evil: The Origins of Genocide and Other Group Violence*, New York, NY: Cambridge University Press.

——(2000) 'Genocide and Mass Killing: Origins, Prevention, Healing and Reconciliation', *Political Psychology*, 21 (2): 367–82.

——(2001) 'Individual and Group Identities in Genocide and Mass Killing', in Ashmore, R. D., Jussim, L. and Wilder, D. (eds) *Social Identity, Intergroup Conflict, and Conflict Reduction*, Oxford: Oxford University Press.

——(2006) 'Reconciliation after Genocide, Mass Killing, or Intractable Conflict', *Political Psychology*, 27 (6): 867–94.

Staub, E. and Bar-Tal, D. (2003) 'Genocide, Mass Killing, and Intractable Conflict: Roots, Evolution, Prevention, and Reconciliation', in Sears, D.O., Huddy, L. and Jervis, R. (eds) *Oxford Handbook of Political Psychology*, Oxford: Oxford University Press.

Stephan, W.G. and Stephan, C.W. (2001) *Improving Intergroup Relations*, London: Sage.

Stover, E. and Weinstein, H.M. (2004) 'A Common Objective: A Universe of Alternatives', in Weinstein, H.M. and Stover, E. (eds) *My Neighbor, My Enemy: Justice and Community in the Aftermath of Mass Atrocity*, Cambridge: Cambridge University Press.

Tausch, N., Hewstone, M., Kenworthy, J., Cairns, E. and Christ, O. (2007) 'Cross-Community Contact, Perceived Status Differences, and Intergroup Attitudes in Northern Ireland', *Political Psychology*, 28 (1): 53–68.

Teitel, R.G. (2002) *Transitional Justice*, Oxford and New York, NY: Oxford University Press.

Vayryen, T. (1999) 'Socially Constructed Ethnic Identities: A Need for Identity Management?' in Wiberg, H. and Scherrer, C.P. (eds) *Ethnicity and Intra-State Conflict: Types, Causes, and Peace Strategies*, Aldershot: Ashgate Publishing.

Villa-Vicencio, C. (2001) 'Restorative Justice in Societal Context: The South African Truth and Reconciliation Commission', in Biggar, N. (ed.) *Burying the Past: Making Peace and Doing Justice after Civil Conflict*, Washington, DC: Georgetown University Press.

——(2006) 'The Politics of Reconciliation', in Borer, T.A. (ed.) *Telling the Truths: Truth Telling and Peace Building in Post-Conflict Societies*, South Bend, IN: University of Notre Dame Press.

Zehr, H. (1990) *Changing Lenses: A New Focus for Crime and Justice*, Scottdale, PA: Herald Press

Chapter 3

The plural justice aims of reparations

Lisa J. Laplante*

Introduction

The subject of reparations for victims of human rights violations now figures prominently in most transitional justice undertakings. While trials and truth-telling tended to dominate the discourse during the early part of the transitional justice movement, in recent times, the idea of reparations has garnered more interest especially in response to the growing number of countries attempting to implement reparations programmes. Reparations generally consist of civil remedies (as opposed to criminal remedies) that are designed to redress harm resulting from an unlawful act that violates the rights of a person. In most domestic national settings reparations are typically awarded pursuant to a court proceeding. In transitional justice settings, however, there are often too many victim-survivors with potential claims for the courts to efficiently and effectively handle, thus prompting governments to resort to administrative solutions. Such programmes, often following a truth commission's recommendations, attempt to provide an array of pecuniary and non-pecuniary measures to respond to the damage caused by conflict, repression, and political violence (Hayner 2001: 171–82).

Often, the stated justification for these reparation programmes rests on moral and ethical grounds, while also pointing to an evolving international legal framework. Indeed, the recognition of the right to reparations has solidified in the last decade, as most notably demonstrated in 2005 by the United Nations General Assembly approving the 'Basic Principles and Guidelines on the Right to a Remedy and Reparation for Survivors of Violations of International Human Rights and Humanitarian Law' (Basic Principles) (United Nations 2006). The Basic Principles (United Nations 2006: Preamble, Section IX) provides a framework predicated on a growing body of jurisprudence arising out of both treaty and customary international law which lays out specific legal contours of the right to reparations.

The infusion of rights into the realm of reparations helps to highlight that, at its core, the concept of reparations revolves around ideas of justice. Thus, in theory, reparations serve as a critical strategy for achieving the central justice aims of transitional justice work. This perspective has led to new empirical field research seeking to assess whether or not reparation programmes, in fact, facilitate or frustrate these overarching justice aims.[1] These findings reveal that the exceptional nature of post-conflict reparation programmes expands traditional notions of redress normally associated with peacetime domestic court settings, requiring a rethinking of what it means to guarantee 'adequate, effective, prompt and appropriate' reparations (United Nations 2006: 2c).

Most notably, transitional justice challenges the more traditional notions of 'reparative' or 'corrective' justice associated with a court calculating the amount of damages that a specific defendant owes for harm caused to an individual plaintiff. This backward looking form of redress seeks to make 'right' a past wrong and usually consists of monetary compensation. Alternatively, transitional justice advocates expect reparation programmes to do much more than simply right a wrong, although viewing corrective justice as a starting point. Reparation scholars – who are often studying what local actors are demanding – speak of perspectives on reparations that invoke various theories of justice, especially given the wide range of rights violations and demographics of victims.

Although reparation programmes implicitly prompt a wide range of justice themes to play out in the real world of transitional justice, the discipline still lacks a cohesive theoretical framework to guide our understanding of the overarching justification, purpose and aims of reparations and how they relate to theories of justice. Most scholarly writing on reparations consists of case studies or appeals on the importance of reparations. A more recent trend sees more critical examinations of reparation programmes and the complicated issues they raise given the sensitive context of post-conflict recovery. While many of these works refer to the concept of justice, few offer a fully developed theory for their exploration.[2]

Thus, this chapter offers a justice-based theory of reparations in transitional justice settings. At the outset it would be reasonable for some readers to ponder, why bother with a theory of reparations? Aside from being mere academic ruminations removed from everyday practical concerns, I would propose that a theoretical framework, like that proposed here, helps to improve the actual implementation of reparations as a justice mechanism. Ultimately, theory guides not only how we think about and understand the role of reparations in transitional justice, but also importantly how to assure the quality control of their design and implementation. Understanding the justice aims of reparations and what they are in theory supposed to achieve is an indispensable starting point for initially choosing the right approaches to pursue. It serves as an important ruler against which the process of implementation can be constantly checked to assure fidelity to promised goals. Lastly, theory allows us to look back and evaluate whether a reparation programme met its proposed purpose.

A 'justice continuum' theory of reparations

As a starting point for constructing a theory of reparations, it is important to recognise that reparations can and should be viewed through a lens of justice. Undoubtedly, the concept of justice is complex and contested, and has inspired generations of theoretical debates, dating back to ancient philosophy, all seeking to understand what constitutes justice and why justice matters. For the purposes of this analysis, I propose that reparations may be understood to function along a 'justice continuum' that moves from a narrower on to a broader theory of justice to explain the aim of reparations. I have selected four theories of justice to plot along the axis of this continuum in order to capture the diversity of reparation approaches taken in transitional justice settings to date. At the left end of the axis, we find the idea of 'reparative justice'. As we move towards the middle of the axis we enter into the general realm of 'restorative justice'. As we continue, we come upon 'civic justice' and then lastly reach 'socioeconomic justice' (see Figure 3.1).

Before I offer a general explanation of each of these theories, it is important to explain the motivation for choosing these four categories for the continuum. Above all else, they seem to best reflect the nascent theories that have begun to be discussed in the academic literature as well as reflect the rationales given by local actors creating and demanding reparation programmes. There are surely other forms of justice that may fit along this continuum, or even form sub-continuums within some of the categories of justice that I have named. To be clear, I do not contend that this is the only or definitive theory, but rather offer it as a template to encourage more discussion and debate as to how we might best articulate the theoretical foundation of reparations. Thus, the theory here is not intended to be exhaustive, but rather to serve as a platform for further development.

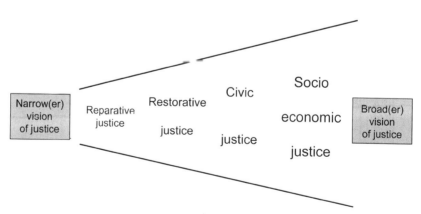

Figure 3.1 Reparation justice continuum

Moreover, the justice continuum is designed to be flexible so as to best capture the choices made locally by those who design and implement reparations. The continuum expands depending on the understanding of what is being repaired and how it should be repaired. As the vision of justice broadens, so does the choice of measures that may be considered to constitute 'reparations'. In particular, the continuum embraces the idea that the perception of victim-survivors will vary on what they believe they need to *feel* repaired, something I describe as the 'felt justice needs' of victims. Therefore, this adaptable model reflects the fact that '[t]he implementation of transitional justice mechanisms in most countries has relied on a pluralist approach to dealing with the multiple needs and expectations for different types of justice' (Lambourne 2009: 33, 46).[3]

Due to their very nature, reparations in transitional justice educe a necessarily dynamic vision of justice, and thus lead me to reject the idea that there is only one unifying basic principle to guide our thinking but rather a pluralistic view of justice. However for the purposes of this chapter, and to some extent for the convenience of explaining a coherent theory, Figure 3.1 attempts to capture the idea of a linear, yet expanding justice continuum while recognising that a linear graph does not fully capture how these theories may operate simultaneously – they may build on one another or take turns on centre stage at different moments during the overall reparation process. Theories may shift due to the officially stated aims of reparation programmes or from the actual input and push-back from local actors who shape the ongoing process (Shaw *et al* 2010). One modality of reparation may even invoke all types of justice aim. Likewise, the continuum reflects the time required for the effectiveness of these measures, with the more narrow theory being more punctual and the broader requiring more space and time. From the planning point of view, the particular theoretical focus will help determine the choice of methods, procedures and measures within a particular localised reparation programme.

In the sections that follow, I give a general overview of each 'stop' along the justice continuum by first discussing existing social or legal theories for each of the justice categories, including classic political philosophy as well as theory from other disciplines. I then consider how the uniqueness of transitional justice may replicate, alter or expand upon these more traditional justice theories in light of actual reparation measures and processes that have been employed in transitional justice experience to date. To some extent, this dialect between the existing theory and the experience of transitional justice may result in a reconstruction of traditional theories as opposed to the development of a wholly original theory. Alternatively, as we continue to use existing theories to critically examine the experience of transitional justice reparation programmes, a new theory may naturally evolve in order to better capture the unique aspects of this contemporary phenomenon. In sum, this exercise in theory construction compels us to look at justice in new ways due in part to the fact that the novelty of reparations in transitional justice raises new issues and concepts to be integrated into older ways of understanding redress.

The justice stops along the justice continuum of reparations

The following sections provide a guided tour along the justice continuum. Limited space does not allow for a full discussion of each theory or an exhaustive catalogue of all the transitional justice examples or literature that fits into each of these theories. Rather select examples are shared to illustrate the various theories.

Reparative justice

The notion of reparations, in particular economic compensation, can be traced back to ancient times. Often discussed in terms of 'corrective justice', the principle of civil remedies enjoys deep roots in classical legal thought (England 2009). Plato said that when a person 'has done a wrong … he must make the damage good to boot' and the law 'must be exact in determining the magnitude of the correction imposed on the particular offense, and … the amount of compensation to be paid' (cited in Pauley 1994: 98). It is Plato's student, Aristotle, however, who receives credit for the theory of corrective justice. He used the metaphor of an arithmetic balance to show that one person who causes harm must compensate another for the resulting injury or damage in order to equalise the equation (Aristotle 1962: 120–23). Thus, the 'reparative' aspect of corrective justice occurs in responding to an injustice by 'righting a wrong' through compensation in order to bring equality back to the relation (Coleman 1995: 53).

Modern day private law embodies the theory of corrective justice, as seen by the use of civil remedies in contract and tort law (Harris *et al* 2002: 21–24, 338–42; Shelton 2006: 60). In these instances, corrective justice also focuses more narrowly on the specific harm and losses that result from an infringement of a right. The general field of international law, which builds off of general principles of municipal law, incorporates reparations but takes on nuances depending on the area of interest or concern it regulates. For example, international human rights tribunals have generated jurisprudence in remedies law by focusing on individualised cases of measurable damages where restitution is not possible or practicable (Roht-Arriaza 2004a: 157–58). Taking the approach of restitution *in integrum*, these decisions adopt a variety of modalities to approximate 'making a victim whole' and restoring the 'status quo ante', while understanding the impossibility of truly rectifying the immeasurable harm caused by torture, extrajudicial killings, disappearances and other serious forms of violence. These plans might include restitution, compensation, rehabilitation, satisfaction and guarantees of non-repetition (United Nations 2006: 19–23; Antkowiak 2008: 351). When international tribunals and monitoring bodies calculate reparations, they take a similar route as their domestic counterparts, assessing the personal harm that the injured party suffered (Malamud-Goti and Grosman 2006: 540). These judgments take on a very legalistic tone, and closely resemble the corrective formula envisioned by Aristotle.

In contrast, most transitional justice undertakings opt for an administrative reparations plan given that situations of mass violence leave many victims to whom traditional judicial venues are not able or willing to provide an effective civil remedy (Roht-Arriaza 2004b: 121, 122, 127). Yet, administrative programmes often encounter technical issues such as the lack of resources to tailor reparation determinations to the specific harms suffered by each victim as would be done in a full civil trial. Thus governments might resort to a unified package for all victims, such as a lump sum figure or access to services already available to indigent populations, and in doing so run counter to the absolute legalistic concepts of corrective and reparative justice.

Chile is an early example of a country that used a pension-like plan to operationalise its reparation programmes (Guembe 2006: 21; Lira 2006: 55). Morocco opted for a lump sum, awarding economic payments pursuant to the recommendations of the Moroccan Indemnity Commission (*Commission d'arbitrage*), which was established following the death of King Hassan II in July 1999 by his son and heir, Mohammed VI, to provide compensation for the victims of arbitrary detention and forced disappearance during the reign of King Hassan II (Slyomovics 2001). Reparations were defined as measures to address the material and moral damage suffered by victims and were granted primarily through financial compensation (Guillerot *et al* 2009: 26) with awards varying from $600 to $300,000 (Hayner 2010: 172). Yet, this reparation programme was criticised for omitting investigations to reveal the truth and its limited mandate in terms of rights violations, and allegedly entailed a process that lacked public outreach and empathy for the beneficiaries (Hayner 2010: 172). Thus, the Moroccan government responded in 2004 by forming the Equity and Reconciliation Commission (*L'Instance Equité et Réconciliation*) whose mission stated, '[t]urning the page on the past and building a modern and democratic state and society in which rights and duties are respected is first and foremost a social issue that engages all Moroccans' (IER 2006: 32). Significantly, responding to the demands of victims this new commission offered a more comprehensive approach to the reparation process which touched upon the broader aims of justice, to be explained next.

Restorative justice

Moving along the justice continuum, the theory of restorative justice, like reparative justice, rests on the basic premise of striving to 'repair the harm'

(Strang and Sherman 2003: 15). Howard Zehr (1990: 37), a forefather of the restorative justice movement, invokes similar language as the rights-based approach commenting that crime 'creates obligations to make things right'. Yet restorative justice responds to the shortcomings of reparative justice by embracing a broader notion of the 'harm' that needs to be repaired. Also, the two theories diverge with regard to restorative justice offering a more creative template for determining the means for achieving this goal, moving beyond a strictly legal rule-based approach to calculating measurable damages.

The philosophical roots of restorative justice traces back to many 'religious and spiritual traditions and to aboriginal practices and customs around the globe' (Eschholz 2003: 147). In its contemporary form, this alternative justice approach coalesced into a global movement in the 1970s through the rising popularity of mediated encounters between victims and offenders. Broadly defined, restorative justice describes '[a] process whereby all the parties with a stake in a particular offense come together to resolve collectively how to deal with the aftermath of the offense and its implications for the future' (Marshall 1999: 5). Restorative justice is often viewed as a direct rejection of a retributive focus on criminal trials to punish offenders and inflicting 'equal and just measure of pain' (Strang and Sherman 2003: 16).

While scholarship on restorative justice historically focused on 'ordinary' interpersonal wrongful acts, there is more recent recognition of how it also can respond to the type of aftermath of mass violence that falls within the parameters of transitional justice (Villa-Vicencio 2000: 68; Cunneen 2006; Menkel-Meadow 2007: 10.10). This new direction accommodates a significant difference from the one-on-one mediation model since the primary 'offender' in transitional justice schemes is the government for either having actively inflicted harm or having failed to protect citizens from third parties. Traditional theories of restorative justice may refer to informal processes occurring beyond the State, whereas transitional justice is usually a State-run initiative. Indeed, it is the same 'offender' State which is expected to facilitate the reparative process (Doolin 2007: 429).

Despite these differences, the theory of restorative justice still contributes to the construction of a transitional justice reparation theory by focusing on the victim (Menkel-Meadow 2007: 10.10; Antkowiak 2011: 279). This approach offers a dynamic view of 'harm' because the beneficiary (i.e. victim-survivor) is the one who can answer the question '"what" must be restored and "how" this restoration is to be fulfilled' (Gabbay 2005: 359; Schneider 2009: 822). Importantly, this focus demands a participatory approach that treats victims as 'stakeholders' in the reparation process (Braithwaite 2002: 11; Waldman 2007: 91).

The participatory focus highlights that 'justice is in the process ... the actualization of the process of doing justice' (Koen 2007: 91). This *process* mends 'relational harms' and fosters self-respect, feelings of safety and empowerment (Doolin 2007: 432). Since human rights violations by definition rob victims of their dignity and their power, reparation processes ideally would address issues of powerlessness through ongoing engagement. Participation helps victims 'to re-define their relationship to the world around them ... [by exercising] some power over the way in which justice is carried out, to have a say in what must be done to "right the wrong"' (Hill 2009: 115).

Restorative justice may also offer a way to ameliorate some of the potential pitfalls of the narrower form of reparative justice that may encounter procedural challenges which can re-victimise the beneficiary populations and place them in a passive, inferior role (Di Giovanni 2005: 25). Such examples include concerns regarding nationwide registry process that place unreasonable burdens on the poor to prove their 'victim status' as well as create new divisions in close-knit communities. In response, restorative justice helps redirect the focus to assure that the implementation *process* is also reparative by respecting the dignity of beneficiaries (King 2008: 1096). The respectful and fair treatment of beneficiaries goes towards repairing the non-material harms associated with human rights violations (Zehr 1990: 14–17).

The flexibility of restorative justice, especially with its reliance on victims to define the parameters of reparations, better captures some of the local customary approaches as a form of microreconciliation (Theidon 2012). Processes like Uganda's *Mato Oput* and Rwanda's *gacacas*, among others, may be viewed as reparative at the community level (Rose 2008: 345–400; Senier 2008; Gordon 2009). Similarly, East Timor resorted to local processes as part of its transitional justice experience, which began after a 1999 referendum led to independence after Indonesian occupation since 1975 (Kent 2011: 435). The United Nations Transitional Administration in East Timor (UNTAET), operating from 2000 to 2002, helped to establish a Commission for Reception, Truth and Reconciliation (*Comissão de Acolhimento, Verdade e Reconciliação de Timor Leste* (CAVR)) to undertake a nationwide truth-seeking process and organised community reconciliation hearings.[4] CAVR included a Community Reconciliation Process aimed at reintegrating estranged members of communities whose commission of politically motivated, 'less serious' crimes (Commission for Reception, Truth and Reconciliation in East Timor 2006: 2). CAVR also held Victims' Hearings and Healing Workshops designed to help restore the dignity of community members. These community-based hearings employed customary rituals such as the *nahe biti boot* which means 'stretching or laying down the mat as a means to facilitate consensus' with the help of ancestors to foster local reconciliation (Babo-Soares 2004: 21, 15). Wendy Lambourne recognises this process as a type of 'symbolic justice' that was 'designed for local conditions and with local ownership, as well as to incorporate culturally relevant symbolism and rituals, in order to support capacity building and meaningful personal and societal transformation' (Lambourne 2009: 46). While some victims felt frustrated that perpetrators did not face criminal prosecution, the CAVR found an overall high rate of satisfaction (Commission for Reception, Truth and Reconciliation in East Timor 2006: 34).

From the experience of East Timor, it is possible to see a more expansive vision of what constitutes reparation that do not per se resemble the narrower concept of only material compensation. The whole transitional justice process can itself become a form of reparation with experiences such as truth-telling and receiving information through trials producing reparative effects (Borer 2006; Kutz 2004; Laplante and Theidon 2007). This wider lens captures a 'responsive justice' spin for reconciling 'often competing justice values simultaneously' (Hill 2009: 151).

Civic justice

Whereas restorative justice refers to a vision of microreconciliation within communities, civic justice refers to a vision of macroreconciliation which mends the relation between the government and the governed. Civic justice has been defined as 'a full opportunity for all citizens to participate in the life of the commonwealth. The simple idea that all citizens must have full and equal opportunities to participate in the public realm is the basis of democratic theory and republican practice' (Trubek and Trubek 1981: 120, 126). This definition echoes the guiding tenants of 'deliberate democracy' which is 'a conception of democratic politics in which decisions and policies are justified in a process of discussion among free and equal citizens or their accountable representatives' (Gutmann and Thompson 2000: 161).

The steps required to both design and then implement government reparation programmes provide critical opportunities for governments to engage and have a dialogue with victim-survivors in their capacity as citizens (Lundy and McGovern 2008). This process itself constitutes a type of 'restitution' since human rights violations by definition trample on citizen rights. Indeed, the basic rights of citizenship (political participation, free speech, freedom of association, equal and fair treatment) tend to be those typically sacrificed during times of conflict and political violence. These experiences may lead victim survivors to feel they were treated as 'second class citizens' or even 'less than human' which is a serious harm that a government must repair to (re)gain the trust of its citizens if it is to effectively govern. Civic justice imagines a type of macro-level 'civil reconciliation' that seeks to mend the relationship between the State and its subjects while lending legitimacy to the new governing enterprise (de Greiff 2006: 460–62).

Civic justice supports the democracy-building aims of transitional justice which understands that violent conflicts can arise when governments systematically fail to respond to the grievances of marginalisation of underrepresented constituencies (Wierzynski 2004: 1934; Stromseth et al 2006: 257). Peacebuilders understand the precarious nature of peace, but also that there are many opportunities for peaceful resolution of disputes along the path to full-blown conflict. Reparation programmes offer one of the first opportunities to start establishing the habits of non-violent dispute resolution by encouraging the social process of 'deliberative politics' and 'communicative action' in which people come together to discuss, modify and agree on laws in a way that accommodates conflicts and is more likely to include minorities (Habermas and Rehg 1998: 5). As Erin Daly observes, '[b]y engaging in a dialogue with the public, the institutional actors can promote the values of the new government. This institutional response is often the earliest and most visible manifestation of the deepest values of the new order. As such, it can begin the transformation of the society at large' (Daly 2002: 75). Daly and others recognise that even if a society has formal legal equality, it suffers from actual divisions and inequalities, thus meaning that '[i]nclusion of the hitherto excluded or marginalised is emphasized' (Hudson 2007: 56). The process of restoring citizen status goes towards cultivating a culture of rights, thus reinforcing the principle that all have a right to 'equal concern and respect' and to be treated 'as an equal' (Dworkin 1977: 132–49; Young 2000) and thus contemplates what Habermas recognised as the symbiosis between democracy and the rule of law (Habermas 1995: 12–20).

Reparations are essential for assuring a cornerstone principle of the rule of law by responding to cultures of impunity and reinforcing a rights-based counter-culture that holds governments accountable for egregious human rights violations especially when pursuant to an official policy. Reparations convey recognition and acknowledgment that the government failed to respect and protect the rights of its citizens, thus symbolising the quintessential check on arbitrary government power, which the rule of law promises to deliver (Doolin 2007: 437). Drawing from classic political theory, this dynamic goes to the core of understanding the consent-based nature of a 'social contract' in which the government serves to protect the fundamental rights of citizens from arbitrary abuse at the hands of its own agents and of non-State actors (Rousseau 1968: 29–30; Gardner 1992: 362; Lyons 2007: 157).

Reparation also serves a form of rights enforcement and reinforces the international human rights law *maxim ubi ius, ibi remedium* (where there is a right, there is a remedy) (Roht-Arriaza 1995: 13–23). Locke recognised this same principle noting that 'Where the laws cannot be executed, it is all one as if there were no laws' (cited in Simmons 1991: 323). Reparations thus aim to compel governments to respect and protect fundamental rights or else pay the cost of failing to have done so. In this way, civic justice may encompass modified retributive justice theory in that civil penalties serve to deter future transgressions (Laplante 2004: 347). As recognised by John Locke, 'a damnified person has this power of appropriating to himself the goods or services of the offender, by right of self-preservation, as every man has a power to punish the crime, to prevent its being committed again, by the right he has of preserving all mankind' (cited in Simmons 1991: 323). Whereas reparations were once viewed as a 'next-best-option' to criminal penalties, they may be regarded as an equally important civil counterpart to criminal justice.

This stop on the justice continuum is necessarily more expansive as it views reparations as part of a wider 'social, political, and judicial reform processes, which together are intended to contribute to "social reconstruction"' (Lykes and Mersky 2006: 590). Reparations become a legitimising moment in which a 'new democratic governments aim to secure their authority and their values ... to transform their societies from ones that tolerated or fostered oppression to ones that respect human rights and democratic values' (Daly 2002: 73). Daly points out that this transformation of culture is necessary since simply changing the governors will not cure the problem.

This vision of political transformation appeared in Peru's transitional justice experience whose transitional government formed its Truth and Reconciliation Commission (PTRC) in 2001 after former authoritarian leader, Alberto Fujimori, fled the country due to corruption scandals. The PTRC worked for two years to investigate a 20-year period (1980–2000) that included both the internal armed conflict between the government and insurgent groups as well as Fujimori's regime. It issued a final report in 2003 that included a comprehensive plan of reparations which were viewed as key components to achieving a type of *macro*reconciliation defined as 'a process of reconstruction of a social and political pact' (Peruvian Truth and Reconciliation Commission 2003: 28, 86).

Consistent with the vision of civic justice, the *Plan Integral de Reparaciones* (PIR) became a key means for national reconciliation. PIR provides a detailed explanation as to why the State has an international obligation to guarantee the right to reparation and that the reconciliation process is intended to 'vindicate the rights of citizens that have been trampled upon' (Peruvian Truth and Reconciliation Commission 2003: 146, 102). PIR is viewed as laying the path towards building an *'estado de derecho'* (rule of law) with an active citizenry that can 'contribute to the reestablishment of civic trust and social solidarity' (Peruvian Truth and Reconciliation Commission 2003: 147).

Although the PTRC viewed all of the components of PIR as contributing to this aim of civic justice, two types of reparation are particularly oriented towards this theoretical ideal. The first form is symbolic and may consist of memorials, official and public gestures, public apologies, letters to families and public ceremonies to clear the name of those unjustly imprisoned for terrorism under Fujimori's draconian national security laws. These acts are aimed at recognising the gravity of the harm caused by the State's failure to protect the victims as well as helping to facilitate a process of recuperating the rights and dignity of citizens.

The second form is the restitution of citizen rights, which calls for 'the return of victims to the state of full citizenship, as a subject of rights ... to remove all legal stigma.' Specific recommendations include expunging criminal records as well as providing families of the disappeared legal declarations to allow inheritance laws to apply instead of existing in 'juridical limbo' (Peruvian Truth and Reconciliation Commission 2003: 182). PIR also re-issued identification documentations that had been destroyed in the war or left behind by fleeing villagers to allow victims to exercise all of their other rights, including accessing reparations. After the PTRC concluded its work, the Peruvian Ombudsman followed up on this recommendation and issued new identification documents to over 500,000 victims of political violence (Defensoria del Pueblo 2008). The objective of these reparations is a type of 'juridical rehabilitation' to establish the full and effective exercise of the person's civil and political rights (Peruvian Truth and Reconciliation Commission 2003: 184).

Socioeconomic justice

Whereas civic justice remedies political inequalities, socioeconomic justice (which sits at the far right end of the justice continuum) seeks to remedy historical social and economic inequalities. In the last five years, this form of justice has gained more currency in transitional justice circles, as scholars and practitioners advocate for recognising the links between transitional justice and development (Mani 2008: 253–65; de Greiff and Duthie 2009). This perspective understands that the causes of violent conflict (which, in turn, cause civil and political human rights violations that need to be remedied) most often arise out of deep-rooted social and economic inequalities. Responding to these structural problems not only repairs the harm suffered by victim-survivors, but also prevents new cycles of violence. Thus socioeconomic justice can be seen to blend 'financial or other material compensation, restitution or reparation for past violations or crimes (historical justice)' with that of 'distributive justice in the future (prospective justice)' (Lambourne 2009: 41).

At first glance, distributive justice appears a separate matter from that of reparations. While the corrective justice aspect of reparations, discussed above, deals with the calculation of specific damages, distributive justice 'is concerned with the best way to allocate the goods of society' (Culhane 2003: 1033). In classic political philosophy, Aristotle instructs that this form of justice is concerned with 'distributions of honour or money or other things that have to be shared among members of the political community' (Aristotle 2000: 85). Modern theorists such as John Rawls offer an utopian ideal in which '[a]ll social values – liberty and opportunity, income and wealth, and the bases of self-respect   are to be distributed equally unless an unequal distribution of any, or all, of these values is to everyone's advantage' (Rawls 1971: 62).

Yet, neither the classic nor modern theories of distributive justice arise from a remedial stance, but are rather forward looking. Yet, philosopher Robert Nozick in his critique of Rawl's theory suggests that the only justification of a distributive scheme of transfer payments would be one based on a 'principle of rectification' that would remedy past injustices (Nozick 1973: 126). Indeed, it is perhaps standing at this interstice that we see how reparations in transitional justice settings can expose the 'artificial realm' between the two types of justice (Culhane 2003: 1033; Wilson 2007).

In transitional justice circles, the confusion with socioeconomic justice may occur because funding for administrative reparation plans usually comes from State coffers, and thus tax dollars from citizens who legally would not be liable for a human rights violation (Segovia 2006). The transfer of public monies resembles more closely that of a distributive wealth policy. Lump sums or access to general public services completely disconnected from an individualised assessment of a victim's damages begins to appear like a form of distributive justice instead of corrective justice (Yepes 2009).

Yet the confusion may be lessened as truth commissions begin to include an analysis of violations of economic, social and cultural rights, and thus propose socioeconomic reparations to respond to these types of rights violation (Laplante 2008). This approach fits in well with a new line of writing in transitional justice which links to the field of sustainable peacebuilding, observing 'the twin objectives of preserving "negative peace" (absence of physical violence) and building "positive peace" (presence of social justice), as well as alleviation, if not elimination, of the underlying causes of conflict' (Lambourne 2009: 34). In fact, Rama Mani (2002) views distributive justice as a critical dimension of reparative justice in post-conflict settings. Empirical studies, including my own, have begun to reveal how reparations beneficiaries desire reparations to help cope with everyday necessities, as opposed to the more narrow focus on repairing actual harm suffered from a human rights violation and may demand this practical assistance in light of their poverty (Laplante 2007). Peacebuilding may offer the holistic and comprehensive approach to responding to war and other situations of mass atrocity since it 'implies a commitment to establishing the security, legal, political, economic, structural, cultural and psychosocial conditions necessary to promote a culture of peace in place of a culture of violence' (Lambourne 2009: 34).

The extensive writing on slavery reparations exposes the distributive justice aspect of reparations, which often propose monetary or 'in-kind transfers from whites to blacks' (Logue 2004: 1320). Aside from the difficulty of assigning blame given that a century has passed from the time of the violations, the proposals for large-scale redistributive transfers are often justified as a way to reduce substantial socioeconomic inequalities between races, thus align closely with the aims of distributive justice (Brophy 2006). Similarly, non-monetary reparations like access to healthcare and education as well as collective reparations can summon the spirit of socioeconomic justice, as was undertaken in Peru (Laplante 2007: 141). An earlier example includes Germany, which granted collective reparations in addition to individual compensation to victims of the Holocaust (Barkan 2000).

Conclusion

As the field of transitional justice moves out of its infancy, it stands at a critical juncture in preserving its own legitimacy as a valid approach to post-conflict recovery. Reflecting upon the theoretical foundations of reparations moves the conversation forward to assure that this justice mechanism deserves to figure so centrally in transitional justice settings. It sharpens the focus on what justice aims to best serve the interests of the intended beneficiaries of reparation programmes.

When seen through the victims' point of view, few reparations programmes are fully satisfactory (Waterhouse 2009: 258) and may even have 'unintended consequences that frustrate or even exacerbate the struggles of communities emerging from mass violence or from a period of repression' (Fletcher 2009: 52). This critique does not automatically justify that reparations be discarded, but rather highlights that they must be carried out with caution.

Given that transitional justice experiences are not per se victim friendly or even victim centric, it is important to institutionalise careful reflection on how to better accommodate the interests and expectations of victims. This policy requires planning to assure their participation in the planning, operation and implementation of justice measures. One first step in managing the expectations and thus the experience of victim-survivors is to identify the guiding justice theory for the design and implementation of reparations. Doing so will allow to cultivate the habit of continuous monitoring for quality control. A country embarking on a transitional justice project that includes reparations must think carefully about what step on the reparation justice continuum they aim to reach, and then clearly articulate these goals. Otherwise, their public message may not match the actual results, resulting in victim frustration and rejection of programmes – a state of affairs that could compromise the overall justice project. The justice continuum model proposed here recognises that while a 'maximalist' approach that encompasses the full range of justice aims would be ideal, at minimum a reparation programme should aim to do no further harm to those it intends to benefit (Rubio-Marín and de Greiff 2007: 331; Laplante 2010; Rubio-Marín 2011: 16). This external reference point assures that post-truth commission reparations, as a justice mechanism, work consistently with the wider aims of transitional justice so as to avoid putting a whole transitional justice enterprise at risk.

Notes

* I would like to thank Kevin Cummings, James Gallagher, Jocelyn Kennedy and Caitlin Peruccio for their research assistance.
1 Some recent examples include J. Miller and R. Kumar (eds) (2006) *Reparations: Interdisciplinary Inquiries*, New York, NY: Oxford University Press; Pablo de Greiff (ed.) (2006) *The Handbook of Reparations*, Oxford: Oxford University Press; E. Doxtader and C. Villa-Vicencio David Philip (eds) (2004) *To Repair the Irreparable: Reparation and Reconstruction in South Africa*, Cape Town: David Philips Publisher; M. Du Plessis and S. Pete (2007) *Repairing the Past? International Perspectives on Reparations for Gross Human Rights Abuses*, Antwerp: Intersentia Publishers; J. Elster (ed.) (2006) *Retribution and Reparation in the Transition to Democracy*, Cambridge, MA: Cambridge University Press; R. Rubio-Marin (ed.) (2006) *What Happened to the Women? Gender and Reparations for Human Rights Violations*, New York, NY: Social Science Research Council; S. Slyomovics and B. Rose Johnston (eds) (2008) *Waging War, Making Peace: Reparations and Human Rights*, Walnut Creek, CA: Left Coast Press; P.C. Bornkamm, *Rwanda's Gacaca Courts: Between Retribution and Reparation*, Oxford Monographs in International Humanitarian and Criminal Law, Oxford: Oxford University Press, 2012.
2 A few of the notable exceptions include R. Teitel (2002) 'Reparatory Justice', in R. Teitel, *Transitional Justice*, New York, NY: Oxford University Press, P. de Greiff (2006) 'Justice and Reparations', in P. de Greiff (ed.) *The Handbook of Reparations*, New York, NY: Oxford University Press, and A. Vermeule (2012) 'Reparations as Rough Justice', in M.S. Williams, R. Nagy and J. Elster (eds) *Transitional Justice*, New York, NY: New York University Press.
3 Wendy Lambourne constructs a theory of justice for transitional justice generally that she feels 'leaves room for cultural interpretation and application' and 'encourages practitioners to be inclusive and mindful of the complexity of human needs and responses in order to avoid the tendency to oversimplify and impose limited or one-size-fits-all solutions' (Lambourne 2009: 46, see also Lambourne, Chapter 1 in this volume). Her experience coupled with my own reflections on this topic lead me to believe that the very nature of transitional justice may, by necessity, require more flexible theoretical models and perhaps multiple models capable of coexisting.
4 The UN also established a hybrid international tribunal, known as the Special Panels for Serious Crimes, to investigate and prosecute cases of war crimes, crimes against humanity, genocide, murder, torture and sexual offences.

Bibliography

Antkowiak, T. (2008) 'Remedial Approaches to Human Rights Violations: The Inter-American Court of Human Rights and Beyond', *Columbia Journal of Transnational Law*, 46 (2): 351–419.

——(2011) 'An Emerging Mandate for International Courts: Victim-Centered Remedies and Restorative Justice', *Stanford Journal of International Law*, 47: 279–332.

Aristotle (1962) *Nicomachean Ethics*, trans. M. Ostwald, New York, NY: Pearson.

——(2000) *Nicomachean Ethics*, trans. R. Crisp, Cambridge: Cambridge University Press.

Babo-Soares, D. (2004) 'Nahe Biti: The Philosophy and Process of Grassroots Reconciliation (and Justice) in East Timor', *Asia Pacific Journal of Anthropology*, 5 (1): 15–33.

Barkan, E. (2000) *The Guilt of Nations: Restitution and Negotiating Historical Injustices*, New York, NY: W.W. Norton & Company.

Borer, T.A. (ed.) (2006) *Telling the Truths: Truth Telling and Peace Building in Post-Conflict Societies*, South Bend, IN: University of Notre Dame Press.

Braithwaite, J. (2002) *Restorative Justice & Responsive Regulation*, New York, NY: Oxford University Press.

Brophy, A. (2006) 'Reconsidering Reparations', *Indiana Law Journal*, 81 (3): 811–50.

Coleman, J. (1995) 'The Practice of Corrective Justice', in Owen, D. (ed.) *Philosophical Foundations of Tort Law*, New York, NY: Oxford University Press.

Commission for Reception, Truth and Reconciliation in East Timor (2006) 'Chega! The Report of the Commission for Reception, Truth and Reconciliation in Timor-Leste (CAVR)'. Available at: <http://www.cavr-timorleste.org/chegaFiles/finalReportEng/09-Community-Reconciliation.pdf> (accessed 24 November 2012).

Culhane, J. (2003) 'Tort, Compensation, and Two Kinds of Justice', *Rutgers Law Review*, 55 (4): 1027–107.

Cunneen, C. (2006) 'Exploring the relationship between reparations, the gross violation of human rights, and restorative justice', in Sullivan, D. and Tifft, L. (eds) *Handbook of Restorative Justice: A Global Perspective*, New York, NY: Routledge.

Daly, E. (2002) 'Transformative Justice: Charting a Path to Reconciliation', *International Legal Perspectives*, 12 (1 and 2): 73–183.

Defensoria del Pueblo (2008) 'Devolverles su identidad es devolverles sus derechos. Supervisión a los registros siniestrados a consecuencia de la violencia política'. Available at: <http://www.defensoria.gob.pe/temas.php?des=9#r> (accessed 24 November 2012).

de Greiff, P. (2006) 'Justice and Reparations', in de Greiff, P. (ed.) *The Handbook of Reparations*, New York, NY: Oxford University Press.

de Greiff, P. and Duthie, R. (eds.) (2009) *Transitional Justice and Development. Making Connections*, New York, NY: Social Science Research Council.

Di Giovanni, A. (2005) 'The Prospect of ICC Reparations in the Case Concerning Northern Uganda: On a Collision Course with Incoherence', *Journal of International Law and International Relations*, 2 (2): 25–64.

Doolin, K. (2007) 'But What does it mean? Seeking Definitional Clarity in Restorative Justice', *Journal of Criminal Law*, 71 (5): 427–40.

Dworkin, R. (1977) *Taking Rights Seriously*, Cambridge, MA: Harvard University Press.

Englard, I. (2009) *Corrective and Distributive Justice: From Aristotle to Modern Times*, New York, NY: Oxford University Press.

Eschholz, S. (2003) 'Restorative Justice: Social Movement, Theory, and Practice', *Criminal Justice Review*, 28 (1): 146–53.

Fletcher, L.E. (2009) 'Institutions from Above and Voices from Below: A Comment on Challenges to Group-Conflict Resolution and Reconciliation', *Law and Contemporary Problems*, 72 (2): 51–55.

Gabbay, Z. (2005) 'Justifying Restorative Justice: A Theoretical Justification for the Use of Restorative Justice Practices', *Journal of Dispute Resolution*, 2: 349–97.

Gardner, E.C. (1992) 'John Locke: Justice and the Social Compact', *Journal of Law and Religion*, 9 (2): 347–71.

Gordon, G. (2009) 'Complementarity and Alternative Justice', *Oregon Law Review*, 88: 101–82.

Guembe, M. (2006) 'Economic Reparations for Grave Human Rights Violations: The Argentinean Experience', in de Greiff, P. (ed.) *The Handbook of Reparations*, New York, NY: Oxford University Press.

Guillerot, J. *et al* (2009) 'The Rabat Report: The Concept and Challenges of Collective Reparations'. Available at: <http://www.ictj.org/sites/default/files/ICTJ-Morocco-Reparations-Report-2009-English.pdf> (accessed 24 November 2012).

Gutmann, A. and Thompson, D. (2000) 'Why Deliberative Democracy is Different', *Social Philosophy and Policy*, 17: 161–80.

Habermas, J. (1995) 'On the Internal Relation between the Rule of Law and Democracy', *European Journal of Philosophy*, 3 (1): 12–20.

Habermas, J. and Rehg, W. (1998) *Between Facts and Norms: Contributions to a Discourse Theory of Law and Democracy*, Cambridge, MA: MIT Press.

Harris, D., Campbell, D. and Halson, R. (eds) (2002) *Remedies in Contract and Tort*, Cambridge: Cambridge University Press.

Hayner, P. (2001) *Unspeakable Truths: Confronting State Terror and Atrocity*, New York, NY: Routledge.

——(2010) *Unspeakable Truths: Transitional Justice and the Challenge of Truth Commissions*, New York, NY: Routledge.

Hill, F. (2009) 'Restorative Justice: Sketching a New Legal Discourse', *Contemporary Readings in Law and Social Justice*, 1 (1): 115–62.

Hudson, B. (2007) 'The Institutionalisation of Restorative Justice: Justice and the Ethics of Discourse', *Acta Juridica*: 56–72.

IER (2006) *Summary of the Final Report*, Casablanca: Imprimerie Najah al-Jadida.

Kent, L. (2011) 'Local Memory Practices in East Timor: Disrupting Transitional Justice Narratives', *International Journal of Transitional Justice*, 5 (3): 434–55.

King, M. (2008) 'Restorative Justice, Therapeutic Jurisprudence and the Rise of Emotionally Intelligent Justice', *Melbourne University Law Review*, 32: 1096–126.

Koen, R. (2007) 'The Antinomies of Restorative Justice', *Acta Juridica: Restorative Justice: Politics, Policies and Prospects*: 247–71.

Kutz, C. (2004), 'Justice in Reparations: The Cost of Memory and the Value of Talk', *Philosophy & Public Affairs*, 32 (3): 277–312.

Lambourne, W. (2009) 'Transitional Justice and Peacebuilding after Mass Violence', *International Journal of Transitional Justice*, 3 (1): 28–48.

Laplante, L.J. (2004) 'Bringing Effective Remedies Home: The Inter-American Human Rights System, Reparations, and the Duty of Prevention', *Netherlands Quarterly of Human Rights*, 22 (3): 347–88.

——(2007) 'On the Indivisibility of Rights: Truth Commissions, Reparations, and the Right to Development', *Yale Human Rights and Development Law Journal*, 10: 141–77.

——(2008) 'Transitional Justice and Peace Building: Diagnosing and Addressing the Socio-economic Roots of Violence through a Human Rights Framework', *International Journal of Transitional Justice*, 2 (3): 331–55.

——(2010) 'Evaluating Truth Commissions and Reparations through the Eyes of Victims', *L'Observateur des Nations Unies*, 28 (1): 167–76.

Laplante, L.J. and Theidon, K. (2007) 'Truth with Consequences: Justice and Reparations in Post-Truth Commission Peru', *Human Rights Quarterly*, 29 (1): 228–50.

Lira, E. (2006) 'The Reparation Policy for Human Rights Violations in Chile', in de Greiff, P. (ed.) *The Handbook of Reparations*, New York, NY: Oxford University Press.

Logue, K. (2004) 'Reparations as Redistribution', *Boston University Law Review*, 84 (5): 1319–74.

Lundy, P. and McGovern, M. (2008) 'Whose Justice? Rethinking Transitional Justice from the Bottom Up', *Journal of Law and Society*, 35 (2): 265–92.

Lykes, M.B. and Mersky, M. (2006) 'Reparations and Mental Health: Psychosocial Interventions Towards Healing, Human Agency, and Rethreading Social Realities', in de Greiff, P. (ed.) *The Handbook of Reparations*, New York, NY: Oxford University Press.

Lyons, E.C. (2007) 'Reason's Freedom and the Dialectic of Ordered Liberty', *Cleveland State Law Review*, 55 (2): 157–234.

Malamud-Goti, J. and Grosman, L. (2006) 'Reparations and Civil Litigation: Compensation for Human Rights Violations in Transitional Democracies', in de Greiff, P. (ed.) *The Handbook of Reparations*, New York, NY: Oxford University Press.

Mani, R. (2002) *Beyond Retribution: Seeking Justice in the Shadows of War*, Cambridge: Polity Press.

——(2008) 'Dilemmas of Expanding Transitional Justice, or Forging the Nexus between Transitional Justice and Development', *International Journal of Transitional Justice*, 2 (3): 253–65.

Marshall, T. (1999). *Restorative Justice: An Overview*, London: Home Office Research Development and Statistics Directorate.

Menkel-Meadow, C. (2007) 'Restorative Justice: What Is it and Does it Work?', *Third Annual Review of Law and Social Science*, 3: 10.1–10.27.

Nozick, R. (1973) 'Distributive Justice', *Philosophy & Public Affairs*, 3 (1): 45–126.

Pauley, M. (1994) 'The Jurisprudence of Crime and Punishment from Plato to Hegel', *American Journal of Jurisprudence*, 39 (1): 97–152.

Peruvian Truth and Reconciliation Commission (2003) 'Peruvian Truth and Reconciliation Commission, Final Report, Vol. 9'. Available at: <http://www.usip.org/files/file/resources/collections/commissions/Peru01-Report/Peru01-Report_Vol9.pdf > (accessed 24 November 2012).

Rawls, J. (1971) *A Theory of Justice*, Cambridge, MA: Harvard University Press.

Roht-Arriaza, N. (1995) 'Punishment, Redress, and Pardon: Theoretical and Psychological Approaches', in Roht-Arriaza, N. (ed.) *Impunity and Human Rights in International Law*, New York, NY: Oxford University Press.

——(2004a) 'Reparations Decisions and Dilemmas', *Hastings International & Comparative Law Review*, 27: 157–219.

——(2004b) 'Reparations in the Aftermath of Repression and Mass Violence', in Stover, E. and Weinstein, H. (eds) *My Neighbor, My Enemy: Justice and Community in the Aftermath of Mass Atrocity*, Cambridge: Cambridge University Press.

Rose, C. (2008) 'Looking beyond Amnesty and Traditional Justice and Reconciliation Mechanisms in Northern Uganda: A Proposal for Truth-Telling and Reparations', *Boston College Third World Law Journal*, 28 (2): 345–400.

Rousseau, J.J (1968) *The Social Contract*, trans. M. Cranston, New York, NY: Penguin Books.

Rubio-Marín, R. (ed.) (2011) *The Gender of Reparations: Unsettling Sexual Hierarchies while Redressing Human Rights Violations*, Cambridge: Cambridge University Press.

Rubio-Marín, R. and de Greiff, P. (2007) 'Women and Reparations', *International Journal of Transitional Justice*, 1 (3): 318–37.

Schneider, A. (2009) 'Bargaining in the Shadow of (International) Law: Why the Normalization of Adjudication in International Governance Regimes Means for Dispute Resolution', *New York University Journal of International Law*, 41: 789–822.

Segovia, A. (2006) 'Financing Reparations Programs: Reflections from International Experience', in de Greiff, P. (ed.) *The Handbook of Reparations*, New York, NY: Oxford University Press.

Senier, A. (2008) 'Traditional Justice as Transitional Justice: A Comparative Case Study of Rwanda and East Timor', *PRAXIS The Fletcher Journal of Human Security*, 233: 67–99.

Shaw, R., Waldorf, L. and Hazan, P. (eds) (2010) *Localizing Transitional Justice*, Stanford, CA: Stanford University Press.

Shelton, D. (2006) *Remedies in International Human Rights Law*, New York, NY: Oxford University Press.

Simmons, J.A. (1991) 'Locke and the Right to Punish', *Philosophy and Public Affairs*, 20 (4): 311–49.

Slyomovics, S. (2001) 'A Truth Commission for Morocco', *Middle East Report*, 218: 18–21.

Strang, H. and Sherman, L. (2003) 'Repairing the Harm: Victims and Restorative Justice', *Utah Law Review*, 15: 15–42.

Stromseth, J., Wippman, D. and Brooks, R. (eds) (2006) *Can Might Make Rights? Building the Rule of Law After Military Interventions*, Cambridge: Cambridge University Press.

Theidon, K. (2012) *Intimate Enemies: Violence and Reconciliation in Peru*, Philadelphia, PA: University of Pennsylvania Press.

Trubek, L. and Trubek, D. (1981) 'Civic Justice Through Civil Justice: A New Approach to Public Interest Advocacy in the United States', in Cappelletti, M. (ed.) *Access to Justice and the Welfare State*, Florence: Sijthoff.

United Nations (2006) 'Basic Principles and Guidelines on the Right to a Remedy and Reparation for Survivors of Violations of International Human Rights and Humanitarian Law', U.N. Doc. A/RES/60/147, 21 March 2006.

Villa-Vicencio, C. (2000) 'Restorative justice: dealing with the past', in Villa-Vicencio, C. and Verwoerd, W. (eds) *Looking Back, Reaching Forward: Reflections on the Truth and Reconciliation Commission of South Africa*, London: Zed Books.

Waldman, E. (2007) 'Restorative Justice and the Pre-Conditions for Grace: Taking Victims' Needs Seriously', *Cardozo Journal of Conflict Resolution*, 9: 91–108.

Waterhouse, C.M. (2009) 'The Good, the Bad and the Ugly: Moral Agency and the Role of Victims in Reparations Programs', *University of Pennsylvania Journal of International Law*, 31 (1): 257–94.

Wierzynski, A. (2004) 'Consolidating Democracy through Transitional Justice: Rwanda's Gacaca Courts', *New York University Law Review*, 79 (5): 1934–69.

Wilson, N. (2007) 'Is Corrective Justice Subsidiary to Distributive Justice? Which Answer Better Captures the Meaning of Tort Law Practice?', *Trinity College Law Review*, 10: 44–59.

Yepes, R.U. (2009) 'Transformative Reparations of Massive Gross Human Rights Violations: Between Corrective and Distributive Justice', *Netherlands Quarterly of Human Rights*, 27 (4): 625–48.

Young, I.M. (2000) *Inclusion and Democracy*, Oxford: Oxford University Press.

Zehr, H. (1990) *Changing Lenses: A New Focus for Crime and Justice*, Scottdale, PA: Herald Press.

Chapter 4

Political liberalism after mass violence

John Rawls and a 'theory' of transitional justice

Kora Andrieu[1]

> What justifies a conception of justice is not its being true to an order antecedent and given to us, but its congruence with our deeper understanding of ourselves and our aspirations, and our realization that, given our history and the traditions embedded in our public life, it is the most reasonable doctrine to us.
>
> John Rawls (1980: 519)

After the fall of the Berlin Wall and witnessing the decline of Marxism as a dominant and institutionalised political ideology, Francis Fukuyama controversially affirmed that the 'end of history' would be marked by liberal democracy as the final, supreme form of human governance. This idea has been widely criticised as being overly naïve in the face of the ongoing emergence of ethno-nationalism and religious fundamentalism. Fukuyama's claim, however, should not be taken as an empirical observation but rather as a normative one. As he himself suggests: 'the assertion that we have reached the end of history is not a statement about the empirical condition of the world, but *a normative argument* concerning the justice or adequacy of liberal democratic political institutions' (Fukuyama 1999: 38). In the thought and practice of the international community, liberalism is indeed the only criterion of political acceptability, the *telos* of any 'normal' political progress. The international outcry when the Libyan National Transitional Council announced its desire to anchor the first post-Gaddafi constitution in the Islamic law and the reluctant acceptance of results in Tunisia's and Egypt's first elections, which were won by Islamic parties, are powerful indicators of this 'normalisation' of liberal democracy.

The goal of this chapter is to read transitional justice through the lens of political philosophy, and to analyse its assumptions in terms of the types of regime it promotes. More specifically, I study the field of transitional justice from the point of view of a Rawlsian understanding of political liberalism, examining possible tensions that may arise between the two, and suggesting ways to overcome them. Indeed, although transitional justice is recognised as a discipline in its own right, very few scholars have attempted to integrate it with a specific philosophy of justice, to think of its goals in terms of *types of regime*, in the light once more of Aristotle's eternal question: 'What is the best form of regime'? Instead, it seems as if the assumption is, naturally, that the goal is liberalisation and democratisation: an open society where no one is excluded because of their ethnicity or beliefs, where citizens can pursue their own happiness and abide the pursuits of their peers, where there is both liberty and opportunity for all. But is transitional justice realistic in its aims? Is it fully equipped for the arduous task of building a liberal democracy? And if not, does this mean that we should re-think the measures, or re-think the goal? I suggest that in the aftermath of dictatorship or mass atrocity, a strictly neutral, procedural understanding of politics, such as defended by Rawlsian theories of liberalism, may seem insufficient to restore meaning and repair social ties. A thicker, more substantial conception of political liberalism may, therefore, be needed.

Liberal theories of justice

John Rawls' 1971 *Theory of Justice* is widely considered as being the foundation for a renewal of political liberalism itself, and sparked important debates in political philosophy. Indeed, Rawls argues for a reconciliation of liberty and equality, and the creation of an ideal condition for parties engaged in the 'circumstances of justice', marked by scarcity and a lack of pure altruism. Rawls constructs a situation of fair choice: an original position, where, under a veil of ignorance that masks all their characteristics and particularities, the parties must agree to binding and universal principles of justice. Rawls thereby suggests that a just society is one where basic rights and liberties are guaranteed to all citizens equally, so that they may pursue their own 'comprehensive doctrine', or conception of the good, as it applies to their individual lives. The just society must, furthermore, rest on a purely political, and not metaphysical, conception of justice. This 'axiological neutrality' is the condition of pluralism, which Rawls regards as fundamental, and the certain result of the exercise of free practical reason. Society must provide a minimum of the 'primary goods', all-purpose means with which individuals may pursue their interests and safeguard their self-respect. Fair competition and equal opportunity should therefore be enshrined in law.

What distinguishes Rawls' account from previous conceptions of liberalism is that it endorses a social consensus without grounding it on any metaphysical foundations – hence the idea of 'political liberalism', as opposed to the more comprehensive, robustly metaphysical liberalism envisioned by Locke or Mill. Rawls seeks to consolidate the potential for liberal consensus in the face of the disparate religious, moral or metaphysical backgrounds specific to the respective parties involved. He calls the result an 'overlapping consensus' – a synthesis of different and often conflicting views of morality, as it applies to the question of governance and the 'basic structure' of society.

Political liberalism is thus defined as strictly neutral in its conception of politics, which distinguishes it from metaphysical conceptions of the Good. This procedural, technocratic conception of politics appears as the condition of a truly open society, ensuring as it does the prevalence of both tolerance and consistency. Neutrality is for Rawls the only option, given what he calls 'the fact of pluralism'. In that, he is sympathetic to a common post-modern feeling concerning the impotence of reason – that it cannot ascertain or devise ultimate meaning or, indeed, be relied upon as a barometer of the 'universal' good. Individual consciousness is left alone to grapple with such complex, and seemingly subjective abstractions. Disagreement and conflict are viewed as being intrinsic to political discourse itself. Indeed, liberals do not consider cultural diversity to be a threat, but rather an asset: 'Under political and social conditions secured by the basic rights and liberties of free institutions', writes Rawls, 'a diversity of conflicting and irreconcilable – and what's more, reasonable – comprehensive doctrines will come about and persist if such diversity does not already obtain' (Rawls 1996: 36). He interestingly adds that 'a continuing shared understanding of one comprehensive religious, moral, or philosophical doctrine can be maintained only by the oppressive use of state power' (Rawls 1996: 37).

Free institutions are therefore defined by pluralism, which is the characteristic of any healthy democracy. The only necessary consensus is the one concerning the value of the institutional framework that preserves basic rights. As Rawls himself states, 'Political liberalism offers a political understanding of justice as an independent theory. It does not give any particular epistemological or metaphysical doctrine beyond what is required by the political conception itself' (Rawls 1995: 35). The right, then, exists prior to the good. The former is neither an extension of the latter, nor its codification in law. This idea is a contentious one, especially among communitarian thinkers, who argue that the total separation of politics and 'comprehensive doctrines' is not possible, and that, in a multicultural society, benevolent neutrality can only ever conceal, in reality, the quiet dominion of one group over another. Other scholars have questioned to what extent Rawls' theory can be applied in concrete spheres of justice, such as minority rights, military interventions, or global poverty (Kymlicka 1995; Beitz 1999). The debates that began in response to Rawls' theory thus seemed to be initiating a new phase in political discourse: by applying concepts and speculations to such concrete issues, political philosophers appeared to forsake the world of ideas and turn back to reality.[2] It was from concrete observation, and empirical debate in the public sphere, that philosophers would derive their norms and principles, not abstract speculation and theoretical contrivance. This form of 'applied practical philosophy' would surely be the best way to use 'the resources of a philosophy, which still has that weakness of believing itself able to contribute, even just a little, to improving the world' (Renaut 2005: 22).

Transitional justice and political liberalism

For a philosophy that looks beyond ideal conditions of justice, or original positions where 'all things are equal', transitional justice represents a particularly rich and interesting sphere of application. The idea of political liberalism, it is worth reminding, was born out of the religious wars that followed the Protestant Reform. In seeking to avoid the eternal and multiform 'war of the gods', liberals proposed that social concord would only be acquired as the result of a moral and epistemological 'neutralisation' of politics. Moreover, a cursory analysis of recent events in the Arab world demonstrates how references to complex concepts of political philosophy are ubiquitous: some call for the 'truth' about past human rights violations to be established, others for a new 'social contract' to be written – these ideas are often cited as a necessary condition of 'reconciliation'. If liberal democracy is indeed the 'end' of history, then it should also be the *telos*, or goal, of any political transitions today. However, in the highly charged and extremely delicate conditions of post-conflict and transitional societies, political liberalism may seem too 'cold', too procedural a conception to assist in the creation of new social foundations. How does one rebuild a liberal society after mass violence? Is it possible, or is a more substantial, 'thicker' conception of politics needed, one with greater meaning and a more sophisticated 'healing' capacity? This is the question I now try to answer.

The UN and other 'experts' in the field of transitional justice, have long, albeit implicitly, defined the end goal of peacebuilding and transitional justice operations as being the cultivation of some form of liberal democracy (see, e.g. Sriram 2007; Richmond and Franks 2009; Andrieu 2010). This tendency is related to a wider trend in peacekeeping practices conceived in the aftermath of the Cold War and defined in Boutros Ghali's 'Agenda for Peace'. According to this idea, peacebuilding operations must employ a wide range of political, developmental and humanitarian programmes and mechanisms in order to prevent the recurrence of violence by promoting democracy, eradicating poverty, guaranteeing sustainable development and promoting the rule of law (United Nations Security Council 2001). The aim is both negative peace (the absence of physical violence) and positive peace (the absence of structural injustices) (Galtung 1990).[3] Notions such as 'dangerous underdevelopment' (Duffield 2001), the 'security/development nexus' (World Bank 2011) and 'human security' are parts of the same holistic and normative approach to peace. Peacemaking thus becomes peacebuilding, linking together development with peace, and peace with democracy: 'There is no development or democracy without peace', writes Boutros Ghali, adding that 'without development, the basis of democracy is lacking and societies will relapse into violence' (United Nations 1992: 43). This positive conception of peace is morally connoted and deeply ethical. According to John-Paul Lederach, peacebuilding includes 'everything that comprehends, generates, and sustains the wide variety of necessary stages and approaches in order to transform conflict situations into pacific and durable relations' (Lederach 1997). This liberal peacebuilding is based on the ideal of the democratic peace: the notion that building stable democracies around the world will bring about 'perpetual peace', as democracies do not go to war against each other. But such a peace cannot happen immediately, and as the recent cases of Tunisia, Egypt and Libya show, people do not become liberal democrats overnight. Transitional justice mechanisms are designed precisely with the purpose of securing the 'transition' of post-conflict States into functional democracies. Their goal is justice, reparations and transformation in the wake of mass violence. These ideals are strongly linked to the assumption that societies need to confront the past in order to move forward: in this new international framework, amnesty and amnesia are no longer normatively acceptable.

The idea of transitional justice as a separate field of research and action was first conceived during the 'third wave' of democratisation in Latin America, as a means of facilitating the evolution of those States involved, from bloody dictatorships to liberal democracies.[4] Transitional justice is thus an application of justice for political change, and includes not only juridical answers to past repressions, but also restorative, administrative and economic measures. It has now become an essential component of any peacebuilding operation, theorised as such by the UN and the World Bank themselves (de Greiff 2011a). The goals of transitional justice are rather ambitious, aiming at nothing less than the transformation, or regeneration, of whole societies. To that end, political, economical, cultural, sociological and psychological actions are taken: prosecutions, TRCs, lustration, the provision of public access to police and governmental records, public apologies, public memorials, reburials, compensation, reparation and literary and historical records are all instruments of this process. It is a notably positive response to mass violence, one contrary to the defeatist argument that views genocide, mass atrocities and the like as crimes that 'transcend the domain of humane affairs' (Arendt 1958: 307) – forever unforgivable and without redress. The teleology of 'transition' in transitional justice is indeed optimistic and seductive – by positing a 'before-and-after narrative of change', it implies that '"after" will necessarily be better'.

Transitional justice has been conceived by the United National Secretary General's Report on 'The Rule of Law and Transitional Justice in Conflict and Post-Conflict Societies' in a rather sophisticated manner, as 'the full range of processes and mechanisms associated with a society's attempts to come to terms with a legacy of large-scale past abuses, in order to ensure accountability, serve justice and achieve reconciliation' (United Nations Secretary General 2004: 1). Such wording gives the impression that transitional justice is a theory of justice in its own right, not an extraordinary form of justice for use in extreme situations, where much compromise is required.

The condition for a real theory, according to transitional justice scholar Pablo de Greiff, is indeed 'a comprehensive conception' which 'articulates the relationship that the different measures have to one another, the relationship between these measures and the normative goals ... the measures should seek, or the relationship between these different goals, some of which may clash' (de Greiff 2011b: 14). Considering that articulating a normative theory entails clarifying its constituent elements, I now try to show how transitional justice's means, and its measures, may ultimately undermine its intention, understood as the formation of a liberal democracy and the (re-) creation of a procedural, neutral, tolerant and open conception of politics and the public sphere: 'to induce former combatants to resolve their differences and to build a society that is representative and tolerant of diverse viewpoints' (Yordan 2009: 61).

I emphasise three main contradictions in the present relation between transitional justice and this liberal peace ideal:

(a)   in its *retributive* sense, transitional justice corresponds to a moral understanding of law that contradicts the legalist impulse of liberalism and its neutral definition of politics as 'non-metaphysical';

(b)   in its *restorative* sense, it presents a conception of the Self that is intrinsically narrative in nature, thereby contradicting the 'disembodied' Self of Rawls' original position; and it defends a thick conception of social unity, that places the community before individuals;

(c)   in its *distributive*, social sense, it revises the liberal model of neutral distribution of economic primary goods (Rawls' second principle of justice) and the Washington consensus on growth, towards a more differentiated, culture-sensitive approach based on recognition and which includes the possibility of collective rights.

Retributive justice: liberalism, morality and the law

Transitional justice is thought of as having been first conceived at the time of the Nuremberg trials, a model of accountability focusing on individual responsibility, which took place in Germany after the Second World War (Teitel 2000). This genealogical link between transitional justice and Nuremberg is revealing in itself. Indeed, Nuremberg was characterised by a highly moral use of the law. The founding idea of the trials was that the crimes committed called for a broader understanding of the law, and exposed the limits of legal positivism. The trials were used as a platform from which to tell a story about the suffering and injustices inflicted by the Nazi regime upon its numerous victims. A cinema screen was introduced into the courtroom for the first time and the prosecutor, Robert Jackson, used these images to confront the perpetrators with their deeds, while survivors and victims testified, often in their presence. It was an encounter designed to restore the moral order. The challenge of Nuremberg was clear: the re-founding of a political and moral community through the narration of past horrors. The law thereby acquired a highly normative and symbolic function.

Similarly, today, in attempts to justify the condemnation of human rights violators, war criminals and dictators, one finds not only the argument that justice must be done for all, but also that trials have many curative powers: they establish truth; they educate the public about the nature of past abuses and they promote a shared retrospective understanding. Furthermore, they help to rebuild the rule of law after mass atrocities, upholding its universality and continuing authority; and reinforce moral norms – forging a nationwide moral consensus regarding the intolerable nature of the atrocities committed. The International Criminal Tribunal for the former Yugoslavia (ICTY, established 1993) and the ICTR (established 1994), as well as the ICC (established 2002), all employed the same retributive model. As in Nuremberg, these trials were also used for larger, more ambitious, purposes: 'ending human rights violations and preventing their recurrence in the future, guaranteeing victim's rights and their dignity, establishing the truth about the past, promoting national reconciliation, re-establishing the rule of law, and helping the building of a sustainable peace' (United Nations Secretary General 2004: 13).

Beyond the fact that these goals are difficult to accomplish and almost impossible to measure, they raise important theoretical difficulties from the point of view of political liberalism, which has traditionally been associated with a form of 'legalism', a doctrine according to which law is fundamentally distinct from politics. On the contrary, advocates of retributive transitional justice approach it from a consequentialist or utilitarian perspective, arguing that justice must be done not just for its own sake, as a legalist would assume, but because it is also socially useful. Retributive justice is thus considered a means towards an end, and trials, containing as they do an expressive and educative function (Osiel 1997), are 'used' for the sake of democratic transition.

This idea is certainly not new, as trials have long been presented as morally important events in the building of a nation's identity. The French sociologist Emile Durkheim saw them as an essential means of reactivating social solidarity by offering society the occasion to gather in common rejection of crime and reaffirmation of moral values. Bruce Ackermann calls trials 'constitutional moments' (Ackerman 1991: 84): they are a show, a sociopolitical drama. Hannah Arendt was aware of that dimension when she assisted in Adolf Eichmann's trial in Jerusalem: Ben Gourion wanted indeed the trial to reunify Israeli society, 'to be a purifying, exciting collective experience: a national catharsis' (Seguev 2000: 328). Punishment is thus supposed to have a pedagogical function for society as a whole: it is a way of restoring a lost social harmony.

For the liberal mind, however, this raises the danger of 'show trials', which are problematic not only because they instrumentalise and moralise the law, but also because they sacrifice the individual right to a fair trial in the name of general, and often partisan political goals. In Rawls' words, they do not respect the distinct character of individual persons. Of course, in Nuremberg and elsewhere, the violation of certain positive rules of due process, such as the principle of non-retroactivity, was justified by the beneficial effects that were expected to flow from the trials. However, for an orthodox liberal, this amounts to sacrificing an individual for the sake of the collective good. In order to avoid such a risk, liberalism relies on an 'ethically pure' and neutral conception of law: legalism, which Judith Shklar defines as 'an ethical attitude that holds moral conduct to be a matter of rule-following, and moral relationships to consist of duties and rights determined by rules' (Shklar 1963: 1). For liberals, the law should therefore operate unimpeded by moral or political interferences.

Restorative justice: truth, forgiveness and the narrative self

As transitional justice evolved, so did its methodology. The adversarial nature of retributive justice has often been criticised for focusing solely on the perpetrators, thereby having little 'healing' power for victims and little effect on social reconciliation. The individualisation of guilt, which is at the foundation of retributive justice, is certainly important to avoid the collective stigmatisation of a whole people, but it also can create large impunity gaps, ignoring the political and legal framework in which these individual transgressions were allowed to occur (Nino 1999: 145). Prosecutions tend indeed to be technical, long and tedious, trivialising the deep, personal suffering under discussion. Their formalism and rigidity has been criticised for not accurately reflecting the experience of victims (Auckerman 2002). As an alternative, restorative justice shifts justice back to the victims and their community, considering that crime is not only an issue of lawbreaking, but also something that impacts harmfully on whole communities and also affects the humanity of the perpetrator.[5] Justice, in this understanding, should aim at reconciling the affected parties and collectively repairing the wrong, rather than simply punishing the perpetrator (Brainswaite 1999; Kiss 2000).

Restorative justice implies a democratisation of the social control of punishment, which was initially applied to small-scale juvenile offenders' crimes. Truth and reconciliation commissions rely on that same paradigm. Their goals are ambitious: to unearth, clarify and acknowledge past violations, to respond to victim's needs and restore their dignity, to create a culture of accountability and respect for the rule of law, to outline institutional responsibility and possible reforms, to advance the prospects of individual and national reconciliation and to reduce historical conflict arising from differing perceptions of the past (Hayner 2002: 24). Truth commissions rest on a participatory understanding of 'truth', and are extra-judicial mechanisms with no power to sanction or subpoena. But their worldview is far removed from the neutral procedures of liberalism. They tend to emphasise the group over the individual, often asking victims to renounce their right to justice and their desire for revenge in the name of national reconciliation. The law is used, here, as a way of emphasising an individual's duty to a larger group, rather than an individual's rights and entitlements.

Truth commissions are also filled with sentimental, ethical notions such as healing, forgiveness and reconciliation, and founded on a thick, narrative understanding of the Self, which is far from the 'disembodied' Self of political liberalism encountered, for instance, in Rawls' original position. In general, the disembodied, or unencumbered Self, seems far from the individualism promoted by advocates of transitional justice. Following Kant, Rawls defines this abstract Self as 'the subject of all possible ends', a 'transcendental subject' which participates in an unconditioned realm of ideas, independent of social and psychological influences. Only by considering ourselves as such, in standing at a distance from our circumstances, can we be agents and not just instruments of the purposes we pursue (Sandel 1984). In itself, this vision is truly liberating: it implies that the human subject can, at any moment, free himself from the impositions of nature and social roles, and be installed as the moral sovereign, free to construct justice unconstrained by any pre-existing moral order.

On the contrary, the assumption of restorative justice is that, in telling one's story in public, individuals can initiate the healing process, as private accounts become woven together into a larger narrative, 'brought from the innermost of the individual to bind us anew to the collective' (Krog 1998). The consequence is remedial, as Juan Mendez confirms: 'official acknowledgment at least begins to heal the wounds' (Mendez 2007: 255). For the liberal mind, however, it is not the role of the politics to heal: to assign such deep, metaphysical goals to an instrument of State is a dangerous proposition. The overemphasis on the therapeutic aspect fails to acknowledge survivors who do not view themselves as 'victims', or as invalids in need of healing, but rather as citizens deserving of justice. For some, recognition may mean punishment rather than storytelling, justice rather than unity. It is significant that many victims' groups in South Africa are now lobbying to revoke the amnesty law and commence with prosecutions, arguing that 'redress is an integral component of reconciliation' (Khulumani Support Group 2007).

Moreover, truth commissions' aim of establishing *the* truth about *the* past appears contrary to the norms of tolerance and pluralism which are so central to political liberalism (see Buckley-Zistel, Chapter 7 in this volume). Individuals need not share a single moral perspective on the past in order to coexist peacefully, and the production of State-sponsored 'truth', established for instance in a truth commission's final report, is also problematic. The notion of a collective memory, faithful to this 'truth', appears as a threat to the liberal *telos*: to what extent will an official version of the past be accepted into people's personal beliefs? The imposition of a top-down historical account of the past may ignore a plurality of individual experiences and memories (Gutman and Thompson 2001). But this pluralism is seen as an essential quality by liberals, and its lack a feature of the totalitarian State. The idea of a reconciliation of all with all, often put forward in the restorative justice paradigm, is a precarious notion that may, in effect, place limits on this plurality. Moreover, restorative justice relies on the concept and virtues of forgiveness, with truth commissions often accompanied by measures of amnesty, a sacrifice justified in the name of abstract goals, such as truth or reconciliation. As Kader Asmal, a South African minister, said: 'We sacrifice justice, because the pains of justice might traumatise our country or affect the transition. We sacrifice justice for truth so as to consolidate democracy, to close the chapter of the past and to avoid confrontation' (cited in Verwoerd 1997).

Two things are problematic here. First, this conception implies that individuals are subordinate to their society. It defends a 'thick' conception of social unity that goes against liberalism, in that it makes individuals mere 'means' for a higher, but rather nebulous aim. For liberals, following Kant again, persons should be considered as 'ends' in themselves, and never solely as means. Second, Asmal's remark implies that confrontation is something to be avoided in the name of consensus and harmony. But liberals think, on the contrary, that politics is based on confrontation, disagreement and differences: the end of conflict is the death of politics, and the beginning of totalitarianism. Lastly, the highly sentimental nature of truth commissions stands in opposition to the strictly procedural, neutral and 'cold' conception of politics in liberalism. As seen above, this aspect was the result of the inevitability of the 'war of Gods', and the need to separate, in order to guarantee social peace, the private from the public spheres. But truth commissions do not truly observe this distinction, promoting instead interpersonal reconciliation and memories, and encouraging emotional outpourings and public grieving. As Justice Albie Sachs of the South Africa Constitutional Court said: 'Tutu cries. A judge does not cry' (cited in Minow 1999). Forgiveness, in particular, is a deeply personal exercise that cannot be dictated, or even coerced, by a State-sponsored institution.

Though seemingly benign, truth commissions' spirit of understanding can ignore a victim's right to legal redress, robbing the victim of his moral power to choose whether or not to forgive. Furthermore, deciding *not* to forgive is not necessarily immoral, nor equivalent to revenge. As philosopher Vladimir Jankelevitch said, talking about the Second World War, 'forgiveness died in the death camps' (Jankelevitch 1986: 21): there is a certain legitimacy in hatred, and anger can play an important role in a victim's healing process. Austrian resistant Jean Améry famously called resentment his 'personal protest against the anti-moral natural process of healing that time brings about' (Améry 1980: 77, my translation). Such points of view could end up being marginalised in the compassionate discourse of restorative justice. Surely, the enormity of some evils should call for societies' resolute refusal to ever again trust the perpetrators involved. Liberals' insistence on tolerance, therefore, does not amount to laxity: a moral community should be defined both by what it comprehends and by what it marks as beyond the pale.

Social justice: recognition, corrective and distributive justice

Claims for reparations have now become a prominent aspect of political transitions, and a constitutive pillar of transitional justice codified in legal documentation.[6] They take various forms, from individual payments to symbolic or collective ones. Their expected outcomes, however, are the same: the rebuilding of institutional trust and the facilitation of social integration in regards to the survivors (de Greiff 2006a). Ernesto Verdeja defines reparations as 'those policies and initiatives that attempt to restore to victims their sense of dignity and moral worth and eliminate the social disparagement and economic marginalization that accompanied their targeting, with the goal of returning their status as citizens' (Verdeja 2008: 1). Financial reparations are meant to restore the balance in the wake of unfair circumstance, through the allocation of a monetary equivalent as a form of compensation and redress. One supposed advantage of reparation policies, as opposed to restorative justice, is that they are morally neutral: the reliance on an economic medium is a way to unhinge the relations from an overwhelming affective and moral weight. Economic exchanges shift things away from their affective signification, transforming the victim versus perpetrator relation into a more neutral relation of debt (Simmel 1999). To that extent, because of their neutral, procedural characteristics, reparations may seem more coherent with the goal of political liberalisation.

Financial payments alone can seem trivial, and incommensurate with the horrors that they are meant to 'compensate' for: how much money is the life of a loved one worth? Cold currency has the effect of 'de-singularising' the event, of rendering it banal. Reparations without truth-telling or punitive measures could therefore be construed by victims as an attempt by the State to 'buy' their silence. The case of Morocco, where reparations were given to victims of repression, but perpetrators remained free and anonymous, is a good example of this problem. Reparative justice without any attempt to reform institutions or punish perpetrators could be viewed as a form of 'payment', or, worse, as hush money.

From a liberal point of view, reparations also raise several issues. First, they imply that individuals are tied to the actions of their predecessors, that they must shoulder responsibility for transgressions committed by their respective nations in the past. 'Political guilt involves liability for the consequences of the deeds of the state whose power governs me and under whose order I live. Everybody is co-responsible for the way he is governed', wrote German philosopher Karl Jaspers (Jaspers 2001: 155). To the extent that citizens benefit from their membership in a community, they must also take responsibility for the historical wrongs perpetrated in its name. But social ties are not so thick in the liberal conception, which presupposes that we can, at any moment, separate ourselves from our society.

The growing importance of economic factors in political violence, and the enduring inequalities found in many post-conflict societies, are signs that individual payments to a certain number of victims are an insufficient means of restoring balance and attaining sustainable peace. Conversely, collective reparations have come to be seen as an effective way to redistribute the goods of society by giving priority to the group that was previously marginalised. They considerably extend the definition of 'victims' to include not only individuals who experienced physical violence directly, but also those whose lives were mutilated in the day-to-day web of regulations in which the atrocities took place. They aim to compensate for the effects of such social ills as corruption, forced displacement, lack of healthcare, hunger or disease. This redefinition of rights, defended by many transitional justice experts, implies a radical break with the way that they have been conceptualised and implemented since their creation (de Greiff 2006b). 'Gross violation of human rights' has indeed almost systematically been understood as including physical violence only: killing, abduction, ill-treatment, rape, torture. Such an amplification of the discipline implies another shift away from the strictly liberal paradigm: political liberalism, indeed, has always defended the pre-eminence of political and civic rights over socioeconomic ones, fearing that making the latter into actual positive *rights* might considerably, and dangerously, extend the power of the State (Honneth and Fraser 2003). Liberals have therefore preferred to carefully separate the field of justice from cultural contexts – against what many communautarians call the 'politics of difference' (Taylor 1994). Lastly, this shift towards recognition would also deeply modify the very definition of a group: liberals tend, indeed, to define groups as voluntary associations, while communautarians see them as comprehensive aggregates that are given rather than chosen (Young 1990).

Rethinking political liberalism through transitional justice

As already seen, transitional justice has a clear teleological nature that seemingly contradicts the traditional, procedural understanding of liberalism that has predominated since the publication of Rawls' *Theory of Justice*.

Transitional justice actors tend to give politics an existential, quasi-romantic dimension that liberals have always been reluctant to admit. I have therefore argued that there is a structural incongruity between the ends of transitional justice and the means used to achieve them. The very notion of transition implies a kind of teleology: we always transit 'towards' something, and in the post-Cold War era in which transitional justice was born, the political horizon was always defined as some form of liberal democracy: a plural, open regime, tolerant of diversity, and not publicly dependent on any metaphysical conception of truth or morality.

The means used by transitional justice, however, tend to contradict this objective, with tools and concepts that undermine some of the fundamental principles and intuitions of political liberalism. For instance, at the retributive level, I study in this chapter the growing confusion between law and morality, and the idea that trials will 'heal' societies, restore the meaning of the past and contribute to building a collective memory. Restorative justice in general, and truth commissions in particular, tend to endorse a form of social holism, a 'sentimentalisation' of the public sphere and a somewhat therapeutic interpretation of rights. The objective of reconciliation itself is strongly embedded morally and religiously, especially when it is defined as engaging a form of social harmony. Reparations, finally, rely on a thick conception of the ties between individuals and their society, and go against the liberal preference for political and civic rights. These elements seem to lend transitional justice a more communautarian complexion, in keeping with Aristotelian perfectionism, rather than the neutral and procedural approach of political liberalism. More research is needed into these areas of tension, so that we might design a more normative approach towards transitional justice and political liberalism. Should we, indeed, reform transitional justice, to allow space for more pluralism, tolerance and recognition? Or should the liberal paradigm itself be revisited in the light of its ethical responsibilities and the limits of its purely neutral, disembodied conception of politics? I try to sketch out two possibilities here, in an effort to determine to what extent the 'extreme case' of post-conflict societies can form a sort of empirical test for our most well-meant intuitions with regard to justice in general. I now suggest two ways of enriching political liberal theories of justice in order to make them more appropriate as the *telos* of transitions: the ethics of dialogue and the capability approach.

Deliberation and democratisation

Dialogue is fundamental to transitional justice: one of its assumptions is indeed that societies and individuals can only 'heal' if past traumas are freely discussed in the public sphere. It therefore stands in stark opposition to the forgetfulness that writers like Nietzsche and Renan thought was an essential human defence against unbearable remembrance. Countries such as France after the Second World War, and Spain after the death of Franco, have chosen a way of mass amnesia, but memory, it seems, persists. The argument in favour of forgetting and moving on is tempting, but even if one accepts it, the question remains: forget what? As Mary Burton, one of the South African TRC chairs, has said: 'We must wipe the slate clean but we haven't even written on the slate yet!' (cited in Boraine 2000: 27) Transitional justice mechanisms at least attempt to define what must be forgotten, if in fact it should be. To that extent, they contribute to restoring the public sphere by liberating communication. Silence is in fact a major danger in the aftermath of mass atrocity, as democracies can only be founded on unfettered communication and a public domain intent on rationale discourse. Jürgen Habermas' concept of 'constitutional patriotism' reflects this idea well: social solidarity, according to the German philosopher, is derived from the citizens' explicit engagement with the moral principles embedded in a liberal constitution. It is the product of a 'civilizing disagreement', ordered by procedural constraints (Habermas 2001: 259).

This model of deliberative politics is philosophically rooted in Habermas' rejection of Rawls' Kantian subjectivist paradigm, which he believes should be replaced by one more intersubjective and communicative, mediated by language. Understood in this way, transitional justice would aim, less ambitiously, at the building of a discursive solidarity in the aftermath of mass atrocity, and at the restoration of lost channels of communication. Indeed, if victim and perpetrator do not share a minimum common language or norm, they will be unable to ask or grant forgiveness. 'Even if I say "I don't forgive you" to someone who asks for my forgiveness, but whom I understand, and who understands me, then the process of reconciliation has started' (Derrida 1999: 7, my translation). Transitional justice is here understood as an intersubjective mode of deliberation, with no mass reconciliatory agenda or desire to establish collective truths or national memories. Rather, the aim is simply to establish conditions wherein peaceful dialogical mechanisms – aimed at building trust while encouraging reasonable differences of opinion – can be put in place. To remain an essential element of liberal peacebuilding, transitional justice should not try to turn the past into a morality play, nor provide a global meta-story about the facts. It should not provide the content as much as the method: a way of looking at the past that authorises discussion and debates. Only then can democratic politics, as peaceful disagreement, be realised.

In this understanding, the solidarity created after mass violence is more procedural and discursive than substantial. It would reflect what Amy Gutman and Dennis Thompson call the 'economy of moral disagreement': seeking a common ground about the past where it exists, and maintaining mutual respect where it does not. This presupposes the notion of reciprocity, 'which asks citizens to try to justify their political views to one another, and to treat with respect those who make ... efforts to engage in this mutual enterprise even when they cannot resolve their disagreements' (Gutman and Thompson 2011: 183). In order for this to be coherent with its liberal *telos*, transitional justice must welcome controversy and avoid final judgments. Its mechanisms should exemplify how people can coexist peacefully and with mutual respect, even as they maintain differing perspectives on the past. It must assume that truth and reconciliation are tentative at best, and are better sought through conflict and controversy than through the manufacturing of a politically authorised consensus. Indeed, one can appreciate another's view as reasonable even if one does not accept its validity. This is even a healthy sign of the willingness of citizens to acknowledge one another as members of a common democracy. The primary function of any transitional mechanism is thus, in Kader Asmal's words, to 'express unwelcome truths, so that inevitable and continuing conflicts and differences stand at least within a single universe of comprehensibility' (Asmal 1999: 46). Only then can politics truly resume.

This deliberative approach to transitional justice would also benefit victims. Indeed, psychological studies have demonstrated that victims of political violence experience difficulties in talking about what happened to them: 'Pain marks the limits of the power of communication', wrote Jean Améry, adding that 'he who wants to make understood his physical pain to someone would have no other choice but to inflict it himself, thereby becoming a perpetrator' (Améry 2005: 82, my translation). Many survivors of mass violence have experienced the same difficulty to articulate their memories and emotions. Simone Veil testifies of the fear of many Auschwitz survivors: that they would not be believed when they told their stories. They therefore chose silence. Primo Levi tells of how these survivors, himself included, experienced 'guilt' and a certain 'disgrace of the world' (Levi 1989: 76). Transitional justice mechanisms, by reactivating lost communication, can contribute to empowering victims and restoring this fundamental trust.

Capabilities and empowerment

This brings us to another way of resolving these theoretical contradictions, this time by modifying not the foundations of transitional justice itself, but that of its *telos*: political liberalism, with reference to Amartya Sen's notion of capability. This theory of capabilities, understood as a means of empowering victims of political violence, will lead me to consider ways, within the liberal paradigm, of reintroducing a certain ethical purpose to those 'ends', which political liberalism, in its traditional Rawlsian form, has abandoned. As we have observed here, transitional justice seems to observe, in its practice, a thicker, more substantial comprehension of 'ends' and meaning: to that extent, it is closer to an Aristotelian form of perfectionism, which considers politics as obligated to make humans *better*, more virtuous, than to a purely procedural execution of justice. Faced with extreme forms of trauma and chronic social pathologies, it seems that political and social organisations need a 'thicker', more substantial, conception of morality and freedom – one that Rawls' strictly procedural liberalism cannot provide. Of course, going too far with this moralisation of politics can also be dangerous: indeed, it was often this very attempt, which, by creating new logistics of exclusion, provided the ideological material of contemporary warfare. Amartya Sen's concept of capability suggests a middle way: neither a cold proceduralism, nor a loaded moral perfectionism. As we can see, transitional justice thereby requires us to assess some of our most cherished assumptions about political liberalism itself.

At the heart of this reconception is the notion of vulnerability, which liberalism fails to truly account for: relying on a strongly autonomous conception of moral and political agents, it does not provide a suitably empathetic space for victims. As seen above, the Self of liberals is 'unencumbered', disembodied, reminiscent of a character out of one of Sartre's novels. Considering that 'transcendental subjects' are free to choose their purposes and ends without observance to any pre-existing moral order, custom, tradition or status, political liberalism neglects to acknowledge the all-too-human dimension of vulnerability. It assumes that one's attributes are accidental, in no way indicative of what one truly is. But things, however, are not that simple when it comes to the victims of political violence, hardwired as they often are with the deep psychological implications of violence. As Jean Améry observed, victims of political violence lose their 'trust in the world', they cannot initially act and be active, as autonomous agents in the public sphere. They cannot, to that extent, take part in Rawls' original positioning: placing this 'victimhood' behind the veil of ignorance appears problematic, as victims of political violence lack the basic capacities that enable partners to agree on principles of justice. Adding further complexity, victims' feeling of fear and powerlessness is not limited to the persons who suffered the violations directly, but applies, by dint of a 'spillover effect', to their whole communities (de Greiff 2009: 43).[7] Human rights violations erase the fundamental normative expectations that make social action possible. As Pablo de Greiff states, these expectations are 'the manifestation of the basic structure, the ground or framework, of our agency' (de Greiff 2009: 43) – things that we feel naturally entitled to: the assistance of other, the protection of the State. When these expectations are disappointed, people experience a deep sense of disorientation, solitude and even resentment. As a consequence, victims and their communities may refrain from participating in public life and engaging in social networks. Transitional justice aims, precisely, at rebuilding the trust that makes such participation possible. It reduces the salience of 'victimness' and attempts to de-politicise the victim's cause by employing a purely moral, emotional and compassionate vocabulary: the premium is on charity, over justice. This is problematic if the goal of transitional justice is to recreate a political community of moral agents. This is where the notion of capability can be truly useful, providing a more positive and substantial conception of freedoms and agency, one that considers the existence of valid vulnerabilities without locking victims into their powerlessness. Integrating Amartya Sen's notion of capability into transitional justice *and* political liberalism may help overcome the contradictions examined in this chapter.

The notion of victim empowerment contains an ethical intention that is not, however, commensurate with political liberalism in its traditional Rawlsian form. Indeed, Sen conceived the capability approach as a way of overcoming the limits inherent to the consideration of economic development only in terms of resources, and replacing the focus on its goal: human well being. Development, he said, should not be thought of in terms of levels of wealth, income or growth, but in terms of what people can do with these assets: more specifically, how they can convert them into well being. It is, therefore, Sen says, 'a process of expanding the real freedoms that people enjoy'. Sen accused Rawls of focusing too much on means (resources) at the expense of ends (well being and positive freedoms). Contrary to Rawls' abstract and disembodied conception of the Self, Sen believes that choices cannot be made independent of material and social factors: to enable the exercise of freedom and capability, society must provide these conditions.

This concreteness is also more consistent with the goals of transitional justice. Indeed, political violence and legacies of mass atrocity undermine capabilities and 'functionings', as Sen understands them: health and longevity, for instance, are clearly affected by physical violence. Emotional development, which Martha Nussbaum lists as one of the fundamental human capabilities, is often interrupted by the fear and anxiety analysed above, as is the capacity to apply practical reason in the pursuit of one's life path.[8]

Viewed in such a light, transitional justice mechanisms could contribute to building long-term capabilities: providing recognition to victims, promoting civic trust, and strengthening the rule of law – all of which are listed by Pablo de Greiff as the primary goals of transitional justice (de Greiff 2009). Transitional justice can thus contribute to rebuilding the fundamental norms that violence erodes. By acting to create *capable* citizens and rational moral agents in the aftermath of mass atrocity, transitional justice could be integrated into the grand project of political liberalism. The theory of capability could thus appear as the missing link between transitional justice mechanisms and political liberalism: it forces a review of its conception of the disembodied Self, in the light of the vulnerabilities created by mass violence; and it gives the discipline a clearer *telos*, one compatible with the type of regime that is expected as the outcome of its ministrations.

Notes

1 The views expressed in this chapter are those of the author and do not reflect the views of her employer, the UN.
2 The title of Thomas Pogge's book *Realizing Rawls* (Pogge 1989) is revealing to that extent.
3 Johann Galtung defines 'peace' as the guarantee of four types of basic needs: survival, well being, identity/meaning, and freedom.
4 See for instance the work of Michel Dobry (2000a, 2000b).
5 To the extent that truth commissions put victims at their heart and do not directly prosecute, they can be labelled restorative. This is different from 'fact-finding commissions', which are more factual and investigative, such as the one in East Germany for instance, or what is known as the 'Bouderbala Commission' in Tunisia, which are not truth commissions per se.
6 For a discussion on how reparations can address different dimensions of justice, see Laplante, Chapter 3 in this volume.
7 Pablo de Greiff elaborates a 'phenomenology of victimhood', to which I refer here.
8 Martha Nussbaum's list of capabilities can be found in Nussbaum 2006 or 1990.

Bibliography

Ackerman, B. (1991) *We the People: Transformations*, Cambridge, MA: Harvard University Press.
Améry, J. (2005) *Par-delà le crime et le châtiment. Essai pour surmonter l'insurmountable*, Paris: Babel.
——(1980) *Par Delà le Crime et le Châtiment. Essai pour Surmonter l'Insurmontable*, Paris: Babel.
Andrieu, K. (2010) 'Civilizing Peacebuilding: Transitional Justice, Civil Society, and the Liberal Paradigm', *Security Dialogue*, 41 (5): 537–58.
Arendt, H. (1958) *The Human Condition*, New York, NY: Penguin.
Asmal, K. (1999) *Reconciliation Through Truth*, New York, NY: David Phillips Publishers.
Auckerman, M. (2002) 'Extraordinary Crime, Ordinary Evil: A Framework for Understanding Transitional Justice', *Harvard Human Rights Journal*, 15 (5): 39–97.
Beitz, C. (1999) *Political Theory and International Relations*, Princeton, NJ: Princeton University Press.
Boraine, A. (2000) *A Country Unmasked: Inside South African Truth and Reconciliation Commission*, Oxford: Oxford University Press.
Brainswaite, J. (1999) 'Restorative Justice: Assessing Optimistic and Pessimistic Accounts', *Crime and Justice*, 25: 1–127.
de Greiff, P. (2006a) 'Truth Telling and the Rule of Law', in Borer, T.A. (ed.) *Telling the Truths, Truth Telling and Peace Building in Post Conflict Societies*, South Bend, IN: Notre Dame University Press.
——(2006b) 'Repairing the Past: Reparations for Victims of Human Rights Violations', in de Greiff, P. (ed.) *Handbook on Reparations*, Oxford: Oxford University Press.
——(2009) 'Articulating the Links between Transitional Justice and Development: Justice and Social Integration' in de Greiff, P. and Duthie, R. (eds) *Transitional Justice and Development. Making Connections*, New York, NY: Social Science Research Council.
——(2011a) 'Theorizing Transitional Justice', in Williams, M., Nagy, R. and Elster, J. (eds) *Transitional Justice*, Nomos L1, New York, NY, and London: University Press.
——(2011b) 'Transitional Justice, Security, and Development', *Security and Justice Thematic Papers*, Washington, DC: World Bank Development Report.

Derrida, J. (1999) *Le Siècle et le Pardon*, Paris: Le Monde des Débats.

Dobry, M. (2000a) 'Les Voies Incertaines de la Transitologie: Choix Stratégiques, Séquences Historiques, Bifurcations et Processus de *Path Dependence*', *Revue Française de Sciences Politiques*, 50 (4): 585–614.

——(2000b) *Democratic and Capitalist Transition in Eastern Europe: Lessons for the Social Sciences*, Dordrecht: Kluwer.

Duffield, M. (2001) *Global Governance and the New Wars*, London: Zed Books.

Fukuyama, F. (1999) 'The End of History, Five Years Later', *History and Theory*, 34 (2): 27–43.

Galtung, J. (1990) 'Cultural Violence', *Journal of Peace Research*, 27 (3): 291–305.

Gutman, A. and Thompson, D. (2001) 'The Moral Foundations of Truth Commissions', in Rotberg, R.I. and Thompson, D. (eds) *Truth v. Justice: The Morality of Truth Commissions*, Princeton, NJ: Princeton University Press.

Habermas, J. (2001) 'Historical Consciousness and the Post-Traditional Identity: the Federal Republic's Orientation to the West', in Nicholsen, S. (ed.) *The New Conservatism, Cultural Criticism and the Historian'Debate*, Boston, MA: MIT Press.

Hayner, P. (2002) *Unspeakable Truth: Confronting State Terror and Atrocity*, New York, NY: Routledge.

Honneth, A. and Fraser, N. (2003) *Redistribution or Recognition? A Political-Philosophical Exchange*, London: Verso.

Jankelevitch, V. (1986) *L'Imprescriptible*, Paris: Seuil.

Jaspers, K. (2001) *The Question of the German Guilt*, Fordham, NY: Fordham University Press.

Khulumani Support Group (2007) *Charter for Redress*. Available at: <http://www.khulumani.net/attachments/212_Final%20Version%20Charter%20for%20Redress2007.pdf> (accessed January 2013).

Kiss, E. (2000) 'Moral Ambition Within and Beyond Political Constrains. Reflections on Restaurative Justice', in Rotberg, R.I. and Thompson, D. (eds) *Truth v. Justice: The Morality of Truth Commissions*, Princeton, NJ: Princeton University Press.

Krog, A. (1998) *Country of my Skull, Guilt, Sorrow, and the Limits of Forgiveness in the New South Africa*, New York, NY: Random House.

Kymlicka, W. (1995) *Multicultural Citizenship. A Liberal Theory of Minority Rights*, Oxford: Clarendon Press.

Lederach, J.P. (1997) *Building Peace: Sustainable Reconciliation in Divided Societies*, Washington, DC: United States Institute of Peace Press.

Levi, P. (1989) *Les Naufrages et les Rescapés: Quarante Ans Après Ausschwitz*, Paris: Gallimard.

Mendez, J. (2007) 'Accountability for Past Abuses', *Human Rights Quarterly*, 19: 255–76.

Minow, M. (1999) *Between Vengeance and Forgiveness. Facing History after Genocide and Mass Violence*, Boston, MA: Beacon Press

Nino, C.S. (1999) *Radical Evil on Trial*, New Haven, CT: Yale University Press.

Nussbaum, M. (1990) 'Aristotelian Social Democracy' in Douglass, R.B., Mara, G.M. and Richardson, H.S. (eds) *Liberalism and the Good*, London: Routledge.

——(2006) *Frontiers of Justice: Disability, Nationality, Species Membership*, Cambridge, MA: Harvard University Press.

Osiel, M. (1997) *Mass Atrocity, Collective Memory and the Law*, New Brunswick, NJ: Transaction Publishers.

Pogge, T. (1989) *Realizing Rawls*, Ithaca, NY: Cornell University Press.

Rawls, J. (1980) 'Kantian Constuctivism in Moral Theory', *Journal of Philosophy*, 77 (9): 515–72.

——(1995) *Libéralisme Politique*, Paris: PUF.

——(1996) *Political Liberalism*, New York, NY: Columbia University Press.

Renaut, A. (2005) *Egalité et Discriminations: Un Essai de Philosophie Politique Appliquée*, Paris: Seuil, coll. 'La Couleur des Idées'.

Richmond, O. and Franks, J. (2009) *Liberal Peace Transitions: Between Peacebuilding and Statebuilding*, Edinburgh: Edinburgh University Press.

Sandel, M. (1984) 'The Procedural Republic and the Unencumbered Self', *Political Theory*, 12 (1): 81–96.

Seguev, T. (2000) *The Seventh Million: The Israeli and the Holocaust*, London: Holt Paperback.

Shklar, J. (1963) *Legalism: Law, Moral and Political Trials*, Cambridge, MA: Harvard University Press.

Simmel, G. (1999) *Philosophie de l'Agent*, Paris: PUF Quadrige.

Sriram, C.L. (2007) 'Justice as Peace? Liberal Peacebuilding and Strategies of Transitional Justice', *Global Society*, 21 (4): 579–91.

Taylor, C. (1994) *Multiculturalism*, Princeton, NJ: Princeton University Press.

Teitel, R.G. (2000) *Transitional Justice*, Oxford and New York, NY: Oxford University Press.

United Nations (1992) 'Agenda for Peace : Preventive Diplomacy, Peacemaking and Peacekeeping', Report of the Secretary General, A/47/277-S/24111, 43. Available at: <http://www.unrol.org/doc.aspx?n=A_47_277.pdf> (accessed January 2013).

United Nations Secretary General (2004) 'The Rule of Law and Transitional Justice in Conflict and Post-Conflict Societies', UN Doc. S/2044/616. Available at: <http://www.unrol.org/doc.aspx?d=3096> (accessed January 2013).

United Nations Security Council (2001), 'Statement by the President of the Security Council', U.N. Doc. S/PRST/2001/5, 20 February 2001.

Verdeja, E. (2008) 'A Critical Theory of Reparative Justice', *Constellations*, 15 (2): 208–22.

Verwoerd, W. (1997) *Justice after Apartheid? Reflections of South African TRC*, Madras: Fifth International Conference on Ethics and Development.

World Bank (2011) *Conflict, Security and Development*, World Development Report, Washington, DC: World Bank.

Yordan, C. (2009) 'Towards the Deliberative Peace: A Habermassian Critique of Contemporary Peace Operations', *Journal of International Relations and Development*, 12 (1): 58–89.

Young, I.M. (1990) *Justice and the Politics of Difference*, Princeton, NJ: Princeton University Press.

Chapter 5

The vertical and horizontal expansion of transitional justice

Explanations and implications for a contested field

*Thomas Obel Hansen**

Introduction

The field of transitional justice has expanded significantly in recent years. Transitional justice is no longer exclusively, or even predominantly, discussed as a matter of whether and how the State ought to deploy various tools aimed at advancing accountability, truth and victims' redress in the context of dealing with human rights violations committed by a prior authoritarian regime. Notably, the State is no longer perceived as the only actor relevant for deciding and implementing transitional justice solutions, and debates about transitional justice now take place in contexts where there has been no regime change, or the transition is not from dictatorship to democracy.

This has led some commentators to speak of a 'normalisation of transitional justice'. This normalisation is said to materialise in an increased prevalence of institutions that pursue accountability, truth, and redress for past human rights violations. Transitional justice, it is argued, is no longer the exception, but the norm (Teitel 2003: 90–93; McEvoy 2008: 16). Teitel notes that the new millennium appears to be associated with a normalisation of transitional justice, whereby 'what was historically viewed as a legal phenomenon associated with extraordinary post-conflict conditions now increasingly appears to be a reflection of ordinary times' (Teitel 2003: 89–90).[1]

While these arguments point to important features of the contemporary field, the perception that transitional justice is now normalised, as opposed to extra-ordinary, does not fully reflect recent developments. Rather than simply speaking of one overarching tendency, such as 'normalisation' or 'globalisation', this chapter suggests that it is more fitting to speak of various forms of expansions – and at least a partial disintegration – of the field.

First, the field has expanded in the sense that actors above and below the State level are increasingly perceived as being relevant for shaping and implementing transitional justice solutions. This chapter proposes the term 'vertical expansion' to refer to the increased importance and attention paid to different actors and levels where transitional justice can take place or be promoted from.

Second, the concept of transitional justice is no longer reserved for analysing justice tools in liberalising political transitions. Instead, justice tools are being conceptualised as transitional justice in highly diverse contexts, including undemocratic political transitions, transitions from violent conflict to a more peaceful order, and situations where apparently there is no ongoing transition, political or otherwise. This chapter discusses this development introducing the term 'horizontal expansion'.

As claims for inclusion multiply in the field of transitional justice, it has become increasingly difficult to operate with one common framework for understanding and evaluating the use of justice tools engineered to deal with violence and repression. Having described the expansions in the field mentioned above, the chapter moves on to discuss how we as observers can approach transitional justice in different contexts. Consequently, the chapter presents a critical account of the concept of transitional justice and developments in the academic field, which aims at laying the ground for a more nuanced understanding of what transitional justice can and should achieve in different contexts and the often complex roles of different actors in promoting these goals.

Current trends in the field of transitional justice

The vertical expansion: the internationalisation and localisation of transitional justice

Some trace the concept of transitional justice back to the Nuremberg trials following the Second World War (Teitel 2003: 70), and some even to Ancient Greece (Elster 2004: 3–23). However, prosecuting those responsible for Nazi atrocities in an international tribunal and other historical attempts at rendering justice for serious crimes were not at the time conceptualised as 'transitional justice'. It is therefore more correct to state that the notion of 'transitional justice' originates in discussions about how the emerging democracies in Latin America should address serious human rights abuses committed by the prior dictatorships (Arthur 2009). With some exceptions, these discussions were based on a State-centric understanding of agents and forums for accountability, truth-seeking and other ways of addressing gross human rights violations committed during the reign of the military dictatorships.[2]

Accordingly, the early field of transitional justice tended to view the State, or more precisely the executive branch of the government, as the key decision-maker concerning transitional justice. Whereas civil society as well as international actors were seen as capable of offering critical input, ultimately the decision to deploy various forms of transitional justice was thought to rest with the new political leadership. Seemingly influenced by the so-called transition to democracy scholarship (Huntington 1991; Linz and Stepan

1996), which had emphasised democratisation as the outcome of elite choices, transitional justice theory similarly implied that the development of transitional justice policies was essentially an elite choice, potentially restrained by other (outgoing) elites. Consequently, the focus in the early literature was primarily on how various forms of political transitions would impact the new leadership's approach to transitional justice, as opposed to how different actors could shape or take control of transitional justice solutions devoid of potential political restraints arising out of the particular nature of the transition. Whereas the early scholarship was characterised by a rich debate concerning the justice decisions made by new democracies, most studies thus took for granted that these tools were to be established at the State level (Kritz 1995a, 1995b; McAdams 1997).

In contrast, contemporary transitional justice discourses perceive the State as only one among several actors with the ability to shape and implement transitional justice. The most obvious indication of this externalisation from the State concerns the rise of criminal justice institutions within the international system. Though Teitel's claim that the entrenchment of the 'Nuremberg Model' of transitional justice turns the prosecution of war crimes, genocide and crimes against humanity into 'a routine matter under international law' may overstate the prevalence of international trials (Teitel 2003: 90), there can be little doubt that international actors, including international tribunals, play an increasingly prominent role in shaping transitional justice solutions. This internationalisation of transitional justice is important because it, in principle, allows that justice be pursued in instances where the political leadership lacks commitment to accountability principles. This has ramifications for the field in that transitional justice obtains new relations with domestic politics through a potential impact on governance and electoral politics which is fundamentally different from State-driven transitional justice. In Kenya, for example, the ICC has charged two prominent politicians of the country, who subsequently created a powerful coalition aimed at ending the ICC process and gaining power in the 2013 presidential elections (Hansen 2011; Sriram and Brown 2012). As a result, transitional justice, in its internationalised form, significantly influences succession politics in the country, while at the same time it has a complex impact on peace and security in the country (Hansen 2011).

Furthermore, the internationalisation of transitional justice is evident from the enhanced role played by international actors, such as UN agencies, international development partners and international NGOs, in supporting and implementing transitional justice tools at various levels, including the local, the national and the international. These actors increasingly see it as their role to provide technical advice and assist governments and others that attempt to create and implement a transitional justice solution. Transitional justice is thus no longer viewed as an exotic task dealt with by specialised departments in 'extra-ordinary' political circumstances, but rather tends to form an integrated part of good governance, human rights and peacebuilding programmes in the developing countries in which these agencies work (Duthie 2008; United Nations Secretary General 2011).

In part due to the strengthened role of international actors in transitional justice processes, some commentators have started to criticise transitional justice solutions that rely overly on international 'best practices' and a 'top-down design', which is said to neglect the voices of victims and the communities affected by violence. Miller, for example, speaks of a 'consistency of language and terminology employed in a wide diversity of post-conflict contexts', which points to a 'global phenomenon and its seemingly successful export/ import from one country or region to another over the course of the past several decades' (Miller 2008: 271). Cavallaro and Albuja identify a similar tendency with respect to truth commissions which, often supported finan- cially and morally by international actors, replicate each other across borders (Cavallaro and Albuja 2008). These and a number of related tendencies make Oomen note that transitional justice has become a 'donor-driven project' (Oomen 2005). The resistance to 'top-down' transitional justice has led segments of the scholarship to call for local-level and participatory approa- ches to transitional justice. Accordingly, consultation and involvement of civil society and local communities are emerging as benchmarks for the legitimacy of transitional justice processes (Lundy and McGovern 2008). The critique of transitional justice as a project that externalises justice from those affected by it has thus produced increased interest for modes of tran- sitional justice that (supposedly) draw on local communities' understandings of justice, often with reference to 'tradition' (Huyse 2008).

While increased attention to the role of international actors as well as local communities' conception of justice presents a positive development for tran- sitional justice, the debate about whether international or local solutions to transitional justice are preferable sometimes takes almost ideological dimen- sions, and is often based on general considerations, as opposed to more contextual deliberations. Before elaborating on when and how different actors should attempt to influence or take control of transitional justice, it is first necessary to describe another trend in the contemporary field, namely the horizontal expansion of transitional justice, which implies a proliferation of transitional justice discourses to cases that are not characterised by a liberalising political transition.

The horizontal expansion: transitional justice beyond liberalising political transitions

As noted above, the field of transitional justice originates in deliberations over how the new democracies of the mid- and late 1980s in Latin America ought to respond to gross human rights violations committed under the prior military dictatorships. The starting point of these discussions was that as much justice as possible should be achieved without endangering the democratic transition – or even better, that justice should contribute to the consolidation of a liberal democratic order (Albon 1995). These premises for the new field of transitional justice were in part the consequence of the conditions of its origin, namely as a merger between the normative frameworks of human rights and the transition to democracy discourses, influenced by scholars such as Huntington, Linz and Stepan (Huntington 1991; Linz and Stepan 1996). To put it simply, the field of transitional justice made the question of justice central to democratic transitions, but also made the question of political transformation central to the agenda of justice.

Because liberalising political transitions were perceived an uncommon phenomenon – as something extraordinary – transitional justice also came to be viewed as something fundamentally apart from other forms of justice. The justice tools in question, it was argued, were utilised in a special, or even unique, political context, and as opposed to 'ordinary justice' these tools should serve essentially political purposes, such as promoting acceptance of the new democracy (Malamud-Goti 1991: 3–13; Nino 1996).

For these reasons, a number of prominent lawyers insisted (and they did so largely unchallenged)[3] that there was a need for a distinctive notion for this form of justice; that transitional justice should be discussed in idiosyncratic terms, rather than in a continuation of general debates about criminal, restorative and other forms of justice. In line with this, Teitel, who claims to have coined the notion, defined transitional justice as 'the conception of justice associated with periods of political change, characterized by legal responses to confront the wrongdoings of repressive predecessor regimes' (Teitel 2003: 69). By political change, Teitel referred to 'the move from less to more democratic regimes' (Teitel 2000: 5).

While these normative dimensions relating to the promotion of liberal democratic values continue to influence transitional justice discourses, it is also clear that the selfsame discourses increasingly analyse and debate justice processes in cases that are fundamentally different from the type of cases around which the field was formed. For example, debates about transitional justice now occur in Uganda, Colombia, Sudan and many other countries that have not (yet?) experienced a fundamental political transition and/or where wide-scale human rights abuses are still ongoing. In other cases, such as Rwanda and Ethiopia, a fundamental political transition has indeed taken place when a transitional justice process is launched, but this transition is not best understood using terms such as 'liberalising'. Transitional justice discourses thus increasingly engage with contexts where there is no liberalising political transition, including illiberal transitions and transitions which seem predominantly to concern an already existing or attempted move from armed conflict, usually of some internal nature, to relative peace.

This expansion of the field from providing a framework for discussing justice in democratic transitions towards a more inclusive, but seemingly less well-defined, perception of 'transition', has led to debates about definitions and how far the borders of the field should extend.

Although attempts to replace the notion of 'transitional justice' with 'post-conflict justice' have by and large been dismissed by the scholarship,[4] some commentators have started to use definitions of transitional justice that embrace justice after authoritarian rule as well as justice after civil war. According to Roht-Arriaza, for example, transitional justice can be understood as a 'set of practices, mechanisms and concerns that arise following a period of conflict, civil strife or repression, and that are aimed directly at confronting and dealing with past violations of human rights and humanitarian law' (Roht-Arriaza 2006: 2). In line with this, some scholars have noted that contemporary 'transitional justice discourses frequently conflate at least two primary kinds of transition: that from authoritarianism to democracy, and that from war to peace' (Aoláin and Campbell 2005: 212).

This perception could be seen to imply that the field has developed simply as a consequence of the fact that legal and quasi-legal measures resembling those used in contexts of liberalising political transitions, such as criminal tribunals, truth commissions and reconciliation efforts, are now utilised in situations like Sierra Leone, Uganda, Colombia and others where the abuses are closely connected to the existence of a past, or sometimes still ongoing, armed conflict. The fact that these measures are debated as transitional justice are thus seen as a kind of generation shift that simply reflects a change in world affairs where serious abuses increasingly take place in the context of civil wars.

However, speaking of two main forms of transition, namely a liberalising political one and one from conflict to peace, does not embrace all the scenarios where debates about transitional justice currently take place. Furthermore, developing new definitions does not necessarily answer the more profound question of whether transitional justice theory is sufficiently equipped to deal with the very diverse set of cases in which some form of justice process is launched to address human rights abuses and/or breaches of international humanitarian law.

On the one hand, some scholars suggest that the dominant normative framework for transitional justice, which emphasises the value of a liberal democratic order, is also suitable for understanding new types of transition dealt with by the scholarship. For example, in their account of transitional justice in 'conflicted democracies', Aoláin and Campbell argue that 'the end goal of transition in conflicted democracies is the same as that in paradigmatic transitions: the achievement of a stable (and therefore peaceful) democracy' (Aoláin and Campbell 2005: 174).

On the other hand, some commentators argue that the expansion of the field also implies, or should imply, an expansion of the goals of transitional justice. Nagy, for example, argues that '[a] narrow, legalistic focus on gross violations of civil and political rights overlooks the ways in which structural violence and gender inequality inform subjective experiences of political conflict, injustice and their consequences', and suggests that transitional justice must address issues like these which are not captured in the dominant conception of transition (Nagy 2008: 287). In a similar vein, Lundy and McGovern argue that dominant ideas about transition may be too narrow because they prioritise a 'liberal and essential Western formulation of democracy', and ignore the 'problem that human rights abuses may continue to take place in circumstances where, in theory at least, the norms of liberal democratic accountability prevail' (Lundy and McGovern 2008: 101). Without explicitly addressing the expansion of the field discussed here, Clark also points to the need for relying on a broader range of goals of transitional justice, including 'reconciliation, peace, justice, healing, forgiveness and truth' (Clark 2008a: 193).

However, there are also those who have started to query whether not the expansions of the field may turn out to threaten the strength of its postulations, noting that the field is now in a sort of 'mid-life crisis'. Most notably, Bell argues that transitional justice has reached a 'paradoxical moment of fieldhood', where increased claims for inclusion cause a confusion, in which it becomes difficult to map out the borders of the field, and it becomes open to criticism that the concept is too vague or is being manipulated by actors with questionable agendas (Bell 2009: 13).

Interrogating the field's expansion and disintegration: legitimate goals and relevant actors in transitional justice processes in different types of case

As opposed to simply broadening the scope of transitional justice goals in general or rejecting the expansion of the field, this chapter suggests a more suitable approach which involves the use of a differentiated framework for understanding and evaluating the highly diverse set of cases where attempts to deal with a legacy of violence or repression are conceptualised as transitional justice. This section outlines the key scenarios in which a justice process may occur to deal with wide-scale human rights abuses and reflects on how we as observers can determine what goals of transitional justice are legitimate and feasible as well as the role of different actors in promoting them. Accordingly, the section investigates the consequences of the vertical and horizontal expansion of the field, and how these two trends interrelate.

Transitional justice in liberalising political transitions

It seems reasonable to suggest that promoting democratisation and the rule of law are central goals of transitional justice in liberalising political transitions, such as in the Latin American countries undergoing profound political transformation in the mid- and late 1980s; Central and Eastern Europe

(CEE) following the collapse of communist rule; and South Africa after the end of Apartheid rule in 1994. Arguably, some of the more recent examples of transitional justice in the Arab world – what was originally labelled the 'Arab Spring', but has often turned out to be a more complex and lengthy process than many had initially hoped for – may also prove to occur in liberalising transitions. Although there are of course very significant differences between these cases, it is a reasonable expectation that new democratically elected leaderships will tend to support transitional justice to the extent that such processes do not conflict with other top priorities of the new regime, including, but not limited to, maintaining stability. This support will typically derive from the new leadership's commitment to the rule of law and human rights; its perceived need to distance itself from the past authoritarian order; its sympathy with victims' calls for justice; and for other reasons which would usually be perceived legitimate. Turned around, the main reason why these new leaderships from time to time oppose (certain modalities of) transitional justice has to do with a perception that justice could jeopardise the consolidation of a new democratic order, for example because if seriously challenged, members of the outgoing regime may have the ability to shake or overthrow the new leadership. In Spain, for example, decisive parts of the new democratic leadership were opposed to transitional justice because it was thought to put at risk the emerging democratic order due to the continued influence of Franco loyalists (Aguilar 2001).

Mainstream transitional justice theory, with its emphasis on liberal democratic values, thus fits relatively well for analysing this type of cases. However, there are at least three major problems with these discourses. First, they tend to rely on an elite conception of decision-making, which means that sufficient attention has not always been paid to the question of how civil society and other actors perceive and try to influence transitional justice (Sharp 2013). Second, these discourses have often failed to analyse whether and how the use of transitional justice actually helps to consolidate a liberal democratic order (Hazan 2006: 19–48). Third, transitional justice theory, especially in the early days of the field, has tended to overlook the question of whether evaluating these cases should not take place using other measures of success, including redistribution of resources and other forms of more structural change (Mani 2002; Nagy 2008).

Though civil society and other non-State actors can and should play an important role in shaping transitional justice solutions in liberalising political transitions, allowing the new political leadership a central role is usually compatible with creating a legitimate transitional justice solution. Importantly, accepting that the State is a central actor in framing transitional justice approaches in these types of transition offers the new political leadership an opportunity for pursuing nation-building (e.g. by creating a shared narrative concerning the wrongdoing of the past) and strengthening the rule of law and democratic ideals (e.g. by showing its commitment to punish those who in the past violated the law as well as supporting the victims' right to justice). To illustrate this point: although it is difficult to empirically verify that Nino was right in arguing that Argentina's transitional justice process – driven by the new leadership but influenced by civil society – helped consolidate democracy, it is certainly a reasonable assumption that the decision to prosecute members of the Junta disseminated a picture of the new political leadership as being committed to the rule of law and may have laid the foundation for creating a more just, albeit not perfect, democratic order (Nino 1996: 145–48).

In part because transitional justice processes created by democratically elected (or clearly democratically oriented) new leadership will tend to involve measures that are acceptable, though not necessarily fully satisfactory, for societies affected by past violence or repression international actors should exercise some level of caution attempting to take control of transitional justice in these situations. Of course, international standards, including accountability norms, fair trial standards, victims' right to a remedy and other norms enshrined in international human rights law, remain important benchmarks for a legitimate transitional justice process. Yet, some compromises to these standards may be acceptable if a new democratic leadership convincingly argues that such compromises are necessary to avoid jeopardising the democratic transition itself, or for other reasons compatible with a liberal democratic order and deemed acceptable by the communities most affected by the decision. Even in cases such as South Africa where many victims of the Apartheid crimes may have been reluctant to accept the new leadership's decision to exclude criminal trials from the transitional justice process, the moral standing and democratic nature of the new leadership makes the 'amnesty for truth' deal an acceptable, though not necessarily ideal, solution to dealing with past human rights abuses (Boraine 2006).

In sum, there should be a preference for a nationally conceived (and driven) transitional justice process in cases of liberalising political transitions. Although international actors may provide valuable assistance to national actors responsible for implementing transitional justice, they should generally refrain from taking control of the processes to the extent a new democratically elected regime creates transitional justice processes in good faith; takes into account the voices of victims and others affected by the past abuses; and shows commitment to fundamental human rights standards.

Transitional justice in non-liberal political transitions

Another type of case that is increasingly debated within a transitional justice framework concerns instances where criminal trials, truth-seeking, reparation schemes and other tools are utilised to deal with past abuses in contexts in which a profound political transition has taken place, but this transformation does not have a democratic nature. In Rwanda, for example, various forms of transitional justice have been pursued following the 1994 Rwandan Patriotic Front (RPF) takeover, but the RPF-led regime can hardly be described as democratic and continues to violate a number of basic rights (Reyntjens 2004).[5] Uzbekistan offers another example of transitional justice in a clearly non-liberal political transition. President Karimov decided to launch a truth commission to deal with abuses committed in the Soviet era, but Karimov's regime is clearly undemocratic and responsible for serious human rights abuses, most well known, perhaps, the massacre of demonstrators in Andizhan in 2005 (Grodsky 2008). The so-called Red Terror trials in Ethiopia, which took place following the overthrow of the highly repressive Mengistu regime, but under the auspices of another authoritarian regime, similarly offers an example that transitional justice can take place in the context of a fundamental political transition that is not liberalising (Harbeson 1998; Tiba 2007). Similarly, the establishment of a truth commission in Chad, under the country's authoritarian president Déby, to deal with the abuses committed during Habré's regime presents an example of how dictators may pursue some kind of justice for the human rights abuses committed by their predecessors (Hayner 2001: 57–59).

Simply debating such cases using a framework that assumes transitional justice is a question of promoting democratisation and rule of law abiding governance is obviously problematic. A key motivation for creating justice processes in such contexts may in fact be the opposite: to silence pro-democratic voices, indoctrinate the population and, ultimately, to consolidate (yet another) non-democratic and repressive regime. For example, Rwanda's Ingando camps, officially claimed to offer a venue for eradicating genocide ideology, are alleged to disseminate a one-sided picture of Rwandan history and indoctrinate its participants according to RPF ideology (Mgbako 2005). Key actors in Rwanda's transitional justice process have stated clearly that democratisation was not seen as a desirable, or at least urgent, outcome of the transition. Then General Secretary of the National Unity and Reconciliation Commission, Aloysia Inyumba (who is also a prominent RPF leader), explained that 'the ordinary citizens are like babies. They will need to be completely educated before we can talk about democracy' (Reyntjens 2004: 183–84). Similarly, transitional justice in Uzbekistan seems to have aimed at consolidating the regime's repressive grip on power. Grodsky notes that 'the very repression that has allowed Karimov to control the state and most of society has created conditions that make transitional justice possible and even likely', in part because Karimov has the need to blame his poor human rights record on something, such as difficulties in overcoming structures put in place during the Soviet era (Grodsky 2008: 289).

Despite these obvious challenges to legitimacy, certain aspects of transitional justice in non-liberal transitions may at the same time promote other, more legitimate goals, such as accountability principles, nation-building, reconciliation and victims' redress. Further, promoting these values may sometimes entail that compromises be made to rule of law standards. In Rwanda, for example, the *gacaca* courts had inherent rule of law flaws and seem partly to have aimed at consolidating the RPF regime's grip on power, but may nonetheless have provided a relevant and partially credible forum for accountability, reconciliation and victims' redress (Clark 2007). Given the importance of these goals, it seems unjustified when some commentators (Sarkin 2001; Fierens 2005) entirely dismiss the legitimacy of the process on the grounds that it does not comply with all human rights standards. By the same token, some scholars have argued that liberal democratic values and human rights are completely irrelevant assessing a transitional justice tool such as the *gacaca* courts (Drumbl 2002: 13–14). This is a far-reaching conclusion because basic fair trial standards may obviously have importance to some, including the suspects.

A number of factors are relevant when assessing the legitimacy of transitional justice processes in non-liberal transitions, including the question of when some compromises to democratic and rule of law standards are acceptable. First, the kind of injustices dealt with by transitional justice must be examined. To the extent the abuses of the past were carried out through mass participation, a more flexible approach to democratic and rule of law standards may be necessary. In Rwanda, for example, the massive participation in the 1994 genocide meant that any transitional justice process inevitably had to balance accountability norms with fair trial standards and other legitimate concerns, such as nation-building and reconciliation (Schabas 2002). Second, attention must be paid to the context in which transitional justice unfolds. To the extent transitional justice takes place in a context defined by an ongoing armed struggle or other highly instable situations, it may be unrealistic to expect that the justice tools utilised primarily aim at promoting liberal democratic values. Achieving stability and security may be seen as more pressing needs in such situations, though of course it must be recognised that the continued rejection of human rights and democratisation are often underlying causes of conflict. Third, the level of poverty as well as the existence of well-functioning State institutions must be taken into account. If transitional justice takes place in a context where the government is commencing a post-conflict reconstruction and no basic judicial infrastructure is in place, compromises to rule of law standards and other liberal values may be more acceptable than in States, such as many of the Latin American, where relatively well-functioning State institutions already existed.

Whereas transitional justice at the State level should therefore not automatically be labelled an entirely illegitimate affair in all instances of a non-liberal political transition, it is important to consider how other actors can promote aspects of change that the government is unlikely to advance. Though the involvement of civil society and the communities affected by violence in transitional justice is desirable, it is often unlikely that these actors can operate in a manner in which they, free of the government's control, can promote accountability, truth-seeking or victims' redress. Still, there are instances where a highly centralised and oppressive government creates space for local communities to shape transitional justice, perhaps unwitting that these communities may utilise the process in ways that the government deems undesirable. Again with the *gacaca* courts as an example, it has been argued that although *gacaca* was re-invented by the State to serve a clearly defined set of partially self-promoting goals, communities have sometimes been able to shape the process and to use it to open democratic space (Clark 2008b: 313). Consequently, despite the government's clear opposition and prohibition (Corey and Joireman 2004: 86–87), *gacaca* hearings, especially at the periphery of the country, have sometimes addressed the serious human rights abuses committed by the RPF in the context and aftermath of the civil war that surrounded the 1994 genocide (Stefanowicz 2011). Though it will usually be difficult for non-State actors to become formally involved in creating transitional justice processes in instances of a non-liberal political transition, an entry point for local communities to influence transitional justice may thus ironically be offered by mechanisms of transitional justice that are essentially conceived by the State to promote its own agenda.

Determining a suitable and feasible role of international actors is equally complex in this type of transitions. On the one hand, international support to transitional justice processes that do not satisfy basic human rights standards and other benchmarks for legitimacy discussed above should in principle be avoided, especially if the support could strengthen a non-democratic regime's ability to oppress the population. On the other hand, international support can take different dimensions, and particular aspects of a transitional justice process may sometimes be worth supporting, even in instances where the overall goals of the transitional justice process may conflict with democratic and rule of law standards and for other reasons be questionable. In Rwanda, for example, international donors supported the training of paralegals (known as Judicial Defenders) to offer legal assistance and representation in the genocide cases pending before the national courts. Although the accountability process itself suffered from serious flaws, the decision to support the paralegals significantly enhanced access to justice, not only with regard to the genocide cases but also in other ways because the paralegals subsequently moved on to deal with various other areas of the law (Hansen 2008). Because attempting to positively influence domestic transitional justice processes may not always be feasible or sufficient for ensuring that important goals are served, international actors can also promote transformation relying on other tools. In particular, international justice could play an important role in dealing with crimes that the State is unwilling to prosecute, in this way strengthening accountability principles and victims' right to justice. From this perspective, it is regrettable that the Arusha-based ICTR has opted to prosecute only genocide crimes, but not the serious crimes committed by the RPF. As noted by Des Forges and Longman, the ICTR's decision to prosecute 'only one party to the Rwandan war has naturally given the impression to some people that the tribunal is working in the interest of one side only' (Des Forges and Longman 2004: 55). In future cases, the ICC could play an important role in non-liberal transitions, where the State may be willing to prosecute certain categories of crimes and offenders, but not others. This could strengthen the Court's potential as a deterrent, while at the same time helping to overcome some of the legitimacy problems facing the ICC itself, including the perception that international justice is biased in favour of those in power.

Transitional justice in the absence of a political transition

Next, there are cases where no fundamental political transition has taken place, at least at the point where the justice processes are launched, but these processes are nonetheless conceptualised within a transitional justice framework. This category of cases is extremely diverse – ranging from societies such as Uganda or Colombia, which were still affected by armed conflict and serious human rights abuses at the point where a transitional justice process was launched, to power-sharing and failed (or at least disputed) transitions such as that in Kenya, and consolidated democracies such as Canada or Australia. Given this diversity, these cases can hardly be understood and evaluated using a single framework, though there may be certain similarities between them, including a disconnection between transitional justice and the pursuit of fundamental political change.

In cases such as Uganda and Colombia, for example, where the main type of transition taking place seems to concern an attempted move from armed conflict to peace, the ruling elites may choose to conceptualise an often limited or half-hearted attempt at addressing past or still ongoing abuses – often committed by various actors, including the incumbent regime itself – as transitional justice. By doing so, the regime may aim at avoiding international interference; shun more profound reforms of the system of governance; disseminate a particular, though not necessarily complete, picture of who is to blame for the abuses; and – perhaps most problematically – in order to target political opponents. For example, it has been argued that Ugandan President Museveni's decision to refer to the ICC the situation relating to the conflict in the northern parts of the country should be seen as one weapon in the arsenal adding pressure on the Lord's Resistance Army, still actively fighting at the time, while designed to avoid prosecutions of atrocities committed by the Ugandan army (Moi 2006; Nouwen and Werner 2011: 946–54). With regard to transitional justice in Colombia, it has been noted that the mechanisms established with the 2005 Justice and Peace Law[6] constitute 'a flawed process of paramilitary disarmament' that has 'arguably not been about the widening, deepening or strengthening of democracy', but rather disseminating a picture that the government is attentive to victim's needs while in reality avoiding more profound political reforms as well as ICC intervention (Diaz 2008: 196). However, transitional justice can have its own dynamics and may end up partially satisfying victims' calls for justice and contribute to reconciliation and peacebuilding. In Colombia, the information provided by ex-combatants in the re-integration process has led to investigations of high-ranking government officials and other positive developments (Human Rights Watch 2008: 36–47). In Uganda, the Juba Agreement, which was arguably conceived in an effort to end ICC prosecutions (once Museveni no longer thought the Court's involvement benefitted his objectives), has contributed to the creation of community-driven reconciliation and re-integration processes in Northern Uganda (Beyond Juba 2009; Greenawalt 2009) as well as the establishment of a special division of the High Court to try the most serious crimes (which so far, however, has had little success advancing accountability principles) (Wegner 2012). Although democratic reforms are certainly relevant for limiting the risks that wide-scale armed conflict continues or reoccurs, it is thus necessary to acknowledge that even if State-driven transitional justice processes in these contexts do not necessarily advance such reforms, these processes can still have some value if they contribute to a peaceful transformation and/or other goals, such as victims' redress. Yet, due to the government's potential interest in manipulating transitional justice, it is important that other actors, both below and above the State level, direct the process. Notably, even if the ICC depends on the cooperation of States, the Court has a responsibility to ensure that international justice is not being captured by national political elites to promote their own narrow agenda, but rather serves to bring justice to the victims and deter new atrocities, irrespectively of the perpetrators' connection to the ruling elites.

In other contexts, accountability, truth-seeking and reform measures are discussed as a matter of transitional justice, but no transition has occurred and the national political leadership has no or limited interest in supporting that these processes bring about meaningful transformation. Yet, due to pressure from civil society and the international community, some of these processes may nonetheless have potential for promoting political and peaceful transformation, for example because they end up targeting members of the political leadership. In Kenya, for example, the attempts made to address the country's legacy of political violence are debated within a transitional justice framework, though the power-sharing deal which ended the 2007/08 post-election violence has not resulted in fundamental political change – and such change seems a prerequisite for creating a more peaceful and just society (Hansen 2013a).

Understanding the case of Kenya requires that attention be paid to the fact that large segments of the political elites remain opposed to a credible and independent transitional justice process because it is seen to jeopardise their privileges and status quo. Consequently, political elites have attempted and partly succeeded capturing and manipulating transitional justice to serve their own agenda and maintain a status quo. Kenya's truth-seeking process, for example, has been almost entirely undermined by political leaders (Hansen 2013a). As a result, the question of how to limit the State's influence on these processes and empower civil society becomes a central concern when creating and implementing transitional justice tools. Further, special attention must be paid to the role of international actors, including how these actors can promote a credible transitional justice process in the absence of political will at the national level. For example, whereas the ICC's decision to intervene in the Kenyan situation presents at positive move for addressing impunity and providing victims with some level of justice, the success of international justice may ultimately depend on whether the Court itself and members of the international community adopts strategies that can circumvent the resistance in the national political leadership (Hansen 2013b). Evaluating the success of transitional justice in a case such as Kenya requires acceptance that strengthening accountability norms and implementing far-reaching legal and institutional reforms are necessary to promote an eventual political transformation as well as to prevent future violence, while at the same time there is a need, as far as possible, to externalise transitional justice from political elites. But it is also necessary to acknowledge that, if pushed into a corner, these elites may have both the will and ability to mobilise masses and trigger new violence (Hansen 2011; Sriram and Brown 2012).

A rather different scenario emerges when consolidated and generally peaceful (at least internally) democracies utilise justice tools to address abuses, which usually took place in a relatively distant past. In Canada and Australia, for example, the governments have established truth-seeking and some measures of reparations to deal with the abuses committed against the indigenous populations. Though these measures are frequently discussed as a matter of transitional justice, they do not seem to aim at achieving a political transition or other forms of fundamental transformation. These measures are nonetheless important because they can serve legitimate purposes, such as providing victims with redress and may lead to public acknowledgement of the past wrongdoing.[7] At the same time, it is necessary to critically analyse how consolidated democracies define their needs to address gross human rights violations. Consolidated democracies often support transitional justice, including criminal accountability processes, in developing countries, but this does not necessarily mean these countries are willing to hold accountable their own nationals for serious ongoing abuses, committed for example in the context of the War against Terrorism. Although it may be unrealistic to expect that the ICC will target powerful states in the West, the selective application of the transitional justice paradigm in some of these countries certainly merits a discussion of how other actors can advance justice for crimes that the State has no interest in addressing.

Conclusions

Discourses on transitional justice have moved to the very forefront of debates about democratisation, conflict prevention and peacebuilding. The enhanced normative power of the transitional justice paradigm seems to reflect an increased belief among important actors that the central question is no longer 'whether something should be done after atrocity but how it should be done' (Nagy 2008: 276). The strengthened position of the field is associated with increased claims for inclusion, but the field's expansion also poses challenges which must be addressed in order to ensure its continued relevance.

As a result of the expansion, transitional justice appears to have lost its connection to 'an exclusive "moment" in time' (McEvoy and McGregor 2008: 6), and conceptions are broadening concerning the kind of cases and actors relevant for the field. The transition, it has been noted, implies a 'journey, with a starting point and a finishing point' (Aoláin and Campbell 2005: 182), but with the expansion of transitional justice discourses, both the starting point and the finishing point of that journey have become increasingly unclear. The fact that ideas about transition are themselves in transition means that there is increased uncertainty concerning the main goals and actors of transitional justice. Specifically, are different goals and actors equally relevant to all types of case where justice processes are considered within a transitional justice paradigm?

Although this chapter dismisses the use of one coherent normative framework, it still acknowledges that the notion of transitional justice can be relevant to other types of case than liberalising political transitions. Certain goals, such as addressing impunity and providing victims with redress, reoccur in many different contexts. Further, transitional justice scholars, often emphasising an inter-disciplinary approach to understanding the law's ability to promote progressive societal change, have created useful tools to analyse accountability processes, truth-seeking and victims' redress – tools that can be used to improve our understanding of justice processes in various contexts. Admittedly, there is a danger that the continued proliferation of transitional justice discourses may, as noted by Bell, result in the field being constructed to mean 'all things to all people' (Bell 2009: 13). Yet, a crucial task of contemporary transitional justice scholarship involves analysing the implications of the field's expansion and partial disintegration, rather than insisting that transitional justice should alone focus on State-level responses to serious human rights abuses committed under a past authoritarian regime. Although this chapter does not claim to offer a conclusive framework for analysing and understanding transitional justice in different contexts, it aims to open the debate on these central issues.

Notes

* The views expressed in this chapter are those of the author only, and do not necessarily reflect the views of the organisations with which the author is affiliated.

1 It should be emphasised that Teitel has later noted: 'At present, we find ourselves in a global phase of transitional justice. The global phase is defined by three significant dimensions: first, the move from exceptional transitional responses to a "steady-state" justice, associated with post-conflict-related phenomena that emerge from a fairly pervasive state of conflict, including ethnic and civil wars; second, a shift from a focus on state-centric obligations to the far broader array of interest in non-state actors associated with globalization; and, lastly, we see an expansion of the law's role in advancing democratization and state-building to the more complex role of transitional justice in the broader purposes of promoting and maintaining peace and human security' (Teitel 2008: 2).

2 See generally the studies in Kritz (1995a, 1995b) and McAdams (1997).

3 For one of the few studies that questioned whether transitional justice should be seen as a special or unique form of justice, see Posner and Vermeule (2004). More recently, Ohlin has conducted a study which examines different conceptions of transitional justice, including the question of whether transitional justice is some other *kind* of justice, fundamentally different from justice during non-transitional moments, or if it is simply *ordinary* justice, a familiar end-state that remains elusive because a society has been ripped apart by mass violence (Ohlin 2007).

4 Such attempts were made in Bassiouni 2002. The notion is dismissed in various studies, including Roht-Arriaza 2006.

5 For different approaches to the Rwandan case, see the essays in Clark and Kaufman 2008. See also Drumbl 2000.

6 For further details on the Law, see Laplante and Theidon (2006).

7 On these two cases, see further the Australian Human Rights Commission 1997 and the International Center for Transitional Justice 2008.

Bibliography

Aguilar, P. (2001) 'Justice, Politics, and Memory in the Spanish Transition', in De Brito, A. B., Gonzalez-Enriques, C. and Aguilar, P. (eds) *The Politics of Memory: Transitional Justice in Democratizing Societies*, Oxford: Oxford University Press.

Albon, M. (1995) 'Project on Justice in Times of Transitions: Report of the Project's Inaugural Meeting', in Kritz, N.J. (ed.) *Transitional Justice: How Emerging Democracies Reckon with Former Regimes*, Vol. I, General Considerations, Washington, DC: United States Institute of Peace Press.

Aoláin, F.N. and Campbell, C. (2005) 'The Paradox of Transition in Conflicted Democracies', *Human Rights Quarterly*, 27 (1): 172–213.

Arthur, P. (2009) 'How "Transitions" Reshaped Human Rights: A Conceptual History of Transitional Justice', *Human Rights Quarterly*, 31(2): 321–67.

Australian Human Rights Commission (1997) *Bringing Them Home: The Stolen Children Report*. Available at: <http//www.hreoc.gov.au/social_justice/bth_report/index.html> (accessed 22 January 2013).

Bassiouni, M.C. (2002) 'Introduction', in Bassiouni, M.C. (ed.) *Post-Conflict Justice*, New York, NY: Transnational Publishers.

Bell, C. (2009) 'Transitional Justice, Interdisciplinarity and the State of the "Field" or "Non-Field"', *International Journal of Transitional Justice*, 3 (1): 5–27.

Beyond Juba (2009) *Tradition in Transition: Drawing on the Old to Develop a New Jurisprudence for Dealing with Uganda's Legacy of Violence (Working Paper No. 1)*. Available at: <http://www.beyondjuba.org/working_papers/BJP.WP1.pdf> (accessed 22 January 2013).

Boraine, A. (2006) 'Truth and Reconciliation Commission in South Africa: The Price of Peace', in Elster, J. (ed.) *Retribution and Reparations in the Transition to Democracy*, Cambridge: Cambridge University Press.

Cavallaro, J.L. and Albuja, S. (2008) 'The Lost Agenda: Economic Crimes and Truth Commissions in Latin America and Beyond', in McEvoy, K. and McGregor, L. (eds) *Transitional Justice from Below. Grassroots Activism and the Struggle for Change* (Human Rights Law in Perspective, Vol. 14), Oxford: Hart Publishing.

Clark, C. (2008a) 'Establishing a Conceptual Framework: Six Key Transitional Justice Themes', in Clark, C. and Kaufman, Z. (eds) *After Genocide: Transitional Justice, Post-Conflict Reconstruction and Reconciliation in Rwanda and Beyond*, New York, NY: Columbia University Press.

——(2008b) 'The Rules (and Politics) of Engagement: The Gacaca Courts and Post-Genocide Justice, Healing and Reconciliation in Rwanda', in Clark, C. and Kaufman, Z. (eds) *After Genocide: Transitional Justice, Post-Conflict Reconstruction and Reconciliation in Rwanda and Beyond*, New York, NY: Columbia University Press.

Clark, P. (2007) 'Hybridity, Holism, and "Traditional" Justice: The Case of the Gacaca Courts in Post-Genocide Rwanda', *George Washington International Law Review*, 39 (4): 765–837.

Clark, P. and Kaufman, Z. (eds) (2008) *After Genocide: Transitional Justice, Post-Conflict Reconstruction and Reconciliation in Rwanda and Beyond*, New York, NY: Columbia University Press.

Corey, A. and Joireman, S.F. (2004) 'Retributive Justice: The Gacaca Courts in Rwanda', *African Affairs*, 103 (410): 73–89.

Des Forges, A. and Longman, T. (2004) 'Legal Responses to Genocide in Rwanda', in Stover, E. and Weinstein, H.M. (eds) *My Neighbor, My Enemy: Justice and Community in the Aftermath of Mass Atrocity*, Cambridge: Cambridge University Press.

Diaz, C. (2008) 'Challenging Impunity from Below: The Contested Ownership of Transitional Justice in Colombia', in McEvoy, K. and McGregor, L. (eds) *Transitional Justice from Below. Grassroots Activism and the Struggle for Change* (Human Rights Law in Perspective, Vol. 14), Oxford: Hart Publishing.

Drumbl, M.A. (2000) 'Sclerosis: Retributive Justice and the Rwandan Genocide', *Punishment and Society*, 2 (3): 287–307.

——(2002) 'Restorative Justice and Collective Responsibility: Lessons for and from the Rwandan Genocide', *Contemporary Justice Reviews*, 5 (1): 5–22.

Duthie, R. (2008) 'Toward a Development-sensitive Approach to Transitional Justice', *International Journal of Transitional Justice*, 2 (3): 292–309.

Elster, J. (2004) *Closing the Books: Transitional Justice in Historical Perspective*, Cambridge: Cambridge University Press.

Fierens, J. (2005) 'Gacaca Courts: Between Fantasy and Reality', *Journal of International Criminal Justice*, 3 (4): 896–919.

Greenawalt, A.K.A. (2009) 'Complementarity in Crisis: Uganda, Alternative Justice, and the International Criminal Court', *Virginia Journal of International Law*, 50 (1): 107–62.

Grodsky, B. (2008) 'Justice Without Transition: Truth Commissions in the Context of Repressive Rule', *Human Rights Review*, 9(3): 281–97.

Hansen, T.O. (2008) 'Human Rights and Transitional Societies: Contemporary Challenges', in Garbutt, R. (ed.) *Activating Human Rights and Peace: Universal Responsibility Conference 2008*, Lismore: Southern Cross University.

——(2011) 'Transitional Justice in Kenya? An Assessment of the Accountability Process in Light of Domestic Politics and Security Concerns', *California Western International Law Journal*, 42 (1): 1–35.

——(2013a) 'Kenya's Power-Sharing Arrangement and its Implications for Transitional Justice', *International Journal of Human Rights*, 17 (2) (forthcoming).

——(2013b) 'The International Criminal Court in Kenya: Three Defining Features of a Contested Accountability Process and Their Implications for the Future of International Justice', *Australian Journal of Human Rights*, 19 (1): 187–217.

Harbeson, J.W. (1998) 'A Bureaucratic Authoritarian Regime', *Journal of Democracy*, 7 (4): 62–69.

Hayner, P.B. (2001) *Unspeakable Truths: Facing the Challenge of Truth Commissions*, New York, NY: Routledge.

Hazan, P. (2006) 'Measuring the Impact of Punishment and Forgiveness: A Framework for Evaluating Transitional Justice', *International Review of the Red Cross*, 88 (861): 19–48.

Human Rights Watch (2008) *Breaking the Grip? Obstacle to Justice for Paramilitary Mafias in Colombia*. Available at: <http://www.hrw.org/sites/default/files/reports/colombia1008web.pdf> (accessed 19 January 2013).

Huntington, S. (1991) *The Third Wave: Democratization in the Late Twentieth Century*, Norman, OK: University of Oklahoma Press.

Huyse, L. (2008) 'Introduction: Tradition-Based Approaches in Peacemaking, Transitional Justice and Reconciliation Policies', in Huyse, L. and Salter, M. (eds) *Traditional Justice and Reconciliation after Violent Conflict: Learning from African Experiences*, Stockholm: International Institute for Democracy and Electoral Assistance.

International Center for Transitional Justice (2008) *Canada's Truth and Reconciliation Commission*, 29 April. Available at: <http://www.ictj.org/publication/canadas-truth-and-reconciliation-commission> (accessed at 22 January 2013).

Kritz, N.J. (ed.) (1995a) *Transitional Justice: How Emerging Democracies Reckon with Former Regimes*, Vol. I, General Considerations, Washington, DC: United States Institute of Peace Press.

——(1995b) *Transitional Justice: How Emerging Democracies Reckon with Former Regimes*, Vol. II, Country Studies, Washington, DC: United States Institute of Peace Press.

Laplante, L.J. and Theidon, K. (2006) 'Transitional Justice in Times of Conflict: Colombia's "Ley de Justicia y Paz"', *Michigan Journal of International Law*, 28 (1): 49–108.

Linz, J.J. and Stepan, A. (1996) *Problems of Democratic Transition and Consolidation: Southern Europe, South America, and Post-Communist Europe*, Baltimore, MD: Johns Hopkins University Press.

Lundy, P. and McGovern, M. (2008) 'The Role of Community in Participatory Transitional Justice', in McEvoy, K. and McGregor, L. (eds) *Transitional Justice from Below. Grassroots Activism and the Struggle for Change* (Human Rights Law in Perspective, Vol. 14), Oxford: Hart Publishing.

McAdams, A.J. (ed.) (1997) *Transitional Justice and the Rule of Law in New Democracies*, South Bend, IN: University of Notre Dame Press.

McEvoy, K. (2008) 'Letting Go of Legalism: Developing a "Thicker" Version of Transitional Justice', in McEvoy, K. and McGregor, L. (eds) *Transitional Justice from Below. Grassroots Activism and the Struggle for Change* (Human Rights Law in Perspective, Vol. 14), Oxford: Hart Publishing.

McEvoy, K. and McGregor, L. (2008) 'Transitional Justice from Below: An Agenda for Research, Policy and Praxis', in McEvoy, K. and McGregor, L. (eds) *Transitional Justice from Below. Grassroots Activism and the Struggle for Change* (Human Rights Law in Perspective, Vol. 14), Oxford: Hart Publishing.

Malamud-Goti, J. (1991) 'Punishment and a Rights-Based Democracy', *Criminal Justice Ethics*, 10 (2): 3–13.

Mani, R. (2002) *Beyond Retribution: Seeking Justice in the Shadows of War*, Cambridge: Polity Press.

Mgbako, C. (2005) 'Ingando Solidarity Camps: Reconciliation and Political Indoctrination in Post-Genocide Rwanda', *Harvard Human Rights Journal*, 18: 201–24.

Miller, Z. (2008) 'Effects of Invisibility: In Search of the Economic in Transitional Justice', *International Journal of Transitional Justice*, 2 (3): 266–91.

Moi, H.A. (2006) 'The International Criminal Court's Arrest Warrants and Uganda's Lord's resistance Army: Renewing the Debate over Amnesty and Complementarity', *Harvard Human Rights Journal*, 19: 267–74.

Nagy, R. (2008) 'Transitional Justice as Global Project: Critical Reflections', *Third World Quarterly*, 29 (2): 275–89.

Nino, C.S. (1996) *Radical Evil on Trial*, New Haven, CT: Yale University Press.

Nouwen, S.M.H. and Werner, W.G. (2011) 'Doing Justice to the Political: The International Criminal Court in Uganda and Sudan', *European Journal of International Law*, 21 (4): 941–65.

Ohlin, J.D. (2007) 'On the Very Idea of Transitional Justice', *Whitehead Journal of Diplomacy and International Relations*, 8 (1): 51–68.

Oomen, B. (2005) 'Donor Driven Justice and Its Discontents: The Case of Rwanda', *Development and Change*, 36, (5): 887–910.

Posner, E.A. and Vermeule, A. (2004) 'Transitional Justice as Ordinary Justice', *Harvard Law Review*, 117 (3): 761–825.

Reyntjens, F. (2004) 'Rwanda, Ten Years on: From Genocide to Dictatorship', *African Affairs*, 103: 177–210.

Roht-Arriaza, N. (2006) 'The New Landscape of Transitional Justice', in Roht-Arriaza, N. and Mariezcurrena, J. (eds) *Transitional Justice in the Twenty-First Century: Beyond Truth versus Justice*, Cambridge: Cambridge University Press.

Sarkin, J. (2001) 'The Tension between Justice and Reconciliation in Rwanda: Politics, Human Rights, Due Process and the Role of Gacaca Courts in Dealing with the Genocide', *Journal of African Law*, 45 (2): 143–72.

Schabas, W.A. (2002) 'The Rwanda Case: Sometimes It's Impossible', in Bassiouni, M.C. (ed.) *Post-Conflict Justice*, New York, NY: Transnational Publishers.

Sharp, D.N. (2013) 'Interrogating the Peripheries; The Preoccupations of Fourth Generation Transitional Justice', *Harvard Human Rights Journal*, 26 (forthcoming, cited with author's permission).

Sriram, C.L. and Brown, S. (2012) 'The Big Fish Won't Fry Themselves: Criminal Accountability for Post-Election Violence in Kenya', *African Affairs*, 111 (443): 244–60.

Stefanowicz, C. (2011) 'Gacaca Highlights Failure to Deal with RPF Crimes', *Think Africa Press*, 8 March 2011. Available at: <http://thinkafricapress.com/node/811> (accessed 19 January 2013).

Teitel, R.G. (2000) *Transitional Justice*, Oxford and New York, NY: Oxford University Press.

——(2003) 'Transitional Justice Genealogy', *Harvard Human Rights Journal*, 16: 69–94.

——(2008) 'Editorial Note – Transitional Justice Globalized', *International Journal of Transitional Justice*, 2 (1): 1–4.

Tiba, F.K. (2007) 'The Mengistu Genocide Trial in Ethiopia', *Journal of International Criminal Justice*, 5 (2): 513–28.

United Nations Secretary General (2011) *The Rule of Law and Transitional Justice in Conflict and Post-Conflict Societies*, U.N. Doc. S/2011/634, 2011.

Wegner, P. (2012) 'Where to With Transitional Justice in Uganda? The Situation After the Extension of the Amnesty Act', *Justice in Conflict*, 22 April 2012. Available at: <http://justiceinconflict.org/2012/04/22/where-to-with-transitional-justice-in-uganda-the-situation-after-the-extension-of-the-amnesty-act/#more-3144> (accessed 19 January 2013).

Part II

Exploring the limits of transitional justice

Chapter 6

Bargaining justice

A theory of transitional justice compliance

Jelena Subotić

A global transitional justice norm has emerged over the past two decades, which prescribes the appropriate way for States to address responsibility for grave human rights abuses. This international norm maintains that, as part of the process of post-conflict or post-authoritarian transition, the most serious human rights violations, such as war crimes, crimes against humanity and genocide, should be adjudicated in a court of law or another type of justice or truth-seeking institution and not left to either victor's justice or forgiveness. While these crimes were historically dealt with by executions or summary trials set up by victors after conflict, or simply remained unpunished, they are now considered just like other crimes that demand a proper trial and due process (Teitel 2003; Roht-Arriaza and Mariezcurrena 2006; Arthur 2009). The international norm of transitional justice was further established, legalised and codified with the creation of, first, the ad hoc ICTY and ICTR, and the Special Court for Sierra Leone, and then the permanent ICC in 1998. The international prestige and publicity of the South African TRC also made this truth-seeking model of transitional justice particularly popular and emulated by dozens of transitioning States (Hayner 2001).

And while the increasing presence and visibility of transitional justice has been followed by the increasing attention of the scholarly literature (Olsen *et al* 2010; Thoms *et al* 2010; Leebaw 2011; Sikkink 2011), not enough attention has been paid to questions of how exactly States go about complying with transitional justice requirements under international pressures, and to what domestic political effect (Peskin 2008; Lamont 2009). In this chapter, I offer a theory of transitional justice compliance. I explain varying breadth and depth of transitional justice adoption by looking at domestic political conditions that motivate local actors to engage with international norms and institutions in different ways. I show how domestic compliance with transitional justice models always faces significant and varied domestic challenges, which often produce unexpected and contradictory policy effects (Boesenecker and Vinjamuri 2011).

I make three principal arguments. First, when States adopt international norms of transitional justice in the absence of broad domestic demand for dealing with crimes of the past, transitional justice mechanisms become a strategic, even subversive, choice for those States that do not have much substantive interest in justice claims. Carrying out a transitional justice project allows domestic elites to signal their respect of international institutions, while using justice mechanisms domestically to achieve other political goals, such as getting rid of domestic political opponents, obtaining financial aid, or gaining membership in prestigious international organisations.

Second, under sustained international pressures, States choose to comply with transitional justice expectations because non-compliance is too costly internationally, and the punishment for non-compliance is severe. At the same time, however, domestic costs of full compliance are also prohibitively high: transitional justice is unpopular at home; powerful domestic anti-justice constituencies can destabilise the new regime; and transitional justice requires fundamental transformation of how domestic political elites understand and interpret the violent past and their role in it. To negotiate the conflicting costs of compliance and non-compliance, domestic political elites often choose to comply with international transitional justice requirements, avoiding sanctions, but repackaging transitional justice normatively to make it more acceptable to the domestic audience.

Lastly, how elites go about engaging in transitional justice is the result of specific domestic power structures and coalitions. The contested process of transitional justice adoption defines domestic elites along three major groups: justice resisters, justice instrumentalists and true believers. Which domestic group comes out on top in the domestic political battle will determine what approach to transitional justice elites undertake and to what policy effect.

This chapter proceeds as follows. I first present evidence of a 'thickening' international environment for transitional justice. I describe how the global environment for human rights generally, and transitional justice specifically, has changed to institutionalise transitional justice as an international norm and make non-compliance with it increasingly difficult for States to manage. I then present three different types of international pressures on States to comply with transitional justice expectations and different domestic coalitions that these pressures embolden. I conclude by analysing the consequences of compliance with transitional justice under international pressure for transitional justice policy outcomes.

The thickening international environment of transitional justice

Over the past two decades, a number of global developments have created new opportunity structures for the expansion of human rights norms more broadly and the transitional justice norm more specifically.[1] The first factor is the presence of the larger norm of global liberalism, which is evident in the increasing legalisation of the international system and reliance on the rule of law as the appropriate model of State practice (Abbott *et al* 2000).

The global trend toward legalisation and 'judicialisation' of politics, in which transitional justice is embedded, is also showing signs of spreading and institutionalisation (Sieder and Schjolden 2005). Solving problems through an institutional or a legal setting is becoming an increasingly internationally accepted practice even for issues that previously were not considered to be in the legal purview, such as legacies of past violence. The increasing visibility of global human rights has also produced increasing public interest in and awareness of transitional justice, as well as an international expectation that some mechanism of accountability is due in the aftermath of mass atrocity and that States can no longer avoid this responsibility. The most recent sign of transitional justice expansion is the notion of universal jurisdiction, according to which national courts can investigate and prosecute alleged perpetrators on their territory, regardless of where the crime was committed or the nationality of the accused or the victim (Roht-Arriaza 2005).

Concerns about human rights, therefore, have become more firmly incorporated into international affairs, especially for democratising or transitional States that are trying hard to shed the legacy of past violence and become full members of the international society. Lastly, great powers have begun promoting institutions of transitional justice, especially foreign and domestic war crimes tribunals, as a way to signal concern for human rights while at the same time avoiding costly humanitarian interventions (Bass 2000). For the great powers, which often foot the bill for international transitional justice projects, it is much less costly to support war crimes tribunals than to risk their own blood and treasure to prevent massacres from occurring in the first place.

For all the reasons mentioned above, the international normative shift toward legalisation as a solution for human rights abuses has led to a massive proliferation of transitional justice initiatives around the world. The institutional designs of transitional justice models are becoming increasingly regulated as professionalised and specialised international organisations supply specific models of policy change for domestic actors to implement (Mattli and Woods 2009; Avant *et al* 2010).

The growing international supply of specific models for dealing with past crimes also creates its own demand from States. States are now expected, encouraged and even coerced by other States, by international organisations and by the growing number of international transitional justice advocacy groups, to conduct transitional justice projects as one of the first steps in post-conflict rebuilding. As a consequence of this unprecedented activism, the international justice experts have succeeded in framing the States' choice as one of which model of justice to adopt, not whether any should be adopted at all.

The normative shift at the international level towards legalisation as a solution for human rights abuses has then been translated and simplified into international policy that makes very specific transitional justice mechanisms, such as, for example, cooperation with war crimes tribunals, a working proxy for respect of human rights. For example, the European Union (EU) had directly tied Serbian and Croatian accession negotiations to full cooperation with the ICTY. Importantly, the EU has chosen this particular policy as a measurement of candidate States' compliance with the larger Copenhagen Criteria of strong democratic institutions and protection of ethnic and human rights. This simplification had significant consequences for international policy-making, as compliance with international justice models increasingly became a marker of domestic human rights policy, opening up a wide space for domestic elites to offer narrow institutional compliance with international justice while continuing to deny responsibility for past human rights violations (Subotić 2009b).

The thickening international environment of global human rights also means that States are increasingly coming under pressure to change their practices in line with changing global norms. While there is abundant evidence that international pressure works in many different ways to bring about positive change in human rights behaviour of States (Keck and Sikkink 1998; Risse-Kappen *et al* 1999), recent research uncovered that this is the case only if certain domestic conditions are met. For example, international demands for States to discontinue certain violations of human rights are most successful if they do not encroach on issues of national security (Cardenas 2004). The real paradox of human rights compliance under pressure, however, is that international actors force States to sign or ratify international human rights treaties they often have neither capacity nor interest in implementing (Avdeyeva 2007; Hafner-Burton and Tsutsui 2007). This makes sense, since if they were fully committed to the international requirement, then no pressure would be necessary in the first place. Therefore, States least interested in international human rights norms they are supposed to accept are the ones most forced into making the dramatic domestic policy shift (Hafner-Burton *et al* 2008).

International pressure, therefore, creates a domestic 'ownership problem' (Checkel 2000). Since policy changes are result of external pressure, domestic incentive to comply is lower as changes are not produced by a domestic political process. It is not surprising, then, that we see 'decoupling' between States' formal commitments and policy practice, or that compliance under pressure will be short lived and shallow (Goodman and Jinks 2005). For example, States can sign international human rights treaties, they can change domestic human rights legislation and even set up new institutions – but they are able to use these institutional markers of compliance as cover for continuing human rights violations at home (Hafner-Burton and Kiyoteru 2005). This is especially the case with autocratic States with weak civil society (Neumayer 2005). Authoritarian leaders will only fulfil international requirements to appease international actors, and even then only when it provides the regime with space and time to further consolidate domestic power and deflect continuing international pressure in other areas (Hawkins 1997). Non-democratic States are just as likely as democracies to commit to human rights treaties if they have poor human rights records, because there is little prospect that the treaties will be enforced (Hathaway 2007). In other words, ratification of international treaties may often be 'costless' to domestic political elites (Hathaway 2002).

Similarly, increasing international pressures on States to comply with transitional justice norms and institutions makes carrying out a transitional justice project an easy way for States to show compliance with international rules without making broader domestic normative changes that these rules require. As a consequence, some of the original goals of transitional justice – truth, justice and reconciliation – become subordinated to ulterior State strategies, as justice becomes hijacked in favour of domestic political needs (Subotić 2009a).

The scope of this chapter, however, encompasses a very specific subset of transitional justice possibilities. It explores compliance with international transitional justice norms under conditions of strong international pressure and limited domestic demand for justice. In other words, it does not include cases of compliance that are clearly domestically driven. When the domestic demand for justice is strong, States comply with international norms because these are the norms they already share or because strong domestic constituencies are able to put pressure on governments to change their behaviour in response to international demands. I also do not discuss cases where international pressures are low or absent and there are no domestic actors pushing for transitional justice. In such cases, we can expect that international justice norms will be soundly rejected or simply ignored.

My argument, then, applies to the universe of cases where both the international pressure for and domestic opposition to transitional justice are strong. International pressures for some transitional justice process are great, but the domestic demand for justice is weak. The theoretical model I present, therefore, is a domestic politics approach to transitional justice compliance under pressure and an analysis of how this international pressure is resisted and appropriated by local political actors.

Varieties of international justice pressures

While the international pressure to comply is a given, it is not a constant. It varies in intensity, internal coherence, sustainability and reliability. It also varies in kind.

Coercion

In States in which the social demand for justice is weak and the State unresponsive to victims' demands, international actors will use issue linkage (tying compliance with international demands to rewards such as foreign aid and investment or membership in international organisations) to effectively coerce the State into complying with or adopting a transitional justice project. States facing international punishments (withholding of aid, imposition of sanctions) or rewards (exclusive club membership, financial investment) will then comply with international transitional justice norms and institutions to ease international coercion and obtain material rewards. Coercive pressure produces a simple political bargaining dynamic: if you comply with our requirements, you will get our benefits. This kind of pressure is most productive if the rules of compliance are clear, the reward is significant, and the threat of withholding the reward is credible (Kelley 2004; Schimmelfennig and Sedelmeier 2004; Schimmelfennig 2008).

As stated earlier, it is in States with domestic policies most out of synch with international norms and standards that international actors use coercive pressure. In such non-compliant or recalcitrant States, the domestic demand for justice is weak, while political support for the abusive regime is strong. This makes the domestic costs of transitional justice appear prohibitively high. There are no powerful domestic constituencies that pressure elites into carrying out a justice project, and the monopoly of force is located with spoilers who have a vested interest in resisting the policy change. Domestic environment, in other words, is greatly inhospitable to transitional justice. However, elites in power are under sustained international pressure to comply with international requirements or else they will be denied international benefits. Therefore, they choose to comply by, for example, extraditing suspects to international courts, but otherwise keep national human rights policies unchanged – they may engage in 'compromise justice' (Grodsky 2009).

Symbolic pressure

States are social actors and as such have a desire to form associational ties with other States (Meyer *et al* 1997). They want to belong to international clubs and to be with other like-minded States. They also want to be perceived as legitimate international actors (Finnemore 1996). In States with a strong desire for international membership and recognition, international actors will use symbolic pressure to entice a reluctant State to comply with domestically unpopular norms (Finnemore 1993), such as norms of transitional justice. Symbolic pressure works based on a simple principle: if you comply, you will become one of us.

While membership in international organisations or clubs, such as the EU or the North Atlantic Treaty Organization (NATO), carries obvious economic and political benefits (alliance military protection, full access to regional markets, economic subsidies and participation or veto power in regional decision-making), there are other pulls for countries to do all they can in order to join (Schimmelfennig and Sedelmeier 2005; Vachudova 2005). Increasingly, State participation in international organisations and other kinds of multilateral behaviour are considered necessary and appropriate if a State is to be considered a good global citizen (March and Olsen 1989; Finnemore 1996). International participation therefore affects State interests and identities. Membership in exclusive clubs such as the EU constitutes what candidate States want to be or what they think they already are – European, liberal, democratic (Barnett and Finnemore 2004). Joining a prestigious international institution or engaging in other types of multilateral behaviour may seem contrary to the immediate national interests of States, but it embodies larger global values that shape strategic choices States make (Ruggie 1993). In other words, States comply with international norms and institutions – such as those of transitional justice – not because of what they do but because of what they signify because of their symbolic and normative properties (DiMaggio and Powell 1983; Powell and DiMaggio 1991).

In this scenario, domestic demand for justice is also weak, but political spoilers of the old regime do not have monopoly of force. Here, transitional ruling elites choose to comply with international justice requirements because they are concerned about international and domestic legitimacy. They do not face broad domestic support for justice, but they also do not have to worry about spoilers destabilising the State. Elites in these circumstances have considerable space in which to move. Unburdened by domestic constraints, they can make policy choices that appeal to their international sponsors, for which they will be rewarded with improvements in reputation and status. Compliance with international justice requirements will be easier for society to 'swallow', as it will be presented as a price of admission to the 'good international society of states'. For this kind of strategic compliance, no normative change is necessary – good international manners will do (Lamont 2010).

Bureaucratic pressure

Under conditions of domestic political uncertainty (such as instability, infighting or unresolved transition), international actors will rely on bureaucratic pressures to ensure compliance with international norms and institutions of transitional justice. If they can find no domestic solution to the justice dilemma and international actors are offering justice solutions that can be easily adopted, some States will choose to comply with international transitional justice models because they believe international actors can solve their domestic problems. Such States are ambiguous about international justice goals and processes, but they are influenced by the neighbourhood effects of international justice diffusion and are likely to respond strongly to the increasing supply of institutional models of transitional justice available to them by mimicking the behaviour of other States. Under bureaucratic pressure, the message international actors send is simple: comply, and we will fix your problems.

Under conditions of political uncertainty, States will adopt the specific institutional solutions of transitional justice that have obtained the most symbolic legitimacy and have the international authority that alternative models lack (Meyer *et al* 1997). These success models serve as a convenient source of best practices the borrowing States will use (DiMaggio and Powell 1983). In fact, it is becoming increasingly clear that a distinguishable 'template' of international transitional justice best practices has emerged that involves prosecutions, truth seeking and domestic legal reforms (McEvoy 2007; Boesenecker and Vinjamuri forthcoming). Transitional justice mechanisms are increasingly viewed as a single multifaceted process, a 'package' composed of truth, justice and reparations (Roht-Arriaza 2006). These best practices have been further institutionalised in UN manuals, such as the 'rule-of-law tools', which explicitly adopt the 'templatisation' model by promoting a holistic or integral approach to transitional justice that includes prosecutions, truth commissions, and vetting.

These transitional justice best practices diffuse across the international system through the activities of a relatively small set of major professionalised international organisations, which present, explain, and sometimes help implement success models to interested States. They help set up and design transitional justice institutions, and provide staff and consulting services. They also act as direct agents of transitional justice projects: they collect witness testimony and evidence, they serve as expert witnesses and advisers, and they help generate the political pressure necessary for the arrest of suspects. They lobby on States' behalf, raise funds, and link transitional justice adoption with other international benefits (Subotić 2012). In the environment of bureaucratic international pressure with limited or mixed domestic demand for justice, States will adopt transitional justice projects that are readily available to them and that carry a certain amount of international prestige.

Compliance with transitional justice norms under these different international pressures is always accompanied by multiple and conflicting points of resistance and support within States. One of the shortcomings of the transnational advocacy network 'boomerang' model (Keck and Sikkink 1998; Simmons 2009) was that it underestimated the strength of domestic elite resistance to international norms and overestimated the power of norm supporters – domestic allies of transnational groups, such as NGOs and civil society (Fletcher *et al* 2009).

The domestic political scene, in fact, tends to be more complicated. While domestic elites in general and government elites in particular may be strongly opposed to transitional justice, what further complicates the process of compliance are frequent differences and domestic political struggles between elite factions, who use transitional justice projects as a domestic wedge issue to score quite localised political points.

International pressures on States, therefore, do not enter a domestic political vacuum. International norms are adapted and interpreted to fit with local beliefs and practices (Acharya 2004, 2011; Merry 2006; Goodale and Merry 2007). They always interact with domestic political conditions to guide State strategies of normative and institutional compliance. The next section of the chapter outlines a number of domestic political factors that influence the manner and outcome of domestic adoption of international transitional justice models.

Domestic political environment of transitional justice adoption

Domestic demand for justice

Domestic demand for justice is the result of the nature of human rights violations and the broad social consensus developed around public beliefs, understandings and commitments the international norm is set to change. Some indicators of societal demand from below include social attitudes toward justice, the political strength of domestic human rights and victims' groups, as well as political support for leaders who carried out human rights violations (Olsen et al 2010). If the domestic demand for justice is high, we can expect the State to engage in a transitional justice project with strong domestic support. Even in States where the demand for justice is low, however, there may still be international pressures to carry out a transitional justice project. It is in such cases that paradoxical outcomes will be most pronounced.

Old regime spoilers

For States transitioning from a violent past, it is important to determine to what extent members and supporters of the previous regime are still involved in policy-making. Do they have access to the apparatus of repression? For example, in States transitioning from an authoritarian rule to democracy, unless the transition was brought on by a massive social revolution, the likelihood is that there are still powerful old-regime elements that are embedded, officially or unofficially, in the transitional State's apparatus of force – the military, police or intelligence agencies. The more 'pacted' the transition was (the stronger the compromise made between the old and incoming regimes), the more power old-regime loyalists have in the new transitional State. If the planned transitional justice project is set to fundamentally alter their place in the new State order by requiring a clean slate and their removal from positions of power and control, and likely arrest and prosecution, the transitional elites will fear political reprisal, even a coup, and will be reluctant to destabilise the country and jeopardise their own power by carrying out a justice project. Transitional justice here is shallow and rewards driven. Under sustained international pressure, governments will sign extradition laws, change domestic legislation and might even arrest suspects – but they will not threaten old-regime loyalists with political extinction. Instead, they will comply with international demands while keeping the domestic balance of power intact.

Domestic political coalitions

While domestic elites in general and government elites in particular may be strongly opposed to transitional justice, what further complicates justice projects are frequent differences and domestic political struggles between elite factions, who use international norms and institutions as domestic wedge issues to score quite localised political points by, for example, instrumentalising a particular international policy intervention in a coming election campaign. The major domestic coalitions whose interaction helps determine the manner of transitional justice compliance can be roughly grouped as justice resisters, justice instrumentalists and justice true believers (Boesenecker and Vinjamuri 2011).

Justice resisters are political elites ideologically, politically or pragmatically opposed to transitional justice. In States with low domestic demand for justice resisters often have strong public support, especially if international transitional justice demands are broadly perceived to be incompatible with shared local values, understanding and practices of human rights. In States where elite legitimacy is based on a particular narrative and interpretation of past events that is fundamentally at odds with the international understanding of the past conflict and proposed justice mechanisms to resolve it, domestic actors are ideologically unable to internalise transitional justice norms because they undermine the basis of their domestic political rule. Nevertheless, these actors will still pursue cosmetic changes to their domestic human rights and transitional justice practices and carry out tactical concessions in order to obtain international benefits and payoffs. At the same time, however, they will send a message to the domestic audience that these moves have to be made in order to appease international coercion, that these attacks on State sovereignty will in fact reap benefits that all can enjoy. They will use international transitional justice norms and institutions to further consolidate their rule instead of undertaking the social transformation transitional justice requires.

Other domestic political elites may be justice instrumentalists. They use transitional justice to distinguish themselves from other political groups and to position themselves as political reformers. Instrumentalists may face serious political challenges from justice resisters and their constituencies. Still, they agree to implement transitional justice projects because they consider them legitimate and necessary if they are to be taken seriously by international actors on whom they depend. International organisation membership and other status incentives therefore lead domestic instrumentalists to rebrand themselves as pro-international and dedicated to compliance with international transitional justice norms. International pressure can also change the domestic balance of power in favour of justice instrumentalists. It can strengthen their domestic position, reaffirm their policy choice, and empower them in relation to their political opponents (Vachudova 2009). Transitional justice compliance, however, is still driven by external incentives – appeals to legitimacy – and not by justice acceptance and internalisation.

Lastly, international transitional justice models are fully accepted by true believers – civil society groups or other political coalitions that are at odds with both justice resisters and instrumentalists. As we know from boomerang and spiral models of human rights diffusion, it is these groups that spearhead human rights policy change by making lasting coalitions with international human rights promoters who put pressure on domestic governments to initiate policy change (Risse-Kappen *et al* 1999). If domestic true believers win the domestic political infighting, we can expect States to fully comply with international norms and institutions of transitional justice.

However, the political environment in which domestic allies of international transitional justice promoters operate is often much more complicated. Civil society in transitional States is just as likely to be bitterly divided over a specific transitional justice model as it is united against a common enemy – the previous regime that carried out human rights abuses (Schmitz 2006). In addition, close alliances with international actors may become a domestic political liability, giving justice resisters an easy way to delegitimate true believers as unpatriotic and dangerous (Mendelson and Glenn 2002). This further distracts domestic groups from spreading international transitional justice norms by making it much more difficult to build effective broad domestic coalitions in an increasingly hostile political environment.

Under conditions of political uncertainty, however, none of the three groups may have a monopoly over domestic legitimacy and authority, and political contestation between resisters and instrumentalists may reach a stalemate. It is in these conditions that international transitional justice promoters have the most room to move and implement various justice projects. They function as transitional justice norm transmitters, providing States with appropriate justice models to choose from, educating them about the benefits of instituting specific transitional justice projects and the proper ways of going about it. In other words, they provide bureaucratic solutions to State problems.

Much of the transnational activism literature oversimplifies the domestic elite impact on compliance by giving the third group, true believers, more agency than to either resisters or instrumentalists. Empirically, however, what happens under international pressure is a genuine domestic competition and contestation between different coalitions about how best to use international institutions to gain political advantage. All groups use posturing, positioning and rhetorical tools to try to amass stronger coalitions among both international and domestic audiences. For example, justice resisters may appeal to a sense of nationalism, sovereignty and independence in rejecting international transitional justice intervention. Justice instrumentalists may stress the benefits to society of being on the international community's good side by accepting international transitional justice models. And justice true believers – domestic as well as international – may appeal to a sense of morality, or the right thing to do, and try to generate support through claims of truth-seeking, righteousness and justice. The more persuasive these different appeals are, the broader the domestic coalitions they are able to build; and the stronger the enforcement mechanisms at their disposal are, the more likely they are to prevail and directly influence the strategy of transitional justice compliance a State will pursue.

Policy outcomes of transitional justice compliance under pressure

Why are different strategies of transitional justice compliance significant? If international actors promoting justice in transitional States observe shifts in elite behaviour, if domestic elites can show institutional or policy changes, if there is a marked improvement in human rights overall – then why does a specific path to transitional justice matter?

As I have shown elsewhere, different strategies of compliance matter centrally because they influence outcomes of international transitional justice projects (Subotić 2009a, 2009b) They shape the effects of international transitional justice norms and institutions both domestically, in terms of political processes that they set in motion, and internationally, in terms of lessons learned for future transitional projects carried out in different political contexts. Although international organisations may initiate transitional justice projects for reasons that emerge out of a larger global concern with respecting human rights, the effects of these projects will differ depending on how they are strategically adopted by local political actors. Refocusing our attention on domestic sources and consequences of international action therefore identifies the limits and opportunities of international transitional justice norms and their policy implications.

If transitional justice norms and institutions are accepted as a result of international coercion, compliance will be shallow and narrow. International actors may see institutional results of their policy interventions – cooperation with international tribunals, setting up of domestic human rights trials or truth commissions – but international transitional justice norms that generated justice projects will not take hold. International policies may also end up providing new space for justice resisters to mobilise, to use international norms and institutions for local political goals. Entrenched elites can adapt quickly to preferences of international actors and develop strategies of quasi-compliance or even outright deception and countermobilisation (Schmitz 2006). Politics in target States will not change. International transitional justice projects will, therefore, at best miss their mark and at worst produce perverse results, as domestic elites use justice models for ulterior political purposes. This domestic move will then delegitimise international transitional justice interventions in other political environments.

If a State complies out of concerns for legitimacy, transitional justice projects adopted will be instrumental and directly tied to international symbols of reputation and status. As long as international actors maintain significant leverage over domestic politics in the target State, domestic elites will comply. If the international policy presence is sustained, concerns for legitimacy will translate into acceptance of international transitional justice norms and institutions, as they will become an integral part of what domestic actors understand constitutes appropriate international behaviour. However, even though international actors may observe the successes of their justice interventions, international normative and institutional change will be only as deep as domestic elites judge is absolutely necessary to maintain international good standing. While transitional justice compliance here is deeper than in the case of coercion, it is still a long way from full adoption and internalisation.

Lastly, if a State adopts transitional justice to resolve political uncertainty through bureaucratic solutions, international norms and institutions will be accepted for a while or until the uncertainty is resolved. Transitional justice projects can then be used to settle domestic political disputes. Furthermore, if primary agents of change are international justice promoters, as soon as they leave the stage, lose their domestic political leverage, or move their attention elsewhere, we can expect politics to return to the way it was prior to the international policy intervention. In other words, transitional justice compliance in response to international bureaucratic pressures will be only as sustainable as the commitment of the international actors promoting it. For all these reasons, international transitional justice projects may get things done in the short term, but they may end up undermining the larger process of substantive acceptance of global justice norms and standards.

The policy implications of a domestic politics approach to transitional justice therefore serve as a cautionary tale for similar international interventions in domestic politics of target States. International pressure is a powerful tool for policy change, but it can produce the opposite effect from the one intended if it is not followed by a comprehensive package of broader social transformation and not mechanistic compliance that ends up being not much more than policy lip service. In the extreme cases, international pressure may collapse, making international actors appear fickle, not serious, and not dedicated to see a policy change go through. This international fatigue allows other target States in future policy interventions to try to 'wait it out', judging that international actors will get tired, distracted and will move on to a new project. In cases of difficult or recalcitrant States, this will make the process of adopting international human rights norms and standards that much more difficult to achieve.

Note

1 This section is adapted from Subotić, J. (2012) 'The Transformation of International Transitional Justice Advocacy', *International Journal of Transitional Justice*, 6: 106–25; reprinted with permission of Oxford University Press.

Bibliography

Abbott, K.W., Keohane, R.O., Moravcsik, A., Slaughter, A.-M. and Snidal, D. (2000) 'The Concept of Legalization', *International Organization*, 54: 401–19.

Acharya, A. (2004) 'How Ideas Spread: Whose Norms Matter? Norm Localization and Institutional Change in Asian Regionalism', *International Organization*, 58: 239–75.

——(2011) 'Norm Subsidiarity and Regional Orders: Sovereignty, Regionalism, and Rule-Making in the Third World', *International Studies Quarterly*, 55: 95–123.

Arthur, P. (2009) 'How "Transitions" Reshaped Human Rights: A Conceptual History of Transitional Justice', *Human Rights Quarterly*, 31 (2): 321–67.

Avant, D.D., Finnemore, M. and Sell, S.K. (2010) *Who Governs the Globe?*, Cambridge: Cambridge University Press.

Avdeyeva, O. (2007) 'When Do States Comply with International Treaties? Policies on Violence against Women in Post-Communist Countries', *International Studies Quarterly*, 51: 877–900.

Barnett, M.N. and Finnemore, M. (2004) *Rules for the World: International Organizations in Global Politics*, Ithaca, NY: Cornell University Press.

Bass, G.J. (2000) *Stay the Hand of Vengeance: The Politics of War Crimes Tribunals*, Princeton, NJ: Princeton University Press.

Boesenecker, A.P. and Vinjamuri, L. (2011) 'Lost in Translation? Civil Society, Faith-Based Organizations and the Negotiation of International Norms', *International Journal of Transitional Justice*, 5: 345–65.

——(forthcoming) 'Charting the Path of Justice in Peacebuilding', in Philpott, D. and Llewellyn, J. (eds) *Restorative Justice, Reconciliation and Peacebuilding*.

Cardenas, S. (2004) 'Norm Collision: Explaining the Effects of International Human Rights Pressure on State Behavior', *International Studies Review*, 6: 213–31.

Checkel, J. (2000) *Compliance and Conditionality*, Oslo: ARENA Centre for European Studies, University of Oslo.

DiMaggio, P. and Powell, W.W. (1983) 'The Iron Cage Revisited: Institutional Isomorphism and Collective Rationality in Organizational Fields', *American Sociological Review*, 48: 147–60.

Finnemore, M. (1993) 'International Organizations as Teachers of Norms', *International Organization*, 47: 565–97.

——(1996) *National Interests in International Society*, Ithaca, NY: Cornell University Press.

Fletcher, L.E., Weinstein, H.M. and Rowen, J. (2009) 'Context, Timing and the Dynamics of Transitional Justice: A Historical Perspective', *Human Rights Quarterly*, 31: 163–220.

Goodale, M. and Merry, S.E. (2007) *The Practice of Human Rights: Tracking Law between the Global and the Local*, Cambridge: Cambridge University Press.

Goodman, R. and Jinks, D. (2005) 'How to Influence States: Socialization and International Human Rights Law', *Duke Law Journal*, 54: 983–98.

Grodsky, B. (2009) 'International Prosecutions and Domestic Politics: The Use of Truth Commissions as Compromise Justice in Serbia and Croatia', *International Studies Review*, 11: 687–706.

Hafner-Burton, E. and Kiyoteru, T. (2005) 'Human Rights in a Globalizing World: The Paradox of Empty Promises', *American Journal of Sociology*, 110: 1373–411.

Hafner-Burton, E. and Tsutsui, K. (2007) 'Justice Lost! The Failure of International Human Rights Law To Matter Where Needed Most', *Journal of Peace Research*, 44: 407–25.

Hafner-Burton, E., Tsutsui, K. and Meyer, J.W. (2008) 'International Human Rights Law and the Politics of Legitimation: Repressive States and Human Rights Treaties', *International Sociology*, 23: 115–41.

Hathaway, O.A. (2002) 'Do Human Rights Treaties Make a Difference?', *Yale Law Journal*, 11: 1935–2042.

——(2007) 'Why Do Countries Commit to Human Rights Treaties?', *Journal of Conflict Resolution*, 51: 588–621.

Hawkins, D. (1997) 'Domestic Responses to International Pressure: Human Rights in Authoritarian Chile', *European Journal of International Relations*, 3: 403–34.

Hayner, P.B. (2001) *Unspeakable Truths: Confronting State Terror and Atrocity*, New York, NY: Routledge.

Keck, M.E. and Sikkink, K. (1998) *Activists beyond Borders: Advocacy Networks in International Politics*, Ithaca, NY: Cornell University Press.

Kelley, J. (2004) 'International Actors on the Domestic Scene: Membership Conditionality and Socialization by International Institutions', *International Organization*, 58: 425–57.

Lamont, C.K. (2009) *International Criminal Justice and the Politics of Compliance*, Burlington, VT: Ashgate Publishing.

——(2010) 'Defiance or Strategic Compliance? The Post-Tudjman Croatian Democratic Union and the International Criminal Tribunal for the former Yugoslavia', *Europe-Asia Studies*, 62: 1683–705.

Leebaw, B.A. (2011) *Judging State-Sponsored Violence, Imagining Political Change*, Cambridge: Cambridge University Press.

McEvoy, K. (2007) 'Beyond Legalism: Towards a Thicker Understanding of Transitional Justice', *Journal of Law and Society*, 34: 411–40.

March, J. and Olsen, J.P. (1989). *Rediscovering Institutions: The Organizational Basis of Politics*, New York, NY: Free Press.

Mattli, W. and Woods, N. (2009) *The Politics of Global Regulation*, Princeton, NJ: Princeton University Press.

Mendelson, S.E. and Glenn, J.K. (2002) *The Power and Limits of NGOs: A Critical Look at Building Democracy in Eastern Europe and Eurasia*, New York, NY: Columbia University Press.

Merry, S.E. (2006) *Human Rights and Gender Violence: Translating International Law into Local Justice*, Chicago, IL: University of Chicago Press.

Meyer, J.W., Boli, J., Thomas, G.M. and Ramirez, F.O. (1997) 'World Society and the Nation State', *American Journal of Sociology*, 103: 144–81.

Neumayer, E. (2005) 'Do International Human Rights Treaties Improve Respect for Human Rights?', *Journal of Conflict Resolution*, 49: 925–53.

Olsen, T.D., Payne, L.A. and Reiter, A.G. (2010) *Transitional Justice in Balance: Comparing Processes, Weighing Efficacy*, Washington, DC: United States Institute of Peace Press.

Peskin, V. (2008) *International Justice in Rwanda and the Balkans: Virtual Trials and the Struggle for State Cooperation*, Cambridge: Cambridge University Press.

Powell, W.W. and DiMaggio, P. (1991) *The New Institutionalism in Organizational Analysis*, Chicago, IL: University of Chicago Press.

Risse-Kappen, T., Ropp, S.C. and Sikkink, K. (1999) *The Power of Human Rights: International Norms and Domestic Change*, New York, NY: Cambridge University Press.

Roht-Arriaza, N. (2005) *The Pinochet Effect: Transnational Justice in the Age of Human Rights*, Philadelphia, PA: University of Pennsylvania Press.

——(2006) 'The New Landscape of Transitional Justice', in Roht-Arriaza, N. and Mariezcurrena, J. (eds) *Transitional Justice in the Twenty-First Century: Beyond Truth versus Justice*, Cambridge: Cambridge University Press.

Roht-Arriaza, N. and Mariezcurrena, J. (eds) (2006) *Transitional Justice in the Twenty-First Century: Beyond Truth versus Justice*, Cambridge: Cambridge University Press.

Ruggie, J.G. (1993) 'Multilateralism: The Anatomy of an Institution', in Ruggie, J.G. (ed.) *Multilateralism Matters: The History and Praxis of an Institutional Form*, New York, NY: Columbia University Press.

Schimmelfennig, F. (2008) 'EU Political Accession Conditionality after the 2004 Enlargement: Consistency and Effectiveness', *Journal of European Public Policy*, 15: 918–37.

Schimmelfennig, F. and Sedelmeier, U. (2004) 'Governance by Conditionality: EU Rule Transfer to the Candidate Countries of Central and Eastern Europe', *Journal of European Public Policy*, 11: 669–87.

——(2005) *The Europeanization of Central and Eastern Europe*, Ithaca, NY: Cornell University Press.

Schmitz, H.P. (2006) *Transnational Mobilization and Domestic Regime Change. Africa in Comparative Perspective*, New York, NY: Palgrave Macmillan.

Sieder, R. and Schjolden, L. (eds) (2005) *The Judicialization of Politics in Latin America*, New York, NY: Palgrave Macmillan.

Sikkink, K. (2011) *The Justice Cascade: How Human Rights Prosecutions are Changing World Politics*, New York, NY: W.W. Norton.

Simmons, B.A. (2009) *Mobilizing for Human Rights: International Law in Domestic Politics*, Cambridge: Cambridge University Press.

Subotić, J. (2009a) *Hijacked Justice: Dealing with the Past in the Balkans*, Ithaca, NY: Cornell University Press.

——(2009b) 'The Paradox of International Justice Compliance', *International Journal of Transitional Justice*, 3: 362–83.

——(2012) 'The Transformation of International Transitional Justice Advocacy', *International Journal of Transitional Justice*, 6: 106–25.

Teitel, R.G. (2003) 'Transitional Justice Genealogy', *Harvard Human Rights Journal*, 16: 69–94.

Thoms, O.N.T., Ron, J. and Paris, R. (2010) 'State-Level Effects of Transitional Justice: What Do We Know?', *International Journal of Transitional Justice*, 4: 329–54.

Vachudova, M.A. (2005) *Europe undivided: Democracy, Leverage, and Integration after Communism*, Oxford: Oxford University Press.

——(2009) 'Democratization in Post-Communist Europe: Illiberal Regimes and the Leverage of the European Union', in Bunce, V., McFaul, M. and Stoner-Weiss, K. (eds) *Democracy and Authoritarianism in the Post-Communist World*, Cambridge: Cambridge University Press.

Chapter 7

Narrative truths

On the construction of the past in truth commissions

Susanne Buckley-Zistel

Truth is a central component of the concept of transitional justice. Truth provides the basis for judgments in court. Truth helps to establish a historical record of human rights abuses during violent conflicts or repressive regimes. It plays a key role in the acknowledgment of victims' suffering. Truth may serve as a foundation for future coexistence. But what is truth and how does it emerge?

To contemplate the notion of truth is by no means a new endeavour but has been subject to philosophical reflections since their beginnings. For my discussion of the notion of truth in transitional justice in this chapter, I draw on contemporary approaches as central to post-positivist epistemologies. With the aid of narrative and discourse theory, I examine how the process of truth-finding informs what kind of truth is revealed, how it is situated into prevailing discourses and – in the process – how it shapes social relations.[1] My specific focus is on truth commissions as institutions aiming at uncovering the truth about massive human rights abuses during violent conflict or repression. I argue that the processes and structures of revealing the truth in the context of these institutions informs and regulates people's interpretation of the past, as mirrored in the stories, or narratives, on which they draw to recount past experiences. Regarding truth, the focus of my chapter is thus not on factual or forensic truth but its social construction through testimonies and witness accounts.

Events belong to the past, narratives about them to the present. This is, of course, highly relevant for transitional justice which is concerned with dealing with this very past. Since the past can never be (re)visited, but only grasped from today, it is important to look at the construction of knowledge – or truth – about this past, as it is central to a narrative approach. This starts from the premise that people use narratives as a strategy to endow events and experiences in their lives – such as human rights violations – with meaning in order to come to terms with them. Exploring narratives therefore asks what is distinctive about a particular narrative, why it is narrated in this way and not another, and how it helps people to make sense of their worlds. Since narratives can only be understood in the context of the prevailing social and political structures in which they are embedded, this is then reflected back onto the question of how narratives produce and reproduce collective social identities.

By now, there is a rather large body of literature discussing the notion of truth in truth commissions.[2] The purpose of this chapter is thus not simply to make a point regarding the ambiguity of truth that emerges in the process, but to introduce narrative theory as a methodology to assess how this production takes place. In order to do so, I begin with the discussion of the notion of narratives and their relevance for analysing the construction of truth. This is followed by an exploration of truth commissions. The main part of the chapter then illustrates the argument by drawing on various empirical studies on truth commissions, divided in sections on institutional embedding, on the one hand, and socio-political, on the other. Importantly, such a division can only be artificial – albeit useful for heuristic purposes – since all these processes are intrinsically intertwined.

Narratives

Many efforts to deal with the past of violent conflicts or repression take place in forums of communication such as truth commissions, courts of law, memorial sites or museums where people come together to exchange views of the past or where objects act as mediums of communication with the onlookers (see also Buckley-Zistel 2013). As a conceptual framework for analysing the interpretation of past crimes and atrocities in the context of one of these forums, truth commissions, this chapter makes use of narrative theory. Narrative theory helps to examine the reproduction of an event – here, past violent crimes – in spoken, written or visual form so that it is not simply confined to the study of literature where it originated but serves as a social science methodology to assess making sense of experiences more broadly.

Why is this relevant for analysing the construction of truth in truth commissions? In her much cited article linking narrative theory with social research, Margaret Somers argues that:

> an energetic engagement with this new ontological narrativity provides an opportunity to infuse the study of identity formation with a relational and historical approach that avoids categorical rigidities by emphasizing the embeddedness of identity in overlapping networks of relations that shift over time and space.
>
> (Somers 1994: 607)

While the analysis of identity formation is a relevant matter in and of itself, it gains particular pertinence in divided societies emerging from a violent past, and particularly in transitional justice processes. The dislocation experienced as a result of violence and repression frequently prompts concerns regarding alternative futures (Norval 1999: 500) and the formation of less rigidly divided group identities in order to prevent a return to violence. This requires some form of social change. In many cases, hence, exerting influence on a collective (national) identity is a stated objective of transitional justice, via strategies such as reconciliation, nation-building, and the like, in particular in commissions which seek to marry truth with reconciliation. Studying the formation of (new, collective) identities in a historical and relational manner – as central to a narrative approach – is thus crucial.

A narrative approach starts from the assumption that the world is not presented to us in the form of 'well-made stories, with central subjects, proper beginnings, middles and ends, and a coherence that permits us to see "the end" in every beginning' (White 1987: 24). Rather, only our desire for coherence, integrity and closure structures events into meaningful actions. This is achieved through 'a clear sequential order that connects events in a meaningful way for a definite audience' (Hinchman and Hinchman 1997: xx). According to Somers, four closely related dimensions are crucial to this process: *relationality of parts, causal emplotment, selective appropriation*, and *temporality, sequence, and place* (Somers 1994: 616). To take each aspect in turn, *relationality of parts* suggests that a single event does not in itself contain meaning but that it only becomes intelligible when considered in relation to other events. This is closely connected to *causal emplotment*, which implies that we do not simply place events in relation to others on the basis of similarities or chronology, but that we order them in a structure that seems meaningful. *Causal emplotment* thus refers to the 'author's storification', that is the transformation of a set of historical events into a structured sequence with a beginning, middle and end (White 1980: 13). Plots can therefore be considered as the logic or syntax of a narrative (Somers 1994: 617). The story is endowed with meaning, often on a continuum of positive or negative morale. Importantly, it is never fixed in time but constantly open to flux through being told and re-told. Moreover, a plot cannot simply take any shape or form but is conditioned by the present spacio-temporal discourse, such as, in the context of a truth commission, efforts to deal with aftermath of violence and repression. This is significant for the aspect of *selective appropriation* indicating that we choose what we consider to be relevant to our story and what can be excluded, providing it with a particular theme. As expressed by Hayden White, 'every narrative, however seemingly "full", is constructed on the basis of a set of events which might have been included but were left out' (White 1980: 14). And, lastly, *temporality, sequence* and *place* makes reference to how events as elements are related to each other within the particular narrative.

This has significant implications for uncovering truth in truth commissions. Based on the above, the sense or meaning of an event – such as the abuse of human rights – cannot simply be unveiled (in a truth commission) but must be created anew by use of a narrative. For White, it follows that '[t]he production of meaning ... can be regarded as a performance, because any given set of real events can be emplotted in a number of ways' (White 1987: 44). There is no simple truth to be uncovered, but truth is the outcome of this process of narration. The truth about a violent past is constructed by the narratives uttered in a truth commission.

This, of course, does not suggest that anything goes, that lies can be told and that narratives are divested from personal biographies and experiences, but rather that there is a:

> dialectic relationship between experience and narrative, between the narrating self and the narrated self. As humans, we draw on our experience to shape narratives about our lives, but equally, our identity and character are shaped by our narratives. People emerge from and as the products of their stories about themselves as much as their stories emerge from their lives.
>
> (Antze and Lambek 1996: vxiii)

Thus, on the one hand, biographical experiences form the tale being told while, on the other hand, these tales form the identity of the narrator.

The strength of a narrative approach, as expressed by Somers, is moreover that it embeds stories historically and relationally in the context in which they emerge, suggesting that it is only within this spacio-temporal framework – discourses – that they can be understood and interpreted. For '[t]he "narrative" dimension of identity there and elsewhere   presumes that action can only be intelligible if we recognise the various ontological and public narratives in which actors are emplotted' (Somers 1994: 625). Thus, how a narrative is told, what is included in the process of selecting and organising events, providing them with meaning, is profoundly affected by the prevailing discursive environment in which the narration takes place. Of particular relevance for the analysis of the present chapter are the institutional framings of truth commissions as well as, on the macro level, the social, political and cultural conditions of the society that emerges from violence more generally. This resonates in the words of Alain Feldman who argues:

> The production of biographical narrative, life history, oral history, and testimony in the aftermath of ethnocidal, genocidal, colonial, and postcolonial violence occurs within specific structural conditions, cognitive constraints, and institutional norms. ... [B]iography emerges as a narrative media within state structures, and within the cultural requirement for jural and political subjects. Historical inquiry must attend to the

conditions under which such narratives arise – the political agency that such narrations refract, replicate, and authorize – and yet also account for the wide-ranging circuits that filter and consume the biographical artefact.

(Feldman 2004: 163)

This leads us to Michel Foucault's argument that the truth about the past and the way in which it is told is determined by 'regimes of truth', which establish what is true or false, who counts as a valid narrator and who does not (and therefore remains silent), and how this affects a process of transition. Regimes of truth, in Foucault's words, correspond to:

> types of disclosure which it [the society] accepts and makes function as true; mechanisms and incidences which enable one to make true and false statements; the techniques and procedures accorded value in the acquisition of truth; the status of those who are charged with saying what counts as true.

(Foucault 1980: 131)

They, therefore, determine how the violent past is uncovered and interpreted, who counts as victim and who as perpetrator, which crimes are named as such, and which patterns of interpretation provide the foundation for the analysis of the violent crimes and the vision of a peaceful future. Which regimes of truth dominate is ultimately a question of power that determines the hegemonic distribution of a particular discourse. Consequently, an analysis of narratives about the past after violent conflict or repression requires an analysis of the political, social and cultural structures into which transitional justice institutions are embedded, and which define the prevailing meta-narrative.

From the above follows that the analysis of statements, such as in truth-seeking processes, always requires an empirical analysis (Somers 1994: 630), i.e. that it is paramount not to assume or take for granted the meaning of individual or collective narratives but to enquire into their mode of construction and production. For '[t]he extent and nature of any given repertoire of narratives available for appropriation is always historically and culturally specific; the particular plots that give meanings to those narratives cannot be determined in advance' (Somers 1994: 630). The objective of the next section is to illustrate this in the context of truth commissions. In doing so, I draw on recent studies that have emerged in the field of transitional justice. Since my references to empirical case studies is limited to available literature many of the arguments focus on the South African TRC (1995–2002), being the best-researched commission thus far. Nevertheless, I contend that this has a much wider applicability.

Truth commissions

As mentioned by way of introduction, truth is a central concern of transitional justice. After human rights abuses, in the words of the think-tank International Center for Transitional Justice, truth-seeking is a basic right:

> Societies and individuals are entitled to know the truth about mass human rights violations in the wake of armed conflict or repression. All cultures recognize the importance of proper mourning to achieve personal and communal healing. International law clearly recognizes the right of victims and survivors to know about the circumstances of serious violations of their human rights and about who was responsible. International law continues to develop in this area and on the concept of a society's right to the truth.
>
> (International Center for Transitional Justice 2012)

Similarly, for the human rights organisation Amnesty International, truth-seeking is an imperative response to crimes such as genocide, crimes against humanity, war crimes, torture, extrajudicial executions and enforced disappearances, rendering it essential for various groups:

> For the direct victims to know the whole truth about the crimes they suffered and the reasons behind it, as well as have their suffering publicly acknowledged. Moreover, truth is necessary to correct any false accusations made against them in the course of the crime.
>
> For family members, particularly of those killed or disappeared, to find out what happened to their loved-one and to establish their whereabouts.
>
> For the affected society to know the circumstances surrounding and reasons that led to violations being committed to ensure that they will not be committed again, and to have their shared experiences acknowledged and preserved.
>
> (Amnesty International 2013)

Both quotations strongly suggest that there is a truth out there that can be uncovered and presented. Consequently, in their advocacy work, the institutions campaign for the establishment of truth commissions in order to fulfil the task.

As an alternative, non-judicial measure of dealing with massive human rights abuses, truth commission have been enjoying much popularity. Depending on source and database, such commissions have been established in 30–40 countries following violent conflicts or repression, at first primarily in Latin America, but increasingly in Asia, Africa and the Arab world.[3] Initially conceived as alternatives to state-centred legal proceedings they have, meanwhile, taken on a complementary role. They can be understood as temporary establishments which, through a multitude of individual testimonies, uncover the crimes of violent regimes or conflicts and expose patterns of repression and discrimination such as persecution of politically, ethnically or racially marginalised groups. Their records seek to impede human rights violations and crimes against humanity by renouncing revisionism, and to establish acceptance of the fact that breaches of the law have taken place even if the origins and causes remain contentious. Truth commissions hence become particularly relevant if the truth – in terms of knowledge and violence – about crimes is unclear or has been suppressed by an earlier regime. Individual witness testimonies become the basis of memory for events that have been struck from the official memory (Humphrey 2000: 8).

While some truth commissions are solely concerned with uncovering human rights abuses, others foster the ambition of contributing to national reconciliation as well, often expressed by the addition of the word reconciliation in their title. For the French philosopher, Jacques Derrida, this becomes a possibility since truth commissions are simultaneously an instrument of remembering and forgetting. Once the truth has been uncovered by a commission, and is archived, it can temporarily be forgotten, for even though it has been safely stored away it remains accessible (Derrida 2001). Thus, a post-violence society does not constantly need to deal with its disturbing past; it can implicitly lay it to rest, draw a line beneath the ugly chapter and look forward to a (common) future.

If one follows Michael Humphrey, truth commissions are composed of two distinct elements: the process and the product (Humphrey 2003: 176). Whiles the process of truth-searching is legitimised by the wide-scale involvement of all parties concerned, often through public staging, the product in form of a final report (including, at times, the promise of reparations) resembles an attempt at shutting down all interpretation of the past. In this sense, the process of speaking the truth serves a performative function, whilst the final report is meant to facilitate closure. This runs counter to the widespread assumption, as implicit in the quotations about the right to truth above, that there is such a thing as 'the truth' that can be revealed through testimonies of witnesses, but instead draws attention to the fact that truth is constructed in the process of social interaction.

Institutional embedding and emplotment

So how is the truth constructed in truth commissions and how does this affect their product, i.e. their outcome? The purpose of this section is to provide some anecdotal and unavoidably sketchy substantiation regarding the narrative construction of truth, drawing on studies on the South African

TRC as well as other commissions. It seeks to link the institutional embedding of narratives to their causal emplotment.

Process

To repeat, in truth commissions, individuals who were victims or witnesses – or, more rarely, perpetrators – of human rights abuses and atrocities testify in front of an officially selected commission. The way a commission approaches the past always already entails certain perceptions and images, informing its leading questions and presuppositions, determining its bias and characterising the nature of the constructed truth (O'Neill 2005: 345). In other words, their accounts of past crimes are embedded into an institutional framework which defines the causal emplotment, selective appropriation and sequencing of their story; it determines the structure which forms thinking and enunciation.

This can be illustrated by the South African TRC where perceptions and images about the past circled *inter alia* around the destruction of a previously harmonious nation (Moon 2004) and the notion of a just war against Apartheid (Bozzoli 1998). Regarding the former, in the discourse of the TRC, victims and perpetrators were presented as if they were violently torn from an originally harmonic relationship, which had to be reconstituted (Moon 2004: 188). The lost harmony – the 'paradise lost' – between white and black South Africans was to be reinstated and mirrored countrywide by national unity. According to a Christian view, as adhered to by the commission, reconciliation emerges when, after a wrongful act, an originally good relationship is restored by the genuine admission of guilt, a show of repentance and a change in the inner attitude (Moon 2004: 188). The notion of reconciliation was thus employed to provide the narratives with meaning, aiming in one particular direction, and to situate the emerging stories on a continuum of a positive or negative morale. By using this moral connotation, the notion served a profoundly political purpose in a country deeply divided as a result of the experiences of Apartheid, as further explored below. Richard Wilson thus argues that:

> [r]econciliation was the Trojan horse used to smuggle an unpleasant aspect of the past (that is, impunity) into the present political order, to transform political compromise into transcendental political principles. Reconciliation structures a field of discourse in order to render commonsensical and acceptable the abjuring of legal retribution against past offenders.
>
> (Wilson 2001: 97)

As a consequence, in South Africa reconciliation became the term that endowed narratives with meaning in order to foster nation-building in the deeply divided society.

How this hegemonic discourse of reconciliation and nation-building affected the emplotment of testimonies and witness accounts – i.e. narratives – is illustrated by the work of Annelies Verdoolaege who shows how the TRC's implicit (and explicit) reconciliation discourse led to the unfailing orientation of narratives about the past toward this superior goal (Verdoolaege 2009: 302), i.e. the authors' storyfication, to return to White's term, transformed the set of historical events into a particular structural sequence. This was achieved by members of the committee placing special emphasis on the word reconciliation in their questions and statements as well as by specifically questioning the victims on aspects of, and their willingness for, reconciliation. For example, it would be elicited whether victims were prepared to meet with the perpetrators, whether they would speak with them or even more directly, whether they were willing to be reconciled (Verdoolaege 2009: 302). According to Verdoolaege, in this way a consciously reconciliation-oriented atmosphere was created in order to convince those testifying that peaceful coexistence in South Africa was a necessity to which they could personally contribute with their actions and testimonies. This led to the majority of the participants in the TRC – whether they were victims, perpetrators, commission members, politicians, scientists or artists – having the sense that they had contributed to the new South Africa (Verdoolaege 2009: 302) and actively helped shaping the new nation. As stated by a former commissioner, the major achievement of the TRC was to put reconciliation into the minds of South Africans.[4]

The overall objective of the commission to contribute to nation-building, the second image referred to above, is well illustrated by Belinda Bozzoli's study of TRC hearings in Alexandra township (Bozzoli 1998: 192–93). She indentifies two narratives that emerged in the course of the hearing: first, the public narratives' causal emplotment situated the anti-Apartheid African National Congress firmly into the context of a just war by naming heroes and martyrs, while fostering a sense of closure since peace and liberation had been attained. As a consequence, reconciliation and forgiveness needed to be granted through the workings of the TRC. In contrast, the private narratives emerging out of individual testimonies were less seamless, with the experiences of the individual witnesses being not so much about participating in a just war but more about suffering from loss, abuse and social repression. Despite the fact that two narratives emerged in Alexandra township, the public narrative assumed hegemony since its coherence, formalised sanctioning and public ownership – i.e. its strength by virtue of institutional embedding – rendered it more powerful. This, Bozzoli concludes, reveals a paradox in the work of the TRC:

> In the very act of defining a public realm, and thus opening up the possibility for the ending of the seclusion of the poor, the hearing oversaw a complex process whereby a *new* silencing and seclusion began to

emerge, through the silences of the hearing and the partial appropriation of what *was* said by a nationalist discourse. Because of this, the commission's newly created public realm could not quite bring to the fore the secluded and excluded 'private' realm of Alexandra township. Instead, a new form of sequestration of the experiences of ordinary Alexandrans was an unexpected result.

(Bozzoli 1998: 193)

Hence, Bozzoli's analysis provides a good example for illustrating how due to an established truth regime and thus power, in the words of Foucault, delineates what can be said and how, what counts as relevant and what as inferior.

A further example of (attempted) causal emplotment on behalf of the TRC as an institution is evident in the observations by Christopher Colvin who analysed its hearings from the perspective of trauma, arguing that its discourse produced particular trauma narratives (Colvin 2003: 155). The way victims were questioned about painful Apartheid experiences, i.e. the manner in which these questions were framed, suggested that their trauma was a thing of the past, and not the present. In doing so, the TRC permanently imposed on victims' narratives that pain and suffering had ended, introducing a sense of closure. This, however, was in conflict with the victims' personal experiences and emotions of pain still lingering and the way it affected their daily lives.

An interesting observation in this context is also the causal emplotment by female witnesses before the TRC. Generally, it has been observed that women mainly testified in their role as wives and mothers and therefore mostly about the crimes committed against their husbands and sons in public (Nesiah 2006: 30). Their own suffering in private, the daily degradation through Apartheid, the structural violence and discrimination from which they suffered, but also the direct attacks in form of sexual or sexualised violence were mostly kept quiet since they did not fit the story line that was expected from them. Not only does this show an androcentric usage of guilt and repentance within the narrative framework of the TRC and a hardly sustainable dichotomy between violence in the public and the private sphere, it also puts into perspective the meaning of the spoken word in itself. Thus, it can be argued that not only speaking out but also keeping quiet became a 'language of pain and grief' (Motsemme 2004: 910), contributing to the narration and thus construction of truth by the TRC.

These insights into the affect of the institutional embedding of the South African TRC on the emplotment of narratives in form of testimonies before the commission resonates in the analysis of truth commissions elsewhere. For instance, Kevin O'Neill's research on truth commissions in Guatemala shows how the official search for truth was formed and structured by Christian images. In the first report about human rights violations, which emanated from the Recovery of the Historic Memory Project of the Catholic Church and was published in 1998, these crimes are presented as an analogy between Guatemala's communal body and the body of the suffering Jesus Christ. The following report of the truth commissions instated by the United Nations (1997–99) reveals different Christian patterns of interpretation based on a Protestant notion according to which the perpetrator, in the sense of reconciliation, lays down a full confession. However, while the Catholic Church was aware of the strong Christian orientation of its work, and acknowledged this in the final report, the report of the official UN commission presented its approach as if it was objective and in the service of the punishment of crimes against human rights (Motsemme 2004: 346).

In addition to the effect of the moral framing of narratives due to the embeddedness in a commission, the content of the revealed truth depends on the mandate of the commission which delineates what can be said, who is entitled to speak, and how the process is to evolve. More practically, it 'can define a commission's investigatory powers, limit or strengthen its investigative reach, define the exact abuses and the perpetrators of abuses that a commission is allowed to investigate, and set the timeline and geographic scope of the commission's investigation' (Hayner 1994: 636). Thus, mandates identify who counts as victim and who as perpetrator, even if this demarcation is empirically hard to sustain, especially in the context of civil wars where both sides were involved in violent activities (see also Moon 2006: 261). This is apparent in a study on the Peruvian Truth and Reconciliation Commission (PTRC), which established a (contested) version of guilt and responsibility regarding crimes committed during the political violence of the 1980s and 1990s. The rural self-defence committees, organised by farmers, played an ambivalent role in the local civil war: on one hand, they were victimised by the guerrilla group *Shining Path*, while, on the other, they joined forces against the guerrilla with the military since the 1990s, thereby contributing to the victory (Garcia-Godos 2008: 82). Thus they were victims as well as perpetrators of crimes. In the reparation programme of the PTRC, however, they were defined exclusively as the victims of crimes committed by the *guerilleros*. In doing so, the commission constructed a particular narrative about the civil war and apported guilt and responsibility, triggering harsh criticism in parts of the population during the course of the truth finding process as well as after the publishing of the final report (Garcia-Godos 2008: 72), and consequently undermined the legitimacy of the constructed truth.

Product

Let us finish this section with some reflections on truth as the product of truth commissions. As argued by way of introduction, truth commissions can be understood as forums of communication. Communication – such as between witnesses and commissioners – never happens in isolation but always involves an audience as well. It has a tripartite structure (Humphrey 2003: 174) including spectators or listeners as recipients. In some cases of truth commissions with public hearings, such as in South Africa, the audience did not just consist of those present in the room but also of viewers and listeners on television and radio sets, receiving much attention. This can also be reported from cases without public hearings such as in Argentina, where the final report of the truth commissions (1983–84) *Nunca Más* turned into a best-seller (Humphrey 2003: 178). With the aid of these public and publicised witness testimonials, truth commissions attempt to objectify and institutionalise truth claims (Humphrey 2003: 176). As many truth commissions attempt to (re)integrate discriminated parts of the population into society by uncovering of the injustices they were subject to, a wide audience is necessary: the narration of the truth does not take place for its own sake but in order to form sustainable structures which are to take a preventive function against future human rights abuses. Social change and nation-building is therefore a purported goal of many truth commissions (and other transitional justice mechanisms), and this requires the presence and inclusion of the population. Nevertheless, speaking truth to and of power remains a challenge in the highly politicised context of a society under transition (Gready 2009a: 175), as discussed in the following section.

That truth is a highly contested concept has not escaped the authors of various truth commission reports. For instance, the first volume of the South African TRC differentiates four different notions of truth: factual or forensic truth; personal or narrative truth; social or dialogue truth and healing and restorative truth (Truth and Reconciliation Commission n.d.). First, factual or forensic truth refers to a legal and positivist notion of presenting evidence gathered by impartial and objective procedures; personal or narrative truth, second, stands for the culmination of individuals stories that provide a multilayered set of experiences; social or dialogue truth, third, is the result of debates and discussions about facts on a collective level, while healing and restorative truth, lastly, derives from giving facts in a particular context in an effort to acknowledge the experiences of individuals. Despite this multifaceted approach, according to Wilson, the account of the truth reflected it the TRC report was rather one sided, focusing mainly on factual and forensic truth to the exclusion of other accounts and the legalist and realist language served to depoliticise and decontextualise events (Wilson 2001: 218). Moreover, the TRC's deliberately strong focus on individual guilt to the exclusion of structural conditions led to some few – the 'rotten apples' – being held responsible for violations of human rights, while the institutionalisation of Apartheid violence in the societal system remained unchallenged (Feldman 2003: 239; Gready 2009a: 178) as it failed to articulate as part of its truth the more encompassing context of violent actions.

Moreover, in the media coverage of the hearings and the TRC's final report, the narratives experienced yet another moment of reduction for their complexity was homogenised into stories of suffering only. According to Fiona Ross:

> [s]uch crystallized forms quickly became formulaic, losing the capacity to hold the attention and restricting the range of expressions through which to give voice to experience. From each testimony, the Commission sought to isolate a coherent chronology, a clear relation between component parts, a climax phrased in terms of the experience of a 'gross violation of human rights'.
>
> (Ross 2003: 329)

This impact of the commission on how the truth was narrated, and the narratives emplotted, was also apparent outside the direct remit of the TRC. In the early days of its hearings, Ross encountered South Africans who felt that the public testimonies on television were undignified since they did not adhere to culturally established norms of shame and blame (Ross 2003: 329). However, after a short period this criticism ebbed and an increasing amount of people looked for opportunities to tell their stories as well, implicitly accepting the TRC's way of eliciting and presenting testimonies. Moreover, and strikingly, she noticed an increasingly strong resemblance in the emplotment of narratives by other interviewees about their past in ways 'that were presented chronologically, structuring narratives temporally and orienting life stories toward events of graphic violence', thus mirroring the narrative structuring of the TRC (Ross 2003: 330).

As this discussion reveals, analysing truth commissions requires paying special attention to the institutional embeddedness for, as the work of Michel Foucault has shown, institutionalised discourses consist of 'grids of specification' (Foucault 1972: 42) that classify and regulate people who operate in them. People internalise actions and practises and adjust their utterances and themes to what is expected from them. They frame what can be said and what has to stay silenced, and who is entitled to speak and who is excluded. Unsurprisingly, this also has implications for the stories people tell with reference to the violent past they experienced – that is the truth that emerges through process and product.

Social and political embedding and emplotment

Truth commissions never exist in isolation but are always embedded in social and political structures that determine their mandate, outreach, set-up, impact (and even their very existence) and that thus have a critical influence on the way the institutional embedding is shaped. They serve a particular function in the society, and respond to certain interests (see Subotić, Chapter 6 in this volume). The objective of this section is thus to sketch how the external social and political contexts in which a commission is embedded shapes its internal, institutional embeddedness and the ensuing emplotment of narratives about the past.

To illustrate this point it is instructive to compare truth-seeking in South Africa and the former East Germany, two vastly different countries regarding their pasts (i.e. the scale, rationale and form of human rights violations) as well as their presence (i.e. their political, economic and social contexts). In contrast to the TRC, as well as other commissions, the objective of the German *Enquete-Kommission*[5] that enquired into State repression was less on individual or collective reconciliation, but on historical correction (Andrews 2003: 51). The public was mostly excluded from the truth-searching process, and the inhabitants of former East Germany – i.e. people affected and/or surrounded by State violence and repression[6] – were not incorporated in the process as a collective. Rather, the approach of the commission resembled much more a scientific investigation into the East German past, mainly based on statements and opinions of specialists. Over the period of two years, the past was analysed by a commission of 16 parliamentarians and 11 external experts, with ten of the 16 parliamentarians being from the former East and the rest, as well as the experts, coming from West Germany. It was therefore critically noted that the newly constructed truth about the East German past was founded on West German interpretations. Due to the composition of the *Enquete-Kommission* and the relatively small number of witnesses who testified (327 witnesses, mainly recruited from a particular part of the population, the victims of the former regime) a narrative of the past was being constructed which had as a goal less national reconciliation – to make the comparison with South Africa – but more to establish a notion of democracy in the way it prevailed in West Germany, and in the then reunified Germany (Andrews 2003: 51).

In order to understand this better it is insightful to compare the social and political embedding of the South African TRC with the *Enquete-Kommission* of the (re-)united Germany (Andrews 2003: 52–53). Even though in both cases the transition from dictatorship to democracy took place peacefully, the security situation of South Africa was highly precarious and the society – due to long-term rigidly determined race affiliation – much deeper divided than East Germany's. Consequently, for the South African TRC, national reconciliation was the highest priority because it was seen as a necessity for the transformation process, making it obligatory to include all parts of the population as witnesses of Apartheid violence by broadcasting the hearings and disseminating the report widely. In contrast, the truth commission for East German State crimes was not concerned with constructing a reconciled, national identity, as the country was joined with West Germany and an internal process of social and political transformation was not regarded to be necessary. Rather, the aim of the commission was to create a democratic consciousness and promote a common political culture (Andrews 2003: 53). As a result, the narratives about (anti-democratic) State crimes constructed in this process turned out to be accusatory and not reconciliatory, and they have not been disseminated widely in the society.

One aspect South Africa and Germany have in common, though, is that most sections of the respective populations were largely in agreement that they wanted to live together peacefully. This is in contrast to political contexts which lack agreement about the future of the country, for instance after violent conflicts from which neither party emerged as a victor. Here, many aspects about future coexistence remain contentious and, instead of contributing to their solution, truth commissions threaten to become the new battleground on which these struggles are fought. In the case of the Guatemalan truth commissions, for example, it was a challenge to find a shared narrative, leaving unresolved who was responsible for the violence, who caused the conflict and who was subjected to it (Ross 2006: 73). This can lead to parts of the population attempting to make their influence on the version of the truth felt rather strongly and to control the selection of the included narrations about atrocities. Here, then, conflict moves from the battleground to the truth commission.

To sum up, the institutional embedding of truth commissions is highly dependent on its surroundings, i.e. the social and political structures that prevail in a society under transition. It is the combination of external and internal forces that shape how narratives are being emplotted, as well as what meaning is created and how. In combination with the internal workings of commissions, this means that the truth established in this process is highly ambivalent.

Conclusions

The objective of this chapter was to explore the production of truth in truth commissions. Drawing on narrative theory it was illustrated how, in truth commissions, narratives are embedded in institutions as well as in the social and political structural proclivities of the respective post-conflict societies, defining the truth. Based on anecdotal insights into the South African TRC, as well as other commissions, it showed the workings of the commissions, how they inform causal emplotment and how they (attempt) to influence the meaning given to events by witnesses in their narratives about the past. More concretely, it showed how the narration of the violent past is conditioned on the dominating institutional embedding in the framework of the truth commissions, as well as (and closely related) how the discourses in the commissions are formed by the social and political contexts into which they are embedded. These 'regimes of truth' (Foucault) determine what may be said where and how, and are therefore fundamentally political. Where the dominant discourse in the public sphere has not yet been consolidated – as can be seen in the example of Guatemala – there is a risk that the battleground of the conflict is transferred into the forum of the truth commission.

Yet, the constructed truth is by no means hermetically sealed and eternal for there are always counter-discourses, dissenting narratives, contingency and flux. Regarding the production of truth in truth commissions Cole observes that:

> [s]ometimes the most potent moments of truth occurred when the commission failed to follow its own protocols and mandates, when the densely congealed layers of truths and untruths became unglued. The dramatic, unruly, ephemeral, and performed aspects of live hearings strongly expressed both the power of the TRC and its limits for truly grappling with the magnitude of the violations of human rights in South Africa's past.
> (Cole 2010: 17–18)

Then, why do we need a methodology to assess the construction of truth in truth commissions? Elsewhere, it has been suggested that truth commissions should be assessed on the basis of what they set out to do, for instance, whether they follow truth as justice, truth as acknowledgment, truth as apology, etc. (Gready 2009b). And yet, this would limit the analysis to the internal – and intentional – logic of a commission obstructing from the view all that is excluded by the institutional embedding of the truth searching process, as well as the social and political embeddedness of the commission itself. It would thus veil the workings of truth regimes and power that include and exclude what can be said and what truth may prevail. This challenges Stanley Cohen's observation that 'as a citizen of South Africa, Ethiopia, Cambodia or Zaire, I would prefer not to have a deconstructivist to be the chairperson of the Truth and Justice Commission. The resulting text would be interesting, but not in my interest' (quoted in Gready 2009b: 161). Surely, it would not be in all people's interest, yet it would open up the space for debate and engagement for those still marginalised by the prevailing social and political structures. It is thus a political project to deconstruct the truth of truth commissions.

There is, however, also a wider insight as a result of this kind of analysis, as relevant for understanding the workings of other transitional justice mechanisms as well. For opening up the black box of transitional justice reveals the ambiguity of their work, it shows how the justice, transition, truth, reconciliation, restoration, reparation and so on are not in and of themselves neutral and unbiased, but the result of the complex context of spacio-temporal agencies and structures both inside and outside the institutions. To return to Feldman, they mirror 'the conditions under which such narratives arise – the political agency that such narrations refract, replicate, and authorize' (Feldman 2004: 163). This is particularly important in societies divided by the experience of violence which endeavour to establish some common traits, or some element of social change to prevent the reoccurrence of violence in the future. Academic analysis thus needs to consider the study of newly forged identities – by the aid of transitional justice mechanisms – with an analysis of their internal, institutional embedding as well as their external, socio-political context.

Notes

1 For other publications using a similar approach, see for instance Andrews 2003; Buckley-Zistel 2009; Gready 2009a, 2009b; Moon 2009 and Wilson 2011.
2 For an overview, see Gready 2009a, 2009b.
3 See for instance Truth Commission 2012; United States Institute of Peace 2012.
4 Remark by Pumla Gobodo-Madikizela at the conference 'Dealing with the Past, Reaching the Future', *Haus der Kulturen der Welt*, Berlin, 29–31 October 2009. I am grateful to Teresa Koloma Beck for this comment.
5 *Enquete-Kommission zur Aufarbeitung von Geschichte und Folgen der SED-Diktatur in Deutschland* (Enquete-Commission for the Reappraisal of the History and Consequences of the SED-Dictatorship in Germany, 1992–94).
6 It is important to note that the experience of living in East Germany was highly diverse and not everybody was subjected to State repression. For a discussion of the multiple forms of remembrance, see Buckley-Zistel 2013.

Bibliography

Amnesty International (2013) *Truth Commissions*. Available at: <http://www.amnesty.org/en/international-justice/issues/truth-commissions> (accessed 9 February 2013).

Andrews, M. (2003) 'Grand National Narratives and the Project of Truth Commissions: A Comparative Analysis', *Media, Culture and Society*, 25: 45–65.

Antze, P. and Lambek, M. (1996) 'Introduction. Forecasting Memory', in Antze, P. and Lambek, M. (eds) *Tense Past. Cultural Essays in Trauma and Memory*, New York, NY, and London: Routledge.

Bozzoli, B. (1998) 'Public Ritual and Private Transition: the Truth Commission in Alexandra Township, South Africa 1996', *African Studies*, 57 (2): 167–95.

Buckley-Zistel, S. (2009) 'Nation, Narration, Unification. The Politics of History Teaching After the Rwandan Genocide', *International Journal of Genocide Research*, 11 (7): 31–53.

——(2013) 'Detained in Hohenschönhausen. Heterotopia, Narratives and Transitions from the Stasi Past in Germany', in Buckley-Zistel, S. and Schäfer, S. (eds) *Memorials of Violence in Times of Transition*, Antwerp: Intersentia (forthcoming).

Cole, C.M. (2010) *Performing South Africa's Truth Commission: Stages of Transition*, Bloomington and Indianapolis, IN: Indiana University Press.

Colvin, C. (2003) 'Brothers and Sisters, Do Not Be Afraid of Me: Trauma, History and the Therapeutic Imagination in the New South Africa', in Hodgkin, K. and Radstone, S. (eds) *Contested pasts: The politics of memory*, London and New York, NY: Routledge.

Derrida, J. (2001) *On Cosmopolitism and Forgiveness*, New York, NY, and London: Routledge.

Feldman, A. (2003) 'Political Terror and the Technologies of Memory: Excuse, Sacrifice, Commodification, and Actuarial Moralities', *Radical Historical Review*, 85: 58–73.

——(2004) 'Memory Theatres, Virtual Witnessing, and the Trauma-Aesthetic', *Biography*, 27 (1): 163–201.

Foucault, M. (1972) *The Archaeology of Knowledge*, New York, NY: Pantheon.

——(1980) *Power/Knowledge. Selected Interviews and Other Things*, Hemel Hempstead: Harvester.

Garcia-Godos, J. (2008) 'Victim Reparations in the Peruvian Truth Commission and the Challenges to Historical Interpretation', *International Journal of Transitional Justice*, 2: 63–82.

Gready, P. (2009a) 'Telling Truth? The Methodological Challenges of Truth Commissions', in Coomans, F., Grünfeld, F. and Kamminga, M. (eds) *Methods of Human Rights Research*, Maastrict Series in Human Rights, Antwerp: Intersentia.

——(2009b) 'Novel Truths: Literature and Truth Commissions', *Comparative Literature Studies*, 46 (1): 156–76.

Hayner, P. (1994) 'Fifteen Truth Commissions – 1974 to 1994: A Comparative Study', *Human Rights Quarterly*, 16 (4): 597–655.

Hinchman, L.P. and Hinchman, S. K. (1997) 'Introduction', in Hinchman, L.P. and Hinchman, S.K. (eds) *Memory, Identity, Community*, Albany, NY: State University of New York Press.

Humphrey, M. (2000) 'From Terror to Trauma: Commissioning Truth for National Reconciliation', *Social Identities*, 6 (1): 7–27.

——(2003) 'From Victim to Victimhood: Truth Commissions and Trials as Rituals of Political Transition and Individual Healing', *Australian Journal of Anthropology*, 14 (2): 171–87.

International Center for Transitional Justice (2012) *Truth and Memory*. Available at: <http://ictj.org/our-work/transitional-justice-issues/truth-and-memory> (accessed 8 March 2012).

Moon, C. (2004) 'Prelapsarian State: Forgiveness and Reconciliation in Transitional Justice', *International Journal for the Semiotics of Law*, 17 (2): 185–97.

——(2006) 'Narrating Political Reconciliation: Truth and Reconciliation in South Africa', *Social & Legal Studies*, 15 (2): 257–75.

——(2009) *Narrating Political Reconciliation: South Africa's Truth and Reconciliation Commission*, Lanham, MD: Lexington Books.

Motsemme, N. (2004) 'The Mute always Speak: On Women's Silence at the Truth and Reconciliation Commission', *Current Sociology*, 52 (5): 909–32.

Nesiah, V. (2006) *Truth Commissions and Gender: Principles, Policies and Procedures*, ICTJ. Available at: <https://ictj.org/sites/default/files/ICTJ-Global-Commissions-Gender-2006-English_0.pdf> (accessed 9 January 2013).

Norval, A. (1999) 'Review Article: Truth and Reconciliation: the Birth of the Present and the Reworking of History', *Journal of Southern African Studies*, 25 (3): 499–519.

O'Neill, K. L. (2005) 'Writing Guatemala's Genocide: Truth and Reconciliation Commission Reports and Christianity', *Journal of Genocide Research*, 7 (3): 331–49.

Ross, A. (2006) 'The Creation and Conduct of the Guatemalan Commission for Historical Clarification', *Geoforum*, 37: 69–81.

Ross, F.C. (2003) 'On Having Voice and Being Heard: Some After-Effects of Testifying Before the South African Truth and Reconciliation Commission', *Anthropological Theory*, 3 (3): 325–41.

Somers, M.R. (1994) 'The Narrative Constitution of Identity: A Relational and Network Approach', *Theory and Society*, 23. 605–49.

Truth Commission (2012) *Strategic Choices in Truth Commissions*. Available at: <http://www.truthcommission.org/> (accessed 8 March 2012).

Truth and Reconciliation Commission (n.d.) 'Report of the Truth and Reconciliation Commission', Vol. 1. Available at: <http://www.justice.gov.za/trc/report/finalreport/Volume%201.pdf> (accessed 20 November 2012).

United States Institute of Peace (2012) *Commission of Inquiry: Honduras 93*. Available at: <http://www.usip.org/publications-tools/latest?filter1=**ALL**&filter0=**ALL**&filter2=2222&filter3=**ALL**&filter4=> (accessed 9 March 2012).

Verdoolaege, A. (2009) 'Dealing with a Traumatic Past: the Victim Hearings of the South African Truth and Reconciliation Commission and their Reconciliation Discourse', *Critical Discourse Studies*, 6 (4): 297–309.

White, H. (1980) 'The Value of Narrativity in the Representation of Reality', *Critical Inquiry*, 7 (1): 5–27.

——(1987) *The Content of the Form: Narrative Discourse and Historical Representation*, Baltimore, MD: Johns Hopkins University Press.

Wilson, R. (2001) *The Politics of Truth and Reconciliation in South Africa: Legitimizing the Post-Apartheid State*, Cambridge: Cambridge University Press.

——(2011) *Writing History in International Criminal Trials*, Cambridge: Cambridge University Press.

Chapter 8

Redressive politics and the nexus of trauma, transitional justice and reconciliation

Magdalena Zolkos

The inquiry into the measures and strategies for addressing mass historical violence within the rubric of transitional justice and reconciliation has coincided with the renewed academic interest in traumatic memory (see e.g. Schwab 2010). The critical study of transitional justice has brought to the forefront the victim-centred view on past violence, in contrast to those juridical and quasi-juridical measures that, as it has been widely argued, fell short of incorporating victims' perspectives and experiences (see e.g. Minow 1999). As a result, it has become a key tenet of the academic inquiry into post-atrocity politics that mitigating the victims' trauma should be considered an important goal of transitional justice and a condition for achieving reconciliation (Hayner 2001).

Given this important nexus of traumatic redress, transitional justice and reconciliation, it is puzzling that in the relevant literature the relation of the last often lacks more elaborate articulation. Is the process of doing justice for the past and achieving reconciliation coterminous with, or conditioned by, the alleviation of trauma among the violence-affected individuals and communities? What is the significance of traumatic memory in redressive politics and post-atrocity societies? This chapter turns to this problematique through critical analysis of the uses and incorporations of the concept of trauma in transitional justice debates, and by mapping the various conceptual constructions of the nexus of traumatic redress, transitional justice and reconciliation. The aim is to investigate critically the meanings and uses of the notion of trauma in the contemporary theorising of transitional justice. Subsequently, the chapter suggests broadening and reframing the concept of trauma in transitional justice scholarship from its clinical rendering as a psychological disorder of individuals and collectives to a cultural understanding of trauma as a breakdown of meaning and of the narratability of experience (cf. Caruth 1995; Felman 2002). The argument is that such framing of trauma illuminates the *limit* of post-atrocity politics to address and do justice for human suffering. Importantly, at stake is not a situational flaw of post-atrocity politics, which could be corrected through appropriate policy amendments and implementations. Rather, this chapter argues that this ultimate impossibility to attend to suffering – always irreducibly singular, subjective, and corporeal – is a *necessary*, and even *constitutive*, limit of post-atrocity politics (and, specifically, of the reconciliatory politics of the past) with regard to individual encounters with historical violence. It must be made clear, however, that the intention is *not* to argue that post-atrocity politics should not attempt to address traumatisation of violence-affected subjects in a pursuit of social justice and redress, or to declare politics impotent in relation to the realm of private experience. Instead, the intention is to elicit a critical reflection about what is currently one of the dogmas in the field transitional justice and reconciliation, namely the therapeutic and confessional engagement with the 'inner lives' of individuals and communities in post-conflict settings.

The dominant human rights discourse of transitional justice is built on the assumption that this field constitutes a complex of plural, but coherent and mutually reinforcing, aims – a logic of 'all good things go together' – which include accountability for human rights violations; reconciliation and forgiveness; public commemoration; alleviation of trauma; prevention of future violence, etc.[1] While some scholars have pointed out tensions and potential incompatibilities between some of these goals (Leebaw 2008), the primary focus of debate in the field has been on 'truth versus justice' and 'justice versus reconciliation' (Roht-Arriaza 2006), rather than on the potentially problematic alignment of psychological trauma with the pursuit of historical justice within a logic of harmony and coherence (see e.g. Mendeloff 2009).

To close this gap, these issues are discussed in this chapter in three distinct steps. First, I map the nexus of trauma, transitional justice and reconciliation, and analyse how the notion of trauma has been incorporated by normative-theoretical approaches to transitional justice. Second, I proceed to therapeutic and clinical uses of trauma in post-atrocity contexts. The suggestion is that while the normative-theoretical approaches engage critically with the assumption of compatibility between the goals of traumatic alleviation and of addressing past human rights abuses, for the most part they remain conflicted about the place of traumatic memory and traumatic redress in post-conflict politics. More specifically, it remains a contested issue whether the question of trauma is specific to the domain of 'private' concerns, or whether it has a bearing on the public processes of transitional justice. In contrast, the therapeutic and clinical approaches have operationalised a richer notion of trauma in terms of the overwhelming effect of catastrophic events on the individual and collective psyche, and in terms of the temporal distortion of inner life (living in the present *as if* it were the past), but for the most part without considering its political dimensions and effects. In the third section, I draw on critical approaches to trauma theory in order to articulate the nexus of trauma, transitional justice and reconciliation beyond the logic of 'all good things go together', and to consider the significance of trauma from the perspective of the subject's breakdown of meaning and historical narratability for redressive politics.

The nexus of trauma, justice and reconciliation: an overview

The contemporary debates on the politics of the past frame the connections of trauma redress, transitional justice and reconciliation primarily in causal terms. They proceed along two main trajectories: first, achieving healing and recovery from trauma through participation in juridical and quasi-juridical fora; and, second, strengthening transitional justice and reconciliatory goals through mitigating people's psychological and emotional trauma. This is exemplified by the so-called 'peace-through-health' approach (Santa Barbara and MacQueen 2004: 385), where therapeutic 'methods of healing and rehabilitation [are] linked to social processes of reconciliation and peace building'. Importantly, that connection is most apparent at the level of *negative argumentation*, i.e. where the lack of therapeutic mechanisms, and thus persistence of the symptoms of psychological trauma in post-conflict populations is claimed to contribute to 'demoralization and lack of initiative, ... and rigid patterns of thinking [and] chronic war' (Santa Barbara and MacQueen 2004: 385). With regard to the mass violation of human rights that transitional justice processes seek to address, traumatisation of individuals and societies is considered the central subjective mediation of historical violence and atrocity. In the discourses of legitimisation of the post-atrocity State, this emphasis on trauma coincides with the emergence of the 'therapeutic modes of governance' (Moon 2009), where the State's *raison d'être* is to achieve the psychosomatic well-being of the State subjects.

According to the literature, addressing trauma through diverse therapeutic measures can have either positive effects on implementing transitional justice and reconciliation or negative effects if it results in re-traumatisation of the victims, or in the so-called 'secondary traumatisation' of witnesses (O'Connell 2005; Kerr and Mobekk 2007). In turn, the failure to address post-conflict traumatisation in the affected populations (collectively or individually) has, as many researchers and policy-makers argue, negative effects (Kritz 1995; Barsalou 2005; Brunner 2008). For instance, drawing on Johan Galtung's well-known distinction between 'negative peace' (as the absence of war) and 'positive peace' (as societal integration), Mendeloff (2009: 611) suggests that the affective components of the experience of victimisation – such as resentment, rage, and mistrust – can have a serious impact on the chances for 'positive peace'. Denied or non-existent access to truth-telling forums for affected populations 'hinders ... psychological healing', and amplifies '[people's] tolerance for violent retribution', which in turn decreases opportunities for social reconciliation (Mendeloff 2009: 599).

In contrast to those approaches that affirm a close and positive co-relation of trauma, historical justice and reconciliation, other scholars have suggested that in selected contexts there might be no obvious connection between organised therapeutic engagements with traumatisation, on the one hand, and successful transitional justice and reconciliation, on the other (see e.g. Summerfield 2002). The proponents of this view offer a critique of the post-conflict 'therapeutic State' by arguing that there is often an *excessive* emphasis on trauma in transitional contexts, which coincides with the institutionalisation of the distinctively Western therapeutic paradigm of post-traumatic stress disorder (PTSD) diagnosis and the so-called 'talking cure', commonly in non-Western contexts. What tends to be overlooked with the institutionalisation of this therapeutic paradigm, they argue, is the socio-culturally specific subjective resilience in catastrophic circumstances. An important confirmation of the validity of these considerations comes from the research on children and adolescent experiences and memories of violent conflict. In *Then They Started Shooting: Growing Up in Wartime Bosnia*, child psychiatrist Lynne Jones (2004) provides evidence that even in the case of direct experiences of conflict and violence, most of the subjects she interviewed after the war did not exhibit symptoms of lasting traumatisation. This approach has led to advocacy of a non-oppositional and integrated conception of human vulnerability and resilience within the rubric of post-atrocity recovery and redress, which does not lock the affected subjects into categories of victims, and acknowledges the oftentimes productive operations of defensive memory mechanisms and forgetting (see also Berk 1998).

Even in research that follows the logic of 'all good things go together' in the conceptual construction of the nexus of trauma, justice and reconciliation, the empirical findings on the contribution of redressive programmes and policies to collective and individual 'healing' are not straightforwardly supportive of a positive direct and causal relation between them, as suggested by Pham *et al* (2010). The authors are critical of asserting a positive causal connectivity between trauma, justice and reconciliation due to the insufficient empirical substantiation of this nexus. What is of particular interest for this chapter is that in spite of the scarcity of affirmative empirical findings, there has been a consistent and strong conceptual and political investment in constructing transitional justice as the way 'to address the effects of war on traumatized communities and bring justice' (Pham *et al* 2010: 98) at the level of policy debates and public health discourses, as well as in selected academic literature (see e.g. Weinstein and Stover 2004; Fletcher *et al* 2009), as illustrated in the following. In particular, the alleviation of societal trauma has been connected to two modalities of transitional justice: first, the operation of TRCs and, second, social reconstruction through reparative, material and/or symbolic, measures, such as monetary payments, non-monetary benefits and public apologies (Pham *et al* 2010: 100). The following discusses both aspects in turn.

Regarding TRCs, Martha Minow (1999) suggests that starting with the South African TRC, the distinctive feature of TRCs has been not only the restorative focus on the victim (rather than the punitive focus on the offender), but also the incorporation of 'reconciliation and healing' as its explicit objectives. Within the often strongly therapeutic discourses of TRCs, the prospects for healing are conditioned upon the subject's willing engagement with the post-conflict *truth regime* through the production of a narrative (i.e. verbalisation of the subjective experience of violence) and through affective submission, including the surrender of vindictive desires and granting forgiveness. As a result, TRCs 'cast ... the consequences of collective violence in terms of trauma; the paradigm of health, rather than justice ... . [T]he formal justice system recurs in discussion of healing as a potential barrier or provocation for renewed trauma' (Minow 1999: 63).

In a similar vein, it has been suggested that TRCs can achieve the therapeutic and reconciliatory objectives insofar as they facilitate confessional and testimonial processes, and provide structures for the narrativisation of the experiences of victimisation and suffering (Hayner 2001: 145–62). They create a platform on which victims, witnesses and perpetrators can 'express [their] feelings' and 'talk out traumatic experience', which preconditions 'recovery and ... psychological health' (Hayner 2001: 146). What emerges in this accumulation of individual memories, stories and affects is referred to as a collective, or communal, traumatic memory, in contrast to such memory formations that remain restricted to the psychic life of individuals (see e.g. Erikson 1994, 1995). However, the emphasis in the design and functioning of TRCs on addressing the participants' psychological need 'to tell one's story', and on generating a sense of relief and a transformative (cathartic) experience, has led some critics to argue that the TRCs' restorative objective rests on 'pillars of optimism' (Acorn 2004: 46). As such, TRCs can be potentially over-ambitious in their therapeutic goals, and, more importantly, they risk subsuming individual experiences of suffering under a uniform paradigm of victimisation. Also, the therapeutic objectives in post-atrocity politics can conflict with other redressive goals (see e.g. Leebaw 2008). Illustrative in this context is a study by Kaminer *et al* aimed at examining 'the degree to which participation in the TRC [in the Western Cape region was] related to current psychiatric status and forgiveness among survivors' (Kaminer *et al* 2001: 373), which found no direct evidence of the connection between individual participation in the TRC and demonstration of 'forgiveness attitudes', or the relief of depression, PTSD and other anxiety disorders. It thus advocated that 'additional therapeutic interventions [which] are culturally appropriate and specifically address the needs of survivors of human rights abuses should supplement the truth commission process' (Kaminer *et al* 2001: 377).

What becomes apparent in the course of the above discussion is that contrary to the normalising logic of 'all good things go together' the nexus of trauma, transitional justice and reconciliation remains highly complex and case specific. It is also riven by potential irreconcilabilities and conflicting logics in that it testifies to the tensions between, on the one hand, the reconciliatory and restorative notions of post-atrocity politics, and, on the other hand, subjective experiences of suffering. In what follows, this chapter looks closer at the clinical conceptualisation of trauma and its incorporation in the transitional justice and reconciliation debates so as to elucidate its implications for questions of post-atrocity redress.

The clinical perspective on trauma in transitional justice

The last two decades have witnessed a proliferation of various medical, psychological and therapeutic initiatives addressed at post-conflict political contexts, aiming at the investigation, management and prevention of mental health consequences of mass political violence. The concept of trauma has been at the core of these initiatives and discussions, as exemplified by the inter-sectional and cross-disciplinary dialogue at the *Global Response: International Conference on Violent Conflict and Health*, organised in 2010 by the Copenhagen-based NGO, Global Doctors. The event consisted of a series of medical professional, academic and public activities, including the publication of special journal issues on public health in conflict and post-conflict societies by *The Lancet, Social Science and Medicine* and the *Journal of the Danish Medical Association*. The conference report extended beyond the inquiry into the impact of violent conflicts on public mental and physical health, and emphasised that dealing with post-conflict trauma needs to be recognised for its direct bearing on the prospects for achieving reconciliation and justice, and for ensuring security and lasting peace (Global Doctors 2010).

Medical humanitarian and relief organisations, such as *Médecins Sans Frontières* (e.g. 2000, 2004, 2012b), International Medical Corps (e.g. 2007) and Medical Relief International (e.g. 2012), have developed strategies of addressing psychological trauma, dating back to the wars of the Yugoslav dissolution in 1990s. As the website of the *Médecins Sans Frontières* (2012a) states, it was 'on the killing fields of Bosnia ... that MSF [*Médecins Sans Frontières*] volunteers recognized that it was not enough to meet the physical needs of people caught up in conflict', since '[t]he psychological and emotional scars of war – wounds that may continue in people's minds long after the fighting has ended – were being neglected.' Importantly, the conceptual framework of their engagement addresses trauma primarily within the rubric of PTSD, and places the process of therapeutic recovery at the cross-section of the individual and collective social realities. This was because, in the words of Kaz De Jong from the *Médecins Sans Frontières* (2012a), '[t]he stigma of weakness, the acknowledgment of suffering, and the shame that so often surrounds traumatized people [becomes] a collective experience'. Also, the organisation has taken a collective approach to emotional and psychological trauma – its programme on mental health in humanitarian crises assumes a causal connection between, on the one hand, 'suffering from mental disorders as a result of conflict or violence' and, on the other, insufficient democratic support for 'reconciliation or peacebuilding efforts' (*Médecins Sans Frontières* 2012a).

Within the field of empirical academic studies that operationalise the concept of trauma, Pham *et al* (2004) have argued that in the post-conflict Rwandan context there has been a strong correspondence between negative popular attitudes towards transitional justice in the juridical framework of the *gacaca* courts, on the one hand, and high levels of traumatisation (defined in terms of the PTSD), on the other. According to the authors, the alleged direct negative correspondence between unaddressed cases of PTSD and prospects for effective post-genocidal redress affirms the causal relationship between the overcoming of individual trauma and successful societal reconciliation. Similarly, focusing on Uganda and the Democratic Republic of Congo, Bayer *et al* (2007) have also concluded that there is a strong situational correspondence between the PTSD symptoms in the war-affected populations, on the one hand, and the 'less openness to reconciliation and more feelings of revenge', on the other. The authors suggest that 'children with PTSD symptoms might regard acts of retaliation as an appropriate way to recover personal integrity and to overcome their traumatic experiences' (Bayer *et al* 2007: 558). Unaddressed PTSD allegedly contributes to 'the cycles of violence found in war-torn regions' (Bayer *et al* 2007: 558). Accordingly, the study links high levels of traumatisation among the affected populations to weakened prospects for democratic consolidation, including introduction of measures for addressing peacefully the legacies of past violence and authoritarianism.

Other studies, however, offer a more sceptical view on the causal relation between the levels of traumatisation and post-atrocity redress. For example, a study investigating the effects of war trauma on segments of post-Yugoslav populations in relation to questions of political accountability and restoration suggested a coincidence of high levels of psychosomatic, affective and mental disorders among the survivors, on the one hand, and a shared public view about insufficient accountability measures for war atrocity, on the other hand (Basoglu *et al* 2005). The study concluded that there was insufficient evidence of a cause-effect relationship between the levels of traumatisation and the socio-political redressive measures, and that more important factors of enduring depression and anxiety were material insecurity and loss of control.

What do these empirical studies suggest about the clinical understanding of trauma? Even this brief look at the studies that operationalise the clinical concept of trauma in relation to post-atrocity redress shows that their definition of trauma remains indebted to the etymology of trauma as 'wound', that is a body-altering injury, which causes the rupture of a protective (psychological or physical) shield (cf. Laplanche and Pontalis 1973: 465). The etymology of wounding connotes 'a spatial model [of trauma], in which the reality of trauma originates "outside" an organism which is violently imposed upon' (Caruth 2002: 107). This is to suggest that the clinical conceptualisations of trauma remain indebted to the imaginary of a violent shock as a 'wound', developed in-depth within psychoanalysis, which occurs as a breach of the ego defences under a surge of intolerable and unexpected psychic stimuli, overflowing strong emotions or accumulated excitations (Laplanche and Pontalis 1973: 466–67).

Integral to the psychoanalytic imaginary of trauma is the idea of the affected subject as 'defenceless', in the sense of the 'incapacity to help [one]self' (Laplanche 1999: 75). This is not to imply the subject's psychic passivity or utter helplessness in the face of the catastrophic occurrence but, rather, existential vulnerability articulated in relation with another person (cf. Erikson 1995: 194). This means that situations of mass violence are considered traumatising insofar as they leave the subject feeling overwhelmed and defenceless – the traumatic effect is not due to 'objective facts' but to the subjective emotional experience. According to the psychoanalytic tradition, traumatisation is brought about by the subjective experience of fright, terror and shock, where the heightened subjective vulnerability in the face of catastrophic experience becomes a characteristic mark of trauma (cf. Laplanche 1999).

Following the mapping of the meanings and uses of trauma in transitional justice debates, this chapter suggests that in understanding the complex effects of past political violence on the *inner life* of the subject, the clinical notion of trauma (where the PTSD rubric figures as the key vocabulary for expression of the subjective experience of pain and suffering) needs to be complemented with a cultural conceptualisation of trauma as a breakdown of meaning and representation. As such, trauma marks not only a psychological and emotional injury, but a 'rupture, discontinuity and disconnection' of the very possibilities of communicating subjective experience of mass violence (Hamber 2009: 75). The cultural conceptualisation of trauma emphasises the 'collapse of language in the face of uncontainable and unintelligible suffering' (Felman 2002: 157). As apparent in the quote by Hamber (2009: 22), 'massive trauma has an amorphous, ahistorical presence, not delimited by place, time, or agency; it precludes its knowing, and not knowing is part of the cycle of destruction'. Accordingly, within the psychoanalytic tradition, the notion of trauma has come to designate those catastrophic experiences of the subject that remain, to some extent, *unassimilated* within the psychic world of the subject. That psychic incapacity to adequately respond to and absorb those experiences indicates their intensity and excessiveness (Laplanche and Pontalis 1973: 465). In regard to the question of communication and narrativisation of experiences of mass violence in reconciliatory and redressive fora, trauma codes not only a trace, or a remnant, of the catastrophic experience on the psyche, but also a rift in, or a breakdown, of meaning and a certain incommunicability and unrepresentability of experience. As this chapter suggests further, the cultural notion of trauma provides resources for critical theorising of transitional justice and post-atrocity politics.

Post-traumatic stress disorder and the collective dimension of trauma

Continuing from the inquiry into the clinical understanding of trauma, as outlined above, this section looks more closely at the concept of PSTD, which, arguably, has been the dominant framework for articulating trauma in post-atrocity contexts. It also links the critical discussion of PTSD to the inquiry into collective dimensions of trauma, which is crucial for mapping the nexus of trauma, transitional justice and reconciliation.

PTSD was first incorporated in the third edition of *Diagnostic and Statistical Manual of Mental Disorders* by the American Psychiatric Association (American Psychiatric Association 1980). It is defined as an anxiety disorder that follows 'a traumatic event which causes intense fear and/or helplessness in an individual' (American Psychiatric Association 1980). Originating in the context of the Vietnam War, and linked to the efforts of anti-war activism, PTSD has replaced older medical descriptors of psychosomatic disturbance caused by combat exposure, such as 'shell shock' or 'combat fatigue' (Jone and Wessely 2005). Within the contemporary humanitarian and therapeutic approaches to post-atrocity politics, PTSD has not only displaced these 'previous [conceptual] incarnations' of war trauma, extending its scope to civilian populations, but it has also been 'more broadly applied [to become] the shorthand by which we understand human responses to a variety of violent experiences ranging from war, genocide, and torture to rape and child abuse' (Moon 2009: 72, 74).

According to Judith Lewis Herman (2001), PTSD needs to be recognised as affecting the whole psychosomatic organisation of the subject (rather than being isolated within it) and as encompassing 'a spectrum of conditions rather than ... a single disorder'. Herman, hence, terms it the 'complex post-traumatic stress disorder'. These alterations occur in 'affect regulation', including dysphoric conditions; in 'consciousness', including memory effects, such as amnesia or hypermnesia; in 'self-perception'; in the 'perception of perpetrator'; in 'relations with others'; and in 'systems of meaning' (Herman 2001: 121). Here the collective dimension of trauma (or what Herman terms 'societal trauma') indicates an aggregate of cases of individual traumatisation, but, importantly, it also acquires a collective or communal dimension that is irreducible to this accumulative result.

This idea of a transitional and post-atrocity society as a collective subject of trauma is modelled upon the dynamics of the inner life of individual trauma victims, and it exhibits three main symptoms: hyper-arousal (permanent alertness of the self-preservation system); intrusion (temporal distortion where the violent past is re-lived as if it were the present and displays of enormous affective capital); and constriction or numbing (emotional detachment, passivity or exaggerated calm in the face of danger). Traumatic intrusion suggests that '[l]ong after the danger is past, traumatized people relive the event as though it were continually recurring in the present. ... It is as if time stops at the moment of trauma. The traumatic moment becomes encoded in an abnormal form of memory' (Herman 2001: 37). This means that in the wake of widespread violence and historical atrocity not only directly affected individuals, but whole communities of victims, bystanders, witnesses and even perpetrators can exhibit PTSD symptoms. Unless such collective trauma is addressed, Herman argues, they remain 'trapped in alternating cycles of numbing and intrusion, silence and reenactment' (Herman 2001: 243). The aim of the therapeutic process, understood in broad terms not only as a clinical intervention, but also as strategic introduction of a variety of social and political practices, is to break that cycle, and to counter repression of the traumatic content within the collective psyche.

According to Herman (2001), the idea of collective trauma enables signification of the contextual features of selected transitional societies in the therapeutic-organicist terms. For instance, the suppression of public discussions around past violent events and the institution of a culture of impunity (or lack of accountability and restitution) become *amnesic symptoms*. This claim draws a parallel between the lack of socio-political and cultural forums to express and work through the painful past, on the one hand, and, on the other hand, the psychic mechanism of amnesia – memory deficit due to psychological traumatisation or brain injury. At stake in the act of suppressing historical memories is not only the forceful attempt at preventing disclosure of potentially subversive, pluralising and critical narratives, but also a collective-psychological defence mechanism where undesirable memories and affects are eliminated from the collective subconscious. In turn, the occurrence of passionate ethno-nationalist investments in transitional societies (accompanied by anti-internationalist attitudes, as well as sacrificial or martyrological national identity) figures as symptomatic of collective paranoia and hypermnesia.

Accordingly, for Herman the process of 'social recovery' has two components: it requires establishment of a 'public forum where victims can speak their truth and their suffering can be formally acknowledged', and 'an organized effort to hold individual perpetrators accountable for their crimes' (Herman 2001: 242). These processes are based on three 'stages of recovery': safety, which includes restoration of control of the situation and of a secure environment; national 'remembrance and mourning'; and 'reconnection', which means an active engagement in the construction of a peaceful future (Herman 2001: 155–74). These components of recovery have important implications for how transitional justice and reconciliation are imagined and practiced insofar as they suggest that in doing justice for the past the State needs to become the locus of security provisions, as well as of therapeutic engagements with (or, to put it in more explicitly Foucauldian terms, management, examination and inspection of) the inner lives of individuals and communities in post-conflict settings.

In a similar vein, according to Hamber, nations, just like individuals, 'have psyches that experience traumas', which means that post-conflict societies need 'a cathartic public process of truth telling' (Hamber 2009: 76). The idea of catharsis, extended in this context to a collective experience, connotes that at stake in redressive and reconciliatory processes is, at least partly, an effect of *purgation* or *purification* achieved through emotional and emphatic engagement of the subjects. In addition to the effect of cleansing, the idea of catharsis also promises *intellectual clarification*, which in the context of post-atrocity politics means that at stake is also formation of shared knowledge about the violent past and constitution of national sites of memory – the way that society 'goes about reading its own past, how it keeps the past alive, [and] commemorates and forgets episodes of its memory' (Rousso 2007: 26). Within this conceptual framework, a post-atrocity society is imagined as a 'living organism … in need of healing' (Hamber 2009: 83). The idea of communal trauma is based on the assumption that 'one can speak of traumatized communities as something distinct from assemblies of traumatized persons' (Erikson 1995: 183). The communal trauma has distinctive socio-political and cultural effects and is irreducible to the sum of traumatic symptoms of affected individuals. It designates a 'blow to the basic tissues of social life that damages the bonds attaching people together and impairs the prevailing sense of community' (Erikson 1994: 233).

These communal and social dimensions of trauma are significant for this chapter's task of mapping the nexus of trauma, transitional justice and reconciliation insofar as, even in those theories that equate trauma with PTSD, there emerges a recognition of a complex relationship between collective memories of mass atrocity and subjective experiences of suffering. The relationship between the social and the singular needs to be differentiated from models of accumulation or collective production of memories as introduced earlier in this chapter. Taking this inference as a reference point, the next section articulates a critical nexus of trauma, transitional justice and reconciliation.

Critique of the nexus of trauma, transitional justice and reconciliation

The above discussion of how trauma has been understood and used in transitional justice discourses gestures towards the internal complexity of its semantic field. Contrary to the logic of 'all good things go together', which views post-atrocity politics in terms of mutually coherent and reinforcing goals, the exposition above suggests that the therapeutic imperative and other redressive aims are potentially conflicting. It also demonstrates that the meanings of trauma can differ substantially across diverse redressive positions.

The critical perspectives on trauma in the debates on transitional justice point out that the uses of the trauma concept contribute to the 'medicalisation' of questions of post-conflict redress, and tend to present the processes at play as 'technical necessities', rather than as political and ethical decisions (Pavlich 2005: 35). The use of PTSD as the key indicator of traumatisation among the violence-affected populations, and thus as the dominant discursive register of subjective human experiences of pain, suffering and loss, has played a significant role in the emergence of the 'therapeutic imperative' of the post-atrocity State formation (Pavlich 2005). The clinical discourse of injury and healing in turn fuels the emergence of the 'therapeutic mandate' of the post-conflict State, where 'the basis of the claim to govern made by some postconflict states, lies in their ability to lay national trauma to rest' (Moon 2009: 72). Within the order of the therapeutic State '[t]he style of justice that [the postconflict states] deploy suggests a radically new mode of state legitimation' (Moon 2009: 86). More specifically, the State is 'legitimate not just because it can forcibly suppress conflict and violence (Hobbes), or because it can deliver justice and protect rights (Locke), but because it can cure people of the pathologies that, on this account, are a potential cause of the resurgence of future violence' (Moon 2009: 86). This transformation of the mandate and operation of the State is significant in the post-atrocity contexts insofar as it legitimises governance of subjectivity and inner life of the populations, including psychic well being, which in the Foucauldian perspective on the State has been addressed within the rubric of pastoral power (the beneficent power of State care). This includes politics of confessionalism, which have been central to redressive and reconciliatory institutions in a variety of contexts, where the subject is urged to publicly disclose one's experiences, feelings and memories for the sake of not only personal healing, but also of communal catharsis (intellectual clarification and affective purgation)

The argument forwarded in this chapter is that the medical and therapeutic presentation of the redressive dilemmas of the post-atrocity State is not specifically due to the use of the notion of trauma in transitional justice and reconciliation, but, rather, to the *equation of trauma with PTSD*. My aim is thus not to suggest that transitional and reconciliatory discourses should be purged of the trauma term per se, but, rather, that alternative understandings of and perspectives on trauma should be considered and brought more centrally into post-atrocity politics. As discussed, the plurality of meanings and the conceptual history of trauma make some of its expressions irreducible to, and often strikingly different from, the clinical and pathological implications of PTSD. For example, a cultural understanding of trauma is neither pathologising nor therapeutically oriented. The remaining part of this section stipulates that such a concept of trauma is potentially productive and illuminative in revisiting the relation between the subjective experience of mass violence and redressive politics.

The above suggestion relies on a critical reflection about what is problematic about the discursive synonymy of trauma and PTSD. It seems namely that the ever increasing number of contemporary PTSD diagnoses has to do with 'changes in the relation between individual "personhood" and modern life', which articulates 'human misery, stress [and] distress' in the clinical vernacular (Summerfield 2001: 95). This rhetoric frames human suffering in 'narrowly deterministic' way, either as a psycho-medical pathology or as a disorder (Summerfield 1996: 376). The diagnosis of PTSD 'does not simply describe a number of symptoms, but, importantly, also determines what has caused them' (Bracken 2003: 75–76). It thus frames historical injustice and mass violence as the intrusion of past memories onto the present, or living in the present as if it were the past (Bracken 2003: 75; see also Prager 2008). In this sense, the epistemic paradigm of the PTSD relies on a linear idea of temporality, which structures past, present and future as separate and sequential.

Moreover, and in broader cultural terms, the equation of trauma with PTSD in transitional justice reflects the Western ontology and value system of the subject and subjective well being, which are individual, secular, medico-therapeutic and technical. As Bracken *et al* (1995) point out, this has resulted in an application of therapeutic techniques or treatment strategies, such as the confessional or testimonial institutionalisations of the emotional life of the subject within the redressive quasi juridical and juridical forums (such as TRCs), in cultural context where they have been inappropriate, intrusive and, perhaps, even violent. This admittedly controversial point is persuasively evidenced by, among others, Acorn, who, in the South African context, has drawn a parallel between the post-Apartheid restorative discourses and institutionalisation of apology, confession and forgiveness on the one hand, and restoration of the 'ex ante state of "conjugal" equality and harmony ... between victims and perpetrators' on the other hand (Acorn 2004: 72). A distinctive inflection of this approach is the ideological register of individualism, which takes as a given that 'heal[ing] the nation requires [healing] of the self, and, consequently, orients the post-atrocity 'public policy ... to the re-inscription of private experience' of violence (Prager 2008: 407).

The suggested need for a critical reflection about the redressive discourses of trauma in terms of their cultural articulations aims thus to achieve greater scholarly awareness in the use of the trauma concept, and thus of its epistemological investments in a particular understanding of what violence is, who the subject of violence is and how mass violence plays out at the level of subjective experience.

Furthermore, such critical reflection can lead to, *inter alia*, taking seriously the gendered and non-Western critiques of the clinical notions of trauma. The project of the so-called 'gendering of trauma' (see e.g. Cubilié 2005) explores the assumedly gender-neutral and gender-inclusive articulations of trauma, and argues instead that the cultural and psychoanalytic conceptual history of trauma has been distinctively gendered, and at times explicitly sexualised. A notable example is the psychological diagnosis of the 'traumatic hysteria', studied at the turn of the nineteenth century and into the twentieth century by Jean-Martin Charcot, Pierre Janet, Sigmund Freud, and others, which was specifically oriented towards women. It thus signified ways of being and feeling considered 'feminine' in the industrial European middle-class, including, primarily, emotional excess and sexual uncontrollability (see Bergo 2009; Roth 2012). This furthermore structured a positivistic relationship between the patient and the therapist, which was inscribed within the binaries male/female, rational/emotional, etc. The clinical uses of trauma coincide with the gendered construction of the non-Western subjects and societies as 'feminine', and thus in need of protection, therapeutic guidance and assistance.

With the outbreak of the First World War, the prototypical traumatic setting was reframed from the psychoanalytic 'scene of seduction' to that of the 'shell shock' or 'battle fatigue' of industrialised warfare. However, the groups of traumatised male soldiers were often described in terms that reflected the initial feminisation of the concept of trauma, namely that of excessive and unmanageable emotionality. For example, the British psychologist Charles Myers described the 'shell shock' of soldiers in the First World War through enumeration of hysterical symptoms: involuntary shivering, crying, spasms, sensory inhibition, amnesia and irrational behaviour (Luckhurst 2008: 54–55). This legacy plays out in contemporary understandings and uses of trauma in redressive settings in which the non-Western victim of trauma is depicted precisely in opposition to the idea of a rational, autonomous and independent Western subject (cf. Prager 2008).

While a more in-depth engagement with the question of gender in the history of trauma is beyond the purview of this chapter, it draws attention to two coinciding tendencies, which have a bearing on the way trauma is theorised and imagined in redressive contexts today: first, the undisclosed and implicit 'feminisation' of the traumatic symptoms belying the purported universal and gender-neutral notion of trauma; and, second, the privileging of particular types of distressing situation as proto-typical of traumatic events (such as direct exposure to violent shock; violence defined as military aggression and a product of industrialised warfare, etc.). This suggests that the clinical notion of trauma tends to exclude from its realm other aspects of mass violence, for example those that visually do not correspond to the ideas and images of traumatisation, such as indirect and socio-material stressors, and that it defines gendered subjects (women and children) as trauma victims in cases of direct physical and sexual violence, but not, for example, of socio-material hardship (Miller and Rasmussen 2010). They remain absent from redressive politics.

Consequently, the critical discussion of trauma in the nexus of transitional justice and reconciliation suggests that the scepticism about the equation of trauma with PTSD could be productively complemented by the inclusion of non-pathologising and cultural articulations of trauma in redressive politics. The following explores one such productive possibility, which originates in the recognition of the ambiguous genesis of trauma as both 'endogenous' and 'exogenous' (cf. Caruth 1995). The theory of 'endogenous trauma' locates traumagenic mechanisms primarily within the operations of the subject's psychic world, whereas 'exogenous trauma' explains traumatic origins in terms of the impact of external forces or events. It suggests that the cultural concept of trauma escapes linear and progressive ideas of time, subject and suffering. This in turn has a bearing on theorising redressive politics in consideration of transitional societies as being 'post' historical violence.

The cultural history of trauma as responsive to, and constitutive of, the 'modern condition' of the Western subject (Micale and Lerner 2001; Luckhurst 2008) situates the origins of the trauma concept, secondary to the medical-surgical ones, in the nineteenth century industrial accidents and the emergence of neurological science. It developed as one of the *maladies de la mémoire* ('maladies of memory') (Roth 2012). One of the proto-traumatic notions was the 'railway spine syndrome', which was reportedly experienced by victims of industrial accidents, and which manifested itself as a shock to the nervous system in the absence of physical injury. The idea of the 'railway spine syndrome' captures the contradictory social reactions to technological progress, including the expansion of the railway system, which appeared to its contemporaries both as a great achievement and as a threat to the existing ways of life. Industrialisation elicited an ambivalent social response insofar as it signified simultaneously 'progress and ruin, liberation and constraint, individualization and massification' (Luckhurst 2008: 20). For these proto-traumatic debates the key question was whether the traumatic reaction was exogenous or endogenous to the nervous system of the subject, that is, whether it occurred outside or within the subject's psychic structure. For example, John Eric Erichsen defined in 1866 the proto-traumatic 'railway spine' in terms of a puzzle or an enigma. Similarly, another neurologist of that era, Herbert Page, described traumatic occurrences in terms of a structural functional disturbance, which is irreducible to the 'organic impact' from the outside (Luckhurst 2008: 23–24). For Page, the 'railway spine' was a form of hysteria (an argument famously advanced in the work of Jean-Martin Charcot within the rubric of *névrose traumatique*, or 'traumatic hysteria', and of young Freud's seduction theory). Traumatic hysteria, defined as 'any experience [that] calls up distressing affects, [including] fright, anxiety, shame, or physical pain' (Freud and Breuer 1982 [1893–85]), became linked to the repression of memory.

These preoccupations appear to be still relevant in the contemporary debates on trauma, including those in redressive and post-atrocity contexts. For example, Caruth (1995: 8) famously locates the origins of trauma both within 'the historical reality of violence' and inside the 'individual's fantasy life'. This seemingly irreconcilable conflict at the heart of the cultural trauma concept has also found its expression in the subsequent debates negotiating between 'structural trauma' (trauma as a trans-historical philosophical concept) an 'historical trauma' (trauma as a consequence of a specific disaster) (LaCapra 1999; Ramadanovic 2002). What is important about this aspect of trauma's conceptual history from the perspective of the critical discussion of trauma in redressive discourses is that it points to some irresolvable ambiguity at the heart of the traumatic concept. Here the concept of trauma cannot be reduced to scientific variables and seamlessly incorporated into the advocacies of societal healing and revitalisation of communal fabric. In contrast, trauma marks a certain excess of the subjective responses of the body in relation to the material conditions of its occurrence – it marks a certain surplus of meaning and incompleteness of scientific explainability. To introduce the non-pathologising and cultural conceptions of trauma into post-atrocity politics, rather than achieve a harmony of reconciliatory and redressive goals and the science of psychic injury, leading to the articulation of a shared progressive and teleological vision of societal healing, means thus to facilitate post-atrocity politics as a space of contestation, conflicting memories, historical ambiguities, and diverse and irreconcilable positions and experiences of violence. In other words, cultural trauma emerges as a concept that resists the tendencies of reconciliatory and redressive politics to strategically *arrest*, *close* or *fix* meanings of historical violence.

Conclusions: cultural trauma, individual suffering, and 'untellability' of experience

This chapter has offered a critical mapping of the nexus of trauma, transitional justice and reconciliation, from the perspective of the clinical discourse of trauma and the therapeutic imperative of the post-atrocity State, which, arguably, has dominated redressive politics in post-atrocity contexts. The aim has been, first, to offer a critical analysis of the meanings and significance of the concept of trauma in the contemporary theorising of transitional justice, and, second, to suggest broadening and diversifying the concept of trauma from its dominant clinical understanding as a psychological disorder to a cultural and non-pathologising notion of trauma as a breakdown of historical meaning and of the narratability of experience. Based on this discussion, the chapter has drawn from the conceptual history of trauma, which troubles causal and linear explanations, and points beyond ideas of clinical injury.

Instead, trauma is understood as carrying an enigmatic or perplexing *remainder* – an indication of something one could not quite grapple with, or explain away, within the available frameworks of knowledge, and, as this chapter suggests, within the frameworks of redressive politics.

What are the implications of this discussion for theorising transitional justice and redressive politics? Cultural and psychoanalytic perspectives on trauma introduce a complex system of mediations of subjective suffering through diverse psychic mechanisms, fantasies, desires, and repressions. As such, it implies that there is a need for thinking about redressive politics *beyond* what Derrida (2001) has called 'therap[ies] of reconciliation'. The non-clinical and non-pathological notion of trauma offers resources for radicalising the questions of post-atrocity politics and ethics insofar as it resists political attempts at closing the space of redressive politics and fixing the meanings of historical violence. Instead, viewed from the cultural traumatic prism, historical violence and injustice are disclosed as something that one cannot, once and for all, satisfactorily do justice for. Cultural trauma institutes a *hiatus* within post-atrocity politics as a site of memory and past experience of loss, suffering, grief and mourning that is 'unintegrable [and] residual, ... that cannot be translated into legal [and political] consciousness and into legal [and political] idiom' (Felman 2002: 162, my emphasis).

This stipulates that, ultimately, at stake is the consideration of the limits of post-atrocity politics in regard to reparative and reconciliatory goals. The disjunction between redressive political aims and the realities of suffering – articulated in this chapter within the rubric of cultural trauma – is not *situational*, and thus cannot be corrected through appropriate policy implementations. Rather, it marks a *necessary* and perhaps even *constitutive* disjunction between the plural and collective goals of politics and the irreducible singularity and corporeality of human suffering (cf. Rothfield 2011).

This furthermore suggests that the cultural perspective on trauma as a breakdown of historical meanings and of narratability of individual suffering signifies a certain recalcitrance of the human experience of violence vis-à-vis the socio-political efforts to come to terms with, and do justice for, the past. At stake in the disjunctive relation between transitional justice and reconciliation as political projects and the narratability of the subjective experience of violence, is, ultimately, the question of the ethics of suffering. In this interpretation, trauma codes what is *un-redressive* and *un-reconciliatory* in redressive and reconciliatory politics, and what incessantly returns, and haunts, the sites of post-atrocity politics, by demarcating its limits, impasses, impossibilities, or what is called in post-structuralist vernacular, *aporeas* (an expression of doubt or irresolvable contradiction) (cf. Derrida 2001; Cubilié 2005). The critical resources within the register of cultural trauma are linked to its articulation of transitional justice and reconciliation as aporetic political projects, that is to say as projects that must face the ultimate impossibility of achieving what they set out to do.

Note

1 An example of the logic of 'all good things go together', in regard to how traumatic redress operates at the level of political practice and democratic consolidation, is the programme of the Peacebuilding Initiative established by the Professionals in Humanitarian Assistance and Protection in collaboration with the UN Peacebuilding Support Office and the Program on Humanitarian Policy and Conflict Research at Harvard University. The Peacebuilding Initiative has included 'psycho-social recovery' among its goals as a way of 'broaden[ing]' conventional perspectives on peacebuilding'. Suggesting that 'transitional justice measures can play a role in healing processes', it has argued that while 'concrete actions to address [the] "invisible wounds" [of trauma] are considered by many experts as still often inadequate, if not entirely missing, from paradigms of assistance and development employed by relief and development organizations in post-conflict transition', there is 'a growing evidence of the individual and collective consequences of trauma' at the level of socio-political change and democratic consolidation. Such discourse confirms that there is a need for more conceptual and political clarity about the ability and the legitimacy of redressive projects to engage with, and to alleviate, the psychological effects of individual and collective trauma.

Bibliography

Acorn, A. (2004) *Compulsory Compassion: A Critique of Restorative Justice*, Seattle, WA: University of Washington Press.

American Psychiatric Association (1980) *Diagnostic and Statistical Manual of Mental Disorders*, Arlington, VA: American Psychiatric Association.

Barsalou, J. (2005) 'Trauma and Transitional Justice in Divided Societies', Special Report 135 of the United States Institute of Peace, Washington, DC: United States Institute of Peace Press.

Basoglu, M., Livanou, M., Crnobaric, C., Franciskovic, T., Suljic, E., Duric, D. and Vranesic, M. (2005) 'Psychiatric and Cognitic Effects of War in Former Yugoslavia. Association of Lack of Redress for Trauma and Posttraumatic Stress Disorder', *Journal of the American Medical Association*, 294 (5): 580–92.

Bayer, C., Klasen, F. and Adam, H. (2007) 'Association of Trauma and PTSD Symptoms With Openness to Reconciliation and Feelings of Revenge Among Former Ugandan and Congolese Child Soldiers', *Journal of the American Medical Association*, 298 (5): 555–59.

Bergo, B. (2009) 'Trauma and Hysteria: A Tale of Passions and Reversal', in Brown Golden, K. and Bergo, B. (eds) *The Trauma Controversy*, New York, NY: SUNY Press.

Berk, J. (1998) 'Trauma and Resilience During War: A Look at the Children and Humanitarian Aid Workers of Bosnia', *Psychoanalytic Review*, 85: 639–58.

Bracken, P. (2003) *Trauma, Culture, Meaning, and Philosophy*, London: Whurr Publishers.

Bracken, P., Giller, J. and Summerfield, D. (1995) 'Psychological Responses to War and Atrocity: The Limitations of Current Concepts', *Social Science and Medicine*, 40 (8): 1073–82.

Brunner, J. (2008) 'Trauma and Justice: the Moral Grammar of Trauma Discourse from Wilhelmine Germany to Post-Apartheid South Africa', in Sarat, A., Davidovitch, N. and Albertstein, M. (eds) *Trauma and Memory. Reading, Healing, and Making Law*, Stanford, CA: Stanford University Press.

Caruth, C. (1995) 'Introduction', in Caruth, C. (ed.) *Trauma. Explorations in Memory*, Baltimore, MD: Johns Hopkins University Press.

——(2002) 'An Interview with Jean Laplanche', in Belau, L. and Ramadanociv, P. (eds), *Topologies of Trauma. Essays on the Limit of Knowledge and Memory*, New York, NY: Other Press.

Cubilié, A. (2005), *Women Witnessing Terror: Testimony and the Cultural Politics of Human Rights*, New York, NY: Fordham University Press.

Derrida, J. (2001) *On Cosmopolitanism and Forgiveness*, New York, NY, and London: Routledge.

Erikson, K. (1994) *A New Species of Trouble: Explorations in Disaster, Trauma, and Community*, London: W.W. Norton.

——(1995) 'Notes on Trauma and Community', in Caruth, C. (ed.) *Trauma: Explorations in Memory*, Baltimore, MD: Johns Hopkins University Press.

Felman, S. (2002) *The Juridical Unconscious. Trials and Trauma in the Twentieth Century*, Cambridge, MA: Harvard University Press.

Fletcher, L., Weinstein, H. and Rowen, J. (2009) 'Context, Timing and the Dynamics of Transitional Justice: A Historical Perspective', *Human Rights Quarterly*, 31 (1): 163–220.

Freud, S. and Breuer, J. (1982) [1895–83], *Studies on Hysteria*, London: Basic Books.

Global Doctors (2010) *Global Response: Conference on Violent Conflict and Health*. Available at: <http://www.global-doctors.org/cms/images/GLdok/GR2010/finalreport1.pdf> (accessed 13 December 2012).

Hamber, B. (2009) *Transforming Societies after Political Violence. Truth, Reconciliation, and Mental Health*, Dordrecht and New York, NY: Springer.

Hayner, P. (2001) *Unspeakable Truths. Transitional Justice and the Challenge of Truth Commissions*, New York, NY: Routledge.

Herman, J. L. (2001) *Trauma and Recovery*, London: Basic Books.

International Medical Corps (2007) 'Reducing Post-War Trauma in Children'. Available at: <http://internationalmedicalcorps.org/page.aspx?pid=041> (accessed 9 December 2012).

Jone, E. and Wessely, S. (2005) *Shell Shock to PTSD: Military Psychology from 1900 to the Gulf War*, London: Psychology Press.

Jones, L. (2004) *Then They Started Shooting: Growing Up in Wartime Bosnia*, Cambridge, MA: Harvard University Press.

Kaminer, D., Stein, D., Mbanga, I. and Zungu-Dirway, N. (2001) 'The Truth and Reconciliation Commission in South Africa: Relation to Psychiatric Status and Forgiveness among Survivors of Human Rights Abuses', *British Journal of Psychiatry*, 178: 373–77.

Kerr, R. and Mobekk, E. (2007) *Peace and Justice. Seeking Accountability After War*, Cambridge: Polity Press.

Kritz, N. (1995) *Transitional Justice. How Emerging Democracies Reckon with Former Regimes*, Washington, DC: United States Institute for Peace.

LaCapra, D. (1999), 'Trauma, Absence, Loss', *Critical Inquiry*, 25: 696–727.

Laplanche, J. (1999) *Essays on Otherness*, New York, NY: Routledge.

Laplanche, J. and Pontalis, J.B. (1973) *The Language of Psycho – Analysis*, London: W.W. Norton.

Leebaw, B. (2008) 'The Irreconcilable Goals of Transitional Justice', *Human Rights Quarterly*, 30 (1): 95–118.

Luckhurst, R. (2008) *The Trauma Question*, London: Routledge.

Médecins Sans Frontières (2000) 'High Levels of Mental Trauma Found in Sierra Leone'. Available at: <http://www.doctorswithoutborders.org/press/release.cfm?id=527> (accessed 9 December 2012).

——(2004) 'The Trauma of Ongoing War in Chechnya'. Available at: <http://www.doctorswithoutborders.org/search.cfm?cx=010337337539629337583%3A-83fbtvg-f0&cof=FOR ID%3A11&q=trauma&sa.x=0&say=0&sa=Go> (accessed 9 December 2012).

——(2012a) 'Mental Health'. Available at: <http://www.doctorswithoutborders.org/news/issue.cfm?id=2399&cat=issue-page> (accessed 9 December 2012).

——(2012b) 'Focusing on People, Not Politics: Providing Trauma Care in the Palestinian Territories'. Available at: <http://www.doctorswithoutborders.org/news/article.cfm?id=60 48&cat=voice-from-the-field> (accessed 9 December 2012).

Medical Relief International (2012) 'Orphan and Widow Programs'. Available at: <http:// medicalri.org/where-we-go/tanzania/item/29-widow-and-orphan-program.html> (accessed 9 December 2012).

Mendeloff, D. (2009) 'Trauma and Vengeance: Assessing the Psychological and Emotional Effects of Post-Conflict Justice', *Human Rights Quarterly*, 31 (3): 592–623.

Micale, M. and Lerner, P. 2001 'Trauma, Psychiatry, and History', in Micale, M. and Lerner, P. (eds) *Traumatic Pasts: History, Psychiatry, and Trauma in the Modern Age*, Cambridge: Cambridge University Press.

Miller, K. and Rasmussen, A. 2010 'War Exposure, Daily Stressors, and Mental Health in Conflict and Post-Conflict Settings', *Social Science and Medicine*, 70: 7–16.

Minow, M. (1999) *Between Vengeance and Forgiveness. Facing History and Genocide after Mass Violence*, Boston, MA: Beacon Press.

Moon, C. (2009) 'Healing Past Violence: Traumatic Assumptions and Therapeutic Interventions in War and Reconciliation', *Journal of Human Rights*, 8 (1): 71–91.

O'Connell, J. (2005) 'Gambling with Psyche: Does Prosecuting Human Rights Violators Console Their Victims?', *Harvard International Law Journal*, 46 (1): 295–345.

Pavlich, G. (2005) *Governing Paradoxes of Restorative Justice*, London: GlassHouse Press.

Pham, H., Weinstein, H. and Longman, T. (2004) 'Trauma and PTSD Symptoms in Rwanda. Implications for Attitudes Towards Justice and Reconciliation', *Journal of the American Medical Association*, 292 (5): 602–12

Pham, N., Vinck, P. and Weinstein, H. (2010) 'Sense of Cohesion and its Association with Exposure to Traumatic Events, Post-Traumatic Stress Disorder, and Depression in Eastern Democratic Republic of the Congo', *Journal of Traumatic Stress*, 23 (3): 313–21.

Prager, J. (2008) 'Healing from History. Psychoanalytic Considerations on Traumatic Pasts and Social Repair', *European Journal of Social Theory*, 11 (3): 405–20.

Ramadanovic, P. (2002) 'In the Future … : On Trauma and Literature', in Belau, L. and Ramadanovic, P. (eds) *Topologies of Trauma*, New York, NY: Other Press.

Roht-Arriaza, N. (2006) 'The New Landscape of Transitional Justice' in Roht-Arriaza, N. and Mariezcurrena, J. (eds) *Transitional Justice in the Twenty-first Century: Beyond Truth versus Justice*, Cambridge: Cambridge University Press.

Roth, M. (2012) *Memory, Trauma, and History*, New York, NY: Columbia University Press.

Rothfield, P. (2011) 'The Singular Case of Jean Améry' in Zolkos, M. (ed.) *On Jean Améry. Philosophy of Catastrophe*, Lanham, MD: Lexington Books.

Rousso, H. (2007) 'History of Memory, Policies of the Past: What For?', in Jarausch, K. and Lindenberger, T. (eds) *Conflicted Memories. Europeanizing Contemporary Histories*, New York, NY: Berghahn Books.

Santa Barbara, J. and MacQueen, G. (2004) 'Peace Through Health: An Opportunity to Join Forces', *The Lancet*, 358 (9288): 384–86.

Schwab, G. (2010) *Haunting Legacies: Violent Histories and Transgenerational Trauma*, New York, NY: Columbia University Press.

Summerfield, D. (1996) 'The Psychological Legacy of War and Atrocity', *Journal of Nervous and Mental Disease*, 184 (6): 375–77.

——(2001) 'The Invention of Post-Traumatic Stress Disorder and the Social Usefulness of a Psychiatric Category', *British Medical Journal*, 322: 95–98.

——(2002) 'Effects of War: Moral Knowledge, Revenge, Reconciliation, and Medicalised Concepts of Recovery', *British Medical Journal*, 325: 1105–7.

Weinstein, H. and Stover, E. (2004) 'Introduction: Conflict, Justice, and Reclamation', in Stover, E. and Weinstein, H. (eds) *My Neighbor, My Enemy: Justice and Community in the Aftermath of Mass Atrocity*, Cambridge: Cambridge University Press.

Chapter 9

Forgetting the embodied past

Body memory in transitional justice

Teresa Koloma Beck

Memory is the modus in which past events make themselves known in the present and, hence, it plays a crucial role in transitional justice processes. The latter addresses, *today*, violence experienced in the *past*, under the conditions of armed conflict or authoritarian rule, in order to facilitate a successful transition towards a more peaceful society. These processes thus act upon the relationship between the past and the present in a post-conflict society – not as the result of some political agenda, but because of the functional logic of memory itself: in the act of remembering, the dimensions of the past and the present are paralleled. Therefore, memory always establishes and (re-)negotiates the relationship between the two dimensions of then and now. From this perspective instruments and mechanisms of transitional justice can be conceived as conscious interventions into the memoryscape of a post-authoritarian or post-war society in an attempt to address injustices and abuses of the violent past.

Yet, although *memory* is a key dimension in the social processes associated with the notion of transitional justice, the understanding of the concept is usually not spelled out. Implicitly, research is founded on the acknowledgement of the mentioned intimacy of the past and the present in processes of remembering;[1] it is because '[r]emembrance is always now' (Steiner 1975), that memories of violence gain political relevance in a post conflict or post-authoritarian situation. Yet, beyond this basic conceptualisation, the understanding of memory in transitional justice thinking remains indistinct, echoing rather general ideas on the matter, which are dominant in Western thought. The most salient characteristic of such ideas is a representation of memory as a faculty of the mind, which neglects its attachment to the bodily aspects of human existence. In Plato's philosophy, for example, the dynamics of memory were compared to a signet ring stamp which is forced into a wax tablet: in the same way the former leaves an imprint on the latter, human experiences leave an imprint on the mind that can be recalled, thus evoking the past in the present (Plato 1997: § 191 c, d). Later, Augustine coined the idea of memory being a storage place in the mind when referring to the 'fields and vast palaces' where images of past experiences are kept (Augustine

2006: 195). Since then, metaphors of memory as a space in the mind for storage and later retrieval run through memory research in the humanities as well as the cognitive sciences[2] with the advent of the computer age further strengthening these analogies.

In the last quarter of the twentieth century, however, the constructivist turn in social sciences and the humanities stimulated a radical re-orientation of the field. Rediscovering the notion of collective memory (Halbwachs 1980, first published 1925), scholars took an interest in the social dimension of memory, more precisely its production *in* society as well as the impact *of* society on processes of remembering and forgetting on the individual level.[3] As a consequence, memory came to be conceptually de-reified. Today, most scholars agree that memory is socially constructed and therefore has to be studied in interpretative frameworks. Yet, these new theoretical approaches, too, continue to conceive memory as something located in minds and consciousnesses and then expressed and negotiated in speech and artefacts; attention only shifts from the single monadic consciousness to the interdependencies of consciousnesses in society.

In transitional justice thinking this understanding of memory is reflected in the emphasis put on the disclosure of cognitive memories about violent events in speech. Especially investigative transitional justice institutions, such as TRCs, commissions of inquiry or trials revolve around the articulation of individual memory images of war, violence and oppression. The well-known (and meanwhile much contested) catchphrase of the South African TRC 'revealing is healing',[4] for example, echoes the storage place metaphor. It suggests that the subject as well as society can be transformed by bringing the light of the public to the darkest corners of the storage room.

Yet, although conceptions of memory as a faculty of minds and consciousnesses continues to dominate in social and cognitive sciences as well as in the humanities, it did not remain unchallenged. Starting in the late nineteenth century, scholars in social theory and philosophy began to question the dichotomy between body and mind, inherited from Ancient philosophy. In doing so, the idea of memory being a uniquely mental capacity was placed under scrutiny. The French philosopher Henri Bergson was the first to propose a radical re-conceptualisation of the subject (Bergson 1903, 1911). He argued that the past is brought to the present not only by imagination, but also through the enactment of habitualised patterns of behaviour. In other words, memory is not only located in the mind, but also in the structures of the body.

Since then, the idea that a theory of memory should distinguish between imaginative or representational memory on the one hand and embodied memory on the other has been further developed and refined, most importantly in the works of the French philosopher and psychologist Maurice Merleau-Ponty (1962, 1976, 2009). In recent years, a number of contemporary scholars, such as the philosopher Edward S. Casey (1987), the sociologists Alois Hahn (2010) and Paul Connerton (1989, 2011) or the philosopher and physician Thomas Fuchs (2008a), have further advanced the knowledge in this field. In transitional justice thinking, however, these insights received but little attention. If at all, the bodily dimension of memory is brought up in analyses of the impact of trauma on transitional justice processes (see e.g. Zolkos, Chapter 8 in this volume). Yet, then, they remain limited to extremely painful memories instead of building on a more general understanding of body memory in transitions and transitional justice.

Against the background of this observation, this chapter explores and discusses the role of body memory in transitional justice. It draws on the distinction introduced above between an imaginative memory, on the one hand, and a repetitive, incorporated memory, on the other. The central question to be asked is: *How does the concept of body memory contribute to theorizing transitional justice?* It is argued that body memories are highly relevant in political transitions, as prolonged states of armed conflict or violent authoritarianism affect not only the sphere of thinking, but also the sphere of acting. They, hence, transform not only patterns of cognition and speech, but also the habitual structures of the body, which are the basis for everyday action. Drawing attention to the latter, the concept of body memory sheds new light on the challenges of dealing with memories of violence in a transitional situation, and it also stimulates questions about the objectives of transitional justice processes in and of themselves.

Based on phenomenological theories of memory and the living body, the first section of this chapter develops the distinction between representational forms of memory, on the one hand, and body memory, on the other. The second section then discusses the particularities of body memories acquired under violent rule, illustrated by accounts from Angola and Mozambique. Lastly, the third section explores the implications of this theoretical approach for theorising transitional justice. It is argued that theories of body memory suggest a re-evaluation of so far peripheral, contested or even rejected transitional justice processes, in particular with a view to civic or socioeconomic transitional justice, so-called indigenous transitional justice rituals as well as silence on past abuses. My theoretical discussion builds on extensive field research in Angola and Mozambique.[5]

Two forms of memory

So far, it has been argued that much of transitional justice thinking employs an implicit understanding of memory which reflects common assumptions on the issue. According to these assumptions, memory is a mental or mental-social phenomenon. The roots of this understanding can be found in the conceptual dichotomy between body and mind, which was introduced by Platonic thinking and has haunted Western thought since then. It is sustained and promoted by the cognitive and neurosciences, which emerged in the late nineteenth century and systematically relate processes of remembering to activity in the brain and the neurosystem (see e.g. Glees, 1988: 106–107).[6] Yet, parallel to the rise of cognitive sciences, an alternative research programme emerged, which was founded on the conviction that the exclusive focus on mental processes obscures the view for the attachment of memory to the bodily aspects of human existence. The French philosopher Henri Bergson was the first to spell out this critique.[7] Writing in the late nineteenth and early twentieth centuries, he was one of the protagonists of the so-called *Lebensphilosophie* (philosophy of life) which emerged in response to the rise of positivism and the related advances in the natural sciences. The aim of this school of thought was to re-conceptualise the processes of life beyond positivist notions of rationality. A-rational, dynamic and creative processes were, hence, at the heart of these writings.

It is within this context that Bergson discusses the problem of memory in his essay *Matière et Mémoire* (Bergson 1903). Based on a critical examination of then recent advances in psychology, he develops a concept of memory which goes beyond cognitive processes. He distinguishes between two interrelated but different forms of memory: *imaginative memory*, on the one hand, and *repetitive memory*, on the other. The concept of imaginative memory refers to imaginal representations of past events; it is, hence, similar to everyday understandings of the notion. The concept of repetitive memory, by contrast, refers to memory that is incorporated, inscribed into the habitual structures of the body by repeated experiences of the same type (Bergson 1903: 75–81). Although being different, the two forms of memory are not independent from each other; instead they are mutually constitutive: experiences lead to memories of the imaginative type, those imaginative memories, however, might introduce changes in the patterns of habitual behaviour and transform repetitive memory (Bergson 1903: 78).

Bergson's ideas did not stall the progress of mainstream neuroscience, but they became influential in the formation of a particular transdisciplinary school of thought, which set out to theorise the body beyond natural scientific understandings in the perspective of the humanities: the so-called *phenomenology of the body*. Seminal in this regard were the works of the French philosopher and psychologist Maurice Merleau-Ponty, who developed the notion of the 'living body' (*le corps propre* in the French original, going back to Heidegger's German notion of the *Leib*)[8] as a philosophical counter-concept to purely physiological understandings of the body. In doing so, he took up Bergson's ideas about habits and habit formation. While Bergson had 'discovered' the body almost accidentally in his philosophical inquiries into the a-rational and spontaneous aspects of human life, Merleau-Ponty set out to establish the philosophical relevance of the living body itself as the mediating interface between the subject and the world. Habits play an important role in this context, as they facilitate the exercise of routinised activities in the everyday world. Merleau-Ponty emphasises the integrated character of habitual structures: acting habitually means to respond to a particular condition in the environment not with a sequence of isolated movements, but with a particular form of action. They are, hence, knowledge incorporated in the body which silently facilitates everyday life activities (Merleau-Ponty 1976: 176–82).

Although Merleau-Ponty was primarily interested in the role played by habitual structures in shaping the relation between the subject and the world, he was already aware of the social implications of habitualised forms of behaviour. As habits emerge and are sustained by repetition, they are crucial in the production and reproduction of social order on an everyday level (Merleau-Ponty 2009: 53). Yet, while Merleau-Ponty's works provide an elaborated theory for what Bergson had preliminarily called repetitive memory or habits, it fails to address the problem of (body) memory as such. Where Bergson's concept of memory lacks a theory of the body, Merleau-Ponty's concept of the living body is myopic for the problem of memory.

In the late twentieth century, however, with the renewed theoretical interest in the topic of memory, some scholars attempted a synthesis of the two approaches. Particularly interesting with a view to the problem of postwar or post-authoritarian transitions are approaches, which take Bergson's and Merleau-Ponty's concepts as starting points for considerations on *body memory* in a more general perspective, for example the works of the US-American philosopher Edward S. Casey (Casey 1987) or the German philosopher and psychiatrist Thomas Fuchs (Fuchs 2008b). These scholars take up the concept of habits as central to Bergson's as well as Merleau-Ponty's work, but draw attention to the fact that the latter is but one aspect of body memory (*Leibgedächtnis* in German) in a larger sense. Broadening the perspective of the early philosophers of the lived body, Casey defines body memory as referring to all processes by which we 'remember in and by and through the body' (Casey 1987: 147). It is the memory intrinsic to the body. Thus, body memory is different from memory *of* the body: while the latter refers to recollections of our body – how it moved, how it felt – during an experience in the past, the former refers to the impact of this experience on the structures of the body itself (Casey 1987. 147).

The privileged conceptual position of habitual memory in the early theories stems from the importance of habitual structures in everyday life. Casey as well as Fuchs point out that habitual memory is the result of repetition. The latter introduces the habitualisation or physiognomisation of behaviour, which facilitates automatised action. Habitual, or in Fuchs' wording *implicit*, memory permits to shift attention from the co-ordination of the body movements necessary to perform a particular action to the objectives of this very action. To illustrate the dynamics of implicit memory, Fuchs uses the example of playing a piece of piano music: it is only when the sequence of movements necessary to play the piece *correctly* has become habitualised through repetition that the musician becomes free to concentrate on playing the piece *beautifully* (Fuchs 2008a: 40). In a broader sense, habitual memory mediates the experience of continuity and, hence, identity, as the same sequences of action are automatically enacted in changing situations. It liberates the individual from the necessity of continuous re-orientation and is therefore crucial for the experience of normality in everyday life (Casey 1987: 151–52; Fuchs 2008a: 39–42).

Yet, despite this importance of habitual structures in everyday activities, habitual body memories are but one form of remembering 'in and by and through the body', to take up Casey's definition once more. Another form are those of traumatic character. Different from habitual body memories which (re-)create the living body as a co-ordinated whole, traumatic memories are associated with the fragmentation of previously integrated structures (Casey 1987: 154–57). While habitual body memory is the past embodied in routinised behaviour, traumatic body memory is the past expressed in an incapacity for 'normal' action – be that in a particular given situation or in general (cf. Casey 1987: 155; Fuchs, 2008a: 60).

Discussing the particularities of body memory in its different manifestations,[9] Casey and Fuchs attempt to analytically distinguish them from representational forms of memory in a broader perspective. The differences are particularly pronounced considering time and identity: the story of one's own life is remembered in representational memory. In other words, representational memory is autobiographic and, hence, constitutive for individual identity. Body memory, by contrast, tends to 'forget' the particular life situations from which it once emerged; in the case of habitual body memory, the emancipation from these origins is even a condition for the spontaneous enactment of a habit. While representational memory is personal and conscious, habitual memory is located at the periphery of the consciousness, it is, in the words of Casey, 'marginal' with regard to our most pressing concerns (Casey 1987: 163–65). Yet, exactly because of this, body memory gains its importance in everyday life: the condition of marginality reverses the logic of time at work in representational memory. The latter brings the past into the present mind; it is thus a movement directed from the present into the past. Body memory, by contrast, embodies a past and thus determines our capacities to turn towards the future; it is, hence, a movement from a past-informed present into the future (Fuchs 2008a: 38).

Yet, as Bergson before them, the contemporary theorists also emphasise the interdependencies between the two forms: sensory perceptions, bodily movements or body-spatial experiences can evoke or liberate memories. Being exposed to a particular sound or smell, performing a certain sequence of movements, or finding yourself in a particular place can bring back memories long forgotten – as in Proust's famous story of the *petites madeleines*, where the sight, smell and taste of these pastries recall the universe of an entire childhood (Fuchs 2008a: 52). From a slightly different theoretical perspective, Casey argues that without body memory there would be no memory at all, as all experience is necessarily bound to the body (Casey 1987: 172–80).

Theories of body memory thus disclose that the past is not only remembered in images or narratives, but also em*bodied*. They draw attention to the fact that past experiences do not only affect the structures of cognition and speech, but also the structures of the living body. Summarising these differences, Fuchs writes: 'We could say that as subjects we *have* our past, while in our bodily existence we *are* our past' (Fuchs 2008a: 43, original emphasis, my translation).

Body memories of violent rule

Yet, how can theories, which distinguish between representational and body memory contribute to a better understanding of transitional justice processes? Most importantly, the distinction introduced in the preceding section leads us to reconsider how the past comes into play in transitional situations. It draws attention to the fact that legacies of armed conflict and violent authoritarian rule are not only represented at the level of cognition and speech, but also incorporated into the structures of the living body and enacted in everyday behaviour. Researching the impact of body memory on post-conflict or post-authoritarian societies, thus, means to look for continuities in the structures of the living bodies, especially in habitual behaviour. It means to identify the contexts in which habits and other body structures, which have been formed in response to armed conflict or violent State oppression, persist in the aftermath of violence; or, more plainly, how habitual everyday life practices of the pre-transitional period are enacted and performed in the new situation.

This implies, however, that we have to understand how body memory is affected by violent conflict or authoritarian rule in the first place; we have to grasp how habits change and how the integrity of the living body is challenged under such conditions. These effects can be manifold, depending on the structure of the conflict, on the strategies employed by the parties to it as well as on the structure of society in general: an intrastate war fought by militias and paramilitary groups with small arms in rural areas inhabited by subsistence farmers has a different impact on habitual everyday life behaviour than an authoritarian regime trying to repress a student opposition movement in urban centres. There is, however, a common trait to all contexts addressed in transitional justice: the importance of experiences of violence. Although wars and violent State oppression can introduce a variety of hardships, which require changes in habitual behaviour and challenge the integrity of the body (e.g. the destruction of infrastructures, hunger and diseases), the necessity to live with the systematic exercise of violence marks all these contexts.

Under the conditions of persistent armed conflict or violent State oppression, habitual behaviour on the individual as well as the collective level changes to cope with experience of violence. In addition, traumatic body memories might emerge from exposure to physical violence, shaking the structures of the living body and distorting orientation in everyday life. In a process of adaption, habitual memories are formed, which facilitate orientation and action in the face of a prevalence of violence in the lifeworld. Yet, these adaptive processes differ, depending on how the respective actors relate to violence itself (Koloma Beck 2011). The difference between combatants and non-combatants is crucial in this regard: armies and police forces as well as non-State armed groups are organisations which deliberately attempt to transform their combatants' living bodies so as to create a readiness for and expertise in *exercising* violence as well as resilience to being exposed to it. Among the so-called civilian population, by contrast, habitual behaviour changes with the objective to maintain necessary and accustomed everyday life activities while being exposed to the risk to *suffer* violence. In the first case, body memory is transformed around the deliberate habitualisation of the exercise of violence. In the second, body memory adapts so as to secure the continuation of everyday life and subsistence activities. In both cases, these changes introduce a *normalisation* of armed conflict or violent oppression, in the sense of a practical habituation to these conditions. The war situation comes to be 'embodied' in the people – combatants and non-combatants alike (Koloma Beck 2012). Sometimes, the expressions 'culture of war' or 'culture of violence' are used to refer to such contexts (see e.g. Waldmann 2007) In the following, I illustrate these dynamics with some examples from Angola and Mozambique.

During field research in Angola three years after the war, I could still observe how people had rearranged the spatial and temporal patterns of everyday activities, such as cultivating fields or trading in the market, so as to sidestep the actions of armed groups. A young man whom I interviewed in the town of Huambo, for example, told me how his mother went to the market always twice a day: first, in the morning to buy food for lunch, and then once more in the afternoon to buy food for dinner. Once, he had asked her, why she did not buy the food for both lunch and dinner in one go. Her answer was that she had acquired this habit of going twice a day at the heights of the war during the siege of the city. In this prolonged period of extreme privation and insecurity, people could not or would not think in the morning about the evening, which one might not even live to see. At this time, she said, people only thought from one meal to the next. Life revolved around one question: 'What are we going to eat?' One went to bed hungry and got up hungry, not knowing how to fill the mouth today. During this time, no thought was spent on *later*, there was not even a sense of time, there was only the necessity to eat. She conceded that, when the war was over, she had continued – without ever thinking about it – to act the way she had become accustomed to during the times of need and insecurity.

An example pointing in a similar direction is presented by Victor Igreja in a study on post-war Mozambique. He describes how one morning an entire village was jolted out of sleep, panicked and collectively flew from the settlement after they had heard what they believed to be shots (Igreja 2012: 408). Although people knew – on a cognitive level – that the war had been over for a while, they responded to the all too familiar sound with a behavioural pattern of survival which their living bodies had acquired during the war: taking a hasty flight. Both examples illustrate how the persistent threat of indiscriminate violence inscribed itself into the structures of the living body; how the condition of war changed patterns of behaviour in everyday life and consequently transformed habitual body memory. Most importantly, however, they also show how these memories outlived the end of the war itself.

In Angola, I could also observe how people had changed everyday practices not only in response to indiscriminate violence, but also to avoid more personalised or discriminate threats. During the conflict, both warring parties had developed measures to sanction sympathisers or supporters of the respective opponent – be they proven or only suspected. In response to this situation, people tried to refrain from any action that would let them appear as being 'one of the enemies'. In a village at the border of a rebel-controlled area, for example, people stopped to publicly stand together in groups for fear that the observing armies might interpret the gathering as a conspiracy against them. In the end, the villagers did not only abandon the custom of village councils, but habitualised the avoidance of any prolonged interaction with others in public more generally – unless the purpose of this interaction was obvious as in collective farming. Modifications in speech were another response to this situation: people did no longer speak frankly as they feared that whatever was said might be used to denunciate them. As a result, a highly encoded language emerged in which nothing was called by its proper name.

Transformations in habitual structures, such as the ones just described, initially emerge as situational responses to particular recurring problems. Habitual body memory transforms as the patterns of everyday behaviour adapt to the situation of the war. Yet, the structures of the body are not independent from the structures of the mind. Therefore, changes in the habitual practices of everyday life are very likely to transform how people think about the world and how they perceive it. For that reason, the transformation of body memory affects social structures and institutions and might alter the value system and the moral order of a society.

The end of violent rule does not by itself reverse these adaptive processes; instead, the habitual structures persist well into the post-conflict or post-authoritarian situation. Some of the typical problems in transitional contexts are frequently indicators for such a persistence, especially the endemisation of violence, the dominance of short-term perspectives or the lack of generalised trust: the spread of non-militant forms of violence (e.g. domestic or criminal violence), which is particularly common in post-war societies, is rooted in the habitualisation of the exercise of violence, especially (but not uniquely) among combatants. The dominance of short-term perspectives in everyday life activities, which frequently risks jeopardising efforts for sustainable post-war development, is the result of the adaptation of everyday life practices to the rhythm of violence. In the same sense, the widespread distrust, which characterises post-war and post-authoritarian societies alike, can be understood as a habit formed under the conditions of war or State oppression, when being denounced as a supporter of the enemy would result in severe if not lethal sanctions. Each of these exemplary problems is, hence, related to body memories of violent rule.

Different from representational forms of memory, which *evoke* the past, body memories *enact* it in the present. This implies that in transitional periods the past persists in so far as the experiences of armed conflict or State oppression have come to be inscribed into the structures of the living bodies. It persists in the habits acquired under the conditions of violence and oppression as well as in the traumatic body memories of the pre-transition period.

Body memory in transitional justice

In the introduction, it was argued that dealing with the past in transitional justice means first and foremost to deal with representational memories of violent events in an aim to redress these abuses and to render justice. The discussion developed in the preceding sections, however, suggests that prolonged periods of violent rule produce injustices or abuses beyond particular outstanding events. Beside the sometimes spectacular crimes, there are uncounted minor but repeated occurrences, which force people to adapt their everyday lives and which, thus, create habitual body memories of war and oppression. Different from the injustices dealt with in trials or commissions, these abuses are not eventive but procedural in their character.[10] As a consequence, they cannot straightforwardly be integrated into classical frameworks of transitional justice. The central problem is that embodied memories of violence cannot easily be expressed in speech. Different from representational memories, they cannot be 'dealt with' in techniques of disclosure and verbal expression or in social processes of re-interpretation. Without being linked to particular marking events, they cannot be brought into a narrative structure, which is the condition for the articulation of abuses in truth commissions or trials (see Buckley-Zistel, Chapter 7 in this volume). In the remainder of this section, I discuss in more detail the implications of these observations, re-considering transitional justice mechanisms in the light of the memory theories presented above.

Discursive versus experiential approaches to transitional justice

Embodied memories of war or State oppression play an important role in transition processes, as their persistence risks jeopardising reconciliation and the construction of peace. Yet, as they are inscribed into the structures of the living body and enacted in everyday life, they cannot be 'forgotten', suppressed or re-interpreted. Being the result of (repeated) experiences, body memories of violent rule can only be transformed by (repeated) experiences of a different kind. Taking body memory into account thus suggests a distinction between discursive transitional justice mechanisms or institutions, on the one hand, and transitional justice processes, which deal with and/or act on everyday experiences, on the other. Body memories resonate in particular with the latter. More precisely, they are addressed by transitional justice processes, which suspend or even eliminate the necessity to enact habitual structures acquired during the period of violence. Looking at the current repertory of transitional justice policies, two types of mechanism stand out in this regard: first, policies aiming at civic or socioeconomic justice; and, second, so-called indigenous forms of transitional justice.

At the centre of initiatives for civic or socioeconomic transitional justice are ideas of political, social and economic inclusion, the possibility of effective participation, and a just distribution of the wealth (see Laplante, Chapter 3 in this volume). Different from the performative logic of trials or truth commissions, these initiatives act upon the structures of everyday life. Their aim is not to 'address' particular injustices of the past, but to contribute to the creation of a just post-war or post-authoritarian society. Typically, arguments in favour of the inclusion of such measures into the repertory of transitional justice policies have been based on normative claims (see e.g. Miller 2008; Pasipanodya 2008). Against the background of the theoretical discussion in the preceding sections, however, a different argument could be made: in prolonged periods of violent conflict or State oppression, people learned to practically 'normalise' emergencies (cf. Koloma Beck 2012). They adapted not only to the recurrence of violence, but also to deprivation and marginalisation. If in the transitional period these emergency features persist, the corresponding body memories persist as well. Where poverty is widespread or discrimination lasts, habitual structures formed during the period of violence continue to be needed or at least useful in the transitional situation. Consequently, the possibilities of transforming the body memories of violent rule are limited, which makes relapses into violence easier and more likely. This observation is particularly relevant when transitional justice processes are implemented in countries with severe socioeconomic problems (Buckley-Zistel et al 2013).

Another mechanism, which acts upon everyday experiences, are so-called indigenous transitional justice institutions. Similar to civic and socio-economic transitional justice, the latter have received growing attention in recent years. With a focus on post-conflict societies mostly in Africa, scholars discussed cleansing rituals, spirit exorcism, or funerals as frequent practices with a significant impact on the individual as well as the community level (see e.g. Boia Junior 1988; Englund 1998; Nordstrom 1998; Granjo 2006; Baines 2010; Igreja et al 2010; Meier 2011; Igreja 2012): for the individual, these rituals may provide a form for dealing with (potentially) traumatising experiences and thus strengthen resilience and mental health. On the community level, they can facilitate the re-integration of returnees. Some scholars and practitioners have praised such indigenous forms for their participatory character, their inclusiveness and their strong focus on the restoration of relationships. It has been argued that these approaches produce more sustainable results because, different from imported 'Western' institutions, they are supported by pre-existing cultural and social structures (for a critical discussion, see MacGinty 2008; see also Boege 2006).

Theories of body memory, however, suggest an entirely different argument in favour of such 'indigenous' institutions – at least for the kinds of ritualistic practice described above: in all cited cases the body is at the centre of the ritual and is supposed to be freed from the burden of the past. They are designed to create transformative experiences so as to overcome body memories of violent conflict: cleansing rituals are meant to wash a person of all evil and to make her or him symbolically born anew. Exorcism rituals attempt to free body and soul from the vengeful spirits of those who have died during the war. Mourning ceremonies and funerals bring the dead to final peace. Different from discursive transitional justice institutions, which rely on the communication of representational memories in speech, transformative rituals are founded upon the idea that the past is immediately present in the here and now. It is *embodied* in the people, it expresses itself through them in everyday life, and hence directly influences the course of current affairs (see also Igreja 2012). The representations of temporality underlying these transformative rituals, thus, correspond to the structures of temporality in the living body, which are characterised by a concurrence of the past and the present. Transformative rituals build on this idea; they aim to free the living body from the distressing presence of the violent past so that the person can move on. While discursive transitional justice institutions aim to bring the past to rest in the present, transformative rituals in their aim to renew the person are unambiguously oriented towards the future.

The virtue of silence

Habitual body memories of war and oppression can transform when the patterns of action and behaviour they are associated with lose their relevance in everyday life. This perspective also suggests a re-evaluation of silence in transitional situations. Dominant transitional justice discourses continue to be critical about the issue. For long, the imperative to explicitly address the past in order to leave it behind has served as a tacit foundation of research and practice. Nevertheless, in recent years, the topics of silence and forgetting gained in importance, especially in critical discussions of transitional justice. Scholars set out to empirically as well as conceptually demonstrate their possible productivity (Buckley-Zistel 2006; Eastmond and Selimovic 2012). Theories of body memory might orient further empirical research to this field.

As people refrain from bringing up the violent past as an issue in day-to-day encounters and act *as if* they had forgotten about it, new patterns of everyday behaviour can emerge or old ones be restored. By facilitating the transformation of habitual body memory, silence, hence, might facilitate the emergence of peaceful everyday life in a transitional situation. With regard to these dynamics, the German philosopher Klaus-Michael Kodalle conceives 'lived normality' as a key mechanism of post-conflict reconciliation. Instead of attempting to explicitly defuse and reconcile the antagonisms which had fuelled the violent conflict, peacefully normal everyday life can become an *incognito of forgiveness* (Kodalle 1994: 14), a pardon which is not pronounced in speech, but expressed through mutual respect and a kind of performative oblivion in everyday interaction. Writing against the background of contemporary European history, Kodalle highlights that especially in post-war situations the return to 'normal' everyday life can never be taken for granted, but should already be understood as an achievement which might pave the way for a consolidation of peace in a mid- or long-term perspective (Kodalle 1994: 14). In the same vein, Eastmond and Selimovic, referring to the case of Bosnia-Herzegovina, write about a 'silence of civility', which tacitly expresses understanding and empathy and is all but detrimental to the process of reconciliation (Eastmond and Selimovic 2012). In a study of Rwanda, Buckley-Zistel speaks of 'chosen amnesia' as the basis for interethnic coexistence in the aftermath of the genocide (Buckley-Zistel 2006). Re-framing these observations in the language of phenomenological memory theory, one might argue that peaceful normal life suspends the necessity to enact habits or other body structures acquired in the period of violence and creates experiences which transform these body memories. This way 'lived normality' can contribute decisively to reconciliation, lowering the likeliness of an easy relapse into violence.

All this, however, only holds in so far as the silence about a violent past is not part of a repressive political project. As Paul Connerton pointed out, there are different types of forgetting in post-conflict societies, some associated with repression, shame and humiliation, and others associated with the restoration of relationships and reconciliation (Connerton 2008). In the latter case, transitional justice initiatives, in particular discursive transitional justice institutions, are likely to disturb these processes as they continuously summon up the past.[11] Drawing attention to the impact of silence on habitual behaviour in everyday life, theories of body memory provide a lens through which to study the problem empirically. In this perspective, the central question is whether silence about the violent past actually contributes to a 'normalisation' of interactions in everyday life. In a broader sense, theories of body memory might help to more clearly distinguish empirical from normative issues in this sensitive area of research and practice.[12]

Conclusion: questioning the normative foundations of transitional justice

Theories of memory, which distinguish between representational and embodied forms, draw attention to the fact that the memoryscapes, into which transitional justice processes intervene, are not only imagined, but also lived in. The memories of violence, around which transitional justice revolves, are located not only in the mind, but they are inscribed as well into the structures of the living body. Due to the particular time structures of body memory (enacting the past in the present), they cannot be undone with the signature of a peace accord or the deposition of an authoritarian regime, but continue to orient behaviour and facilitate action in the transitional situation. Dealing with the past as an incorporated reality means to facilitate the transformation of these body memories. Introducing the distinction between discursive and experiential forms of transitional justice, this chapter has shown how peripheral, contested, or even rejected sub-areas of transitional justice (civic and socioeconomic transitional justice, transformative rituals as well as silence) gain in importance, once body memory is taken into account.

This discussion, however, has pretended that the lack of awareness for the remembering body in transitional justice would be due to a lack of knowledge in the field. If this would be the case, transitional justice research and practice could be 'improved' by further studies and the diffusion of the knowledge produced to practitioners. From a more political perspective, however, the absence of body memory from transitional justice thinking and the apprehensiveness in the field to include experiential transitional justice mechanisms (see e.g. Hansen, Chapter 5 in this volume), prompts a more radical interrogation about the actual objectives of transitional justice processes. The lack-of-knowledge perspective is founded upon the assumption that the transformative engagement with memories of war and violence would be an objective of transitional justice processes. The discursive intimacy between transitional justice and reconciliation seems to support such a view. Yet, some scholars have proposed an alternative reading of transitional justice, at the heart of which is not the notion of reconciliation but that of power (see e.g. Buckley-Zistel, Chapter 7, and Subotic, Chapter 6 in this volume). In this perspective, transitional justice is not an instrument of individual healing and social repair, but part and parcel of the political struggles over the discursive and material set-up of the post-transitional State. In this context, the exigencies of (re-)creating the nation prime over those of building peace. Discursive measures of transitional justice can serve these political goals because in public debates about guilt, accountability and victimhood, the value system of the transitional society as well as the future status of its former elites is re-negotiated. Experiential transitional justice measures, by contrast, are usually less public and, to be successful, have to function rather noiselessly. In this sense, they cannot be politically exploited, as they lack the feature of discursiveness. What follows, for transitional justice research and practice, from the discussion of body memory developed in this chapter, hence, is contingent upon the understanding of transitional justice itself and the objectives associated to it.

Notes

1 This intimate relationship between the past and the present has been first discussed in philosophical inquiries into the dynamics of psychoanalysis. See for example Ricœur 1965 and Lacan 1966.

2 For an overview of the development of memory metaphors, see Roediger 1980. For classical positions, see also Hume 1962 and Locke 1975.

3 An important contribution was, for example, Aleida Assmann's concept of cultural memory (Assmann 1999).

4 For a critical discussion of this formula, see for example Hamber 2009 or Fletcher and Weinstein 2002.

5 In 2005/06, I spent seven months in Angola in the course of the collaborative research project 'Micropolitics of Armed Groups' at Humboldt University Berlin, funded by the Volkswagen Foundation. In 2010, I conducted five months of field research in Mozambique as part of the research project 'The Politics of Building Peace' at Philipps University Marburg, which was funded by the German Research Foundation.

6 Historically, the development of brain research is related to the rise of positivism as the new paradigm of scientific research in the mid-nineteenth century. In this context, the 'discovery' of the brain is of major importance: being conceived as the organ whose function is to orient and coordinate human behaviour, it serves to replace the hitherto powerful and functionally equivalent concept of the soul (cf. Zimmer 2004).

7 A more recent challenge to the concept of memory being exclusively a brain or neuronal activity comes from advances in genetics. In particular, epigenetics, which researches the impact of environmental stimuli on the hereditary information, has demonstrated the plasticity and the associated memory qualities of the genome (Bird 2002; Powledge 2009).

8 The concept 'Leib' was introduced to conceive the body not in a physiological perspective, but as it is experienced by the subject in the interplay between organic functions and the consciousness (e.g. Husserl 1970: 217).

9 Casey introduces *erotic memory* as a third sub-type of body memory. Yet, as this plays no role for the question at hand, it is omitted from the present discussion (Casey 1987: 157–62).

10 Legal thinking is not unfamiliar with violations of legally protected rights through a process rather than through distinct events. Today, for example, criminal law in many countries considers child neglect as a punishable crime. See for example Myers 2006.

11 For an empirical discussion of these dynamics, see Buckley-Zistel's case study on the introduction of Gacaca tribunals in Rwanda (Buckley-Zistel 2005).

12 A researcher might, for example, empirically observe the emergence of restorative silence and still find it normatively problematic.

Bibliography

Assmann, A. (1999) *Erinnerungsräume. Formen und Wandlungen des kulturellen Gedächtnisses*, München: Beck.

Augustine (2006) *Confessions*, ed. M.P. Foley, Indianapolis, IN: Hackett.

Baines, E. (2010) 'Spirits and Social Reconstruction After Mass Violence. Rethinking Transitional Justice', *African Affairs*, 109: 409–30.

Bergson, H. (1903) *Matière et Mémoire. Essai sur la Relation du Corps à l'Esprit*, Paris: Félix Alcan.

——(1911) *Matter and Memory*, London: George Allen & Unwin.

Bird, A. (2002) 'DNA Methylation Patterns and Epigenetic Memory', *Genes & Development Genes & Development*, 16: 6–21.

Boege, V. (2006) *Traditional Approaches to Conflict Transformation. Potentials and Limits*, Berlin: Berghof Research.

Boia Junior, E. (1998), 'Die Geister können Schmerzen lindern. Traditionelle Riten in der Therapiearbeit mit ehemaligen Kindersoldaten in Mosambik', *Der Überblick*, 4: 52–57.

Buckley-Zistel, S. (2005), '"Die Wahrheit heilt"? Gacaca-Tribunale und Friedenskonsolidierung in Ruanda', *Friedens-Warte*, 80: 113–29.

——(2006) 'Remembering to Forget. Chosen Amnesia as a Strategy for Local Coexistence in Post-Genocide Rwanda', *Africa*, 76: 131–50.

Buckley-Zistel, S., Koloma Beck, T., Mieth, F., Viebach, J. (2013) 'Redressing Violence in Africa', in Arrigo, B. and Bersot, H. (eds) *The Routledge Handbook of International Crime and Justice Studies*, London: Routledge.

Casey, E.S. (1987) *Remembering. A Phenomenological Study*, Bloomington, IN: Indiana University Press.

Connerton, P. (1989) *How Societies Remember*, Cambridge and New York, NY: Cambridge University Press.

——(2008) 'Seven Types of Forgetting', *Memory Studies*, 1: 59–71.

——(2011) *The Spirit of Mourning. History, Memory and the Body*, Cambridge. Cambridge University Press

Eastmond, M. and Selimovic, J.M. (2012) 'Silence As Possibility in Postwar Everyday Life', *International Journal of Transitional Justice*, 6: 502–24.

Englund, H. (1998) 'Death, Trauma and Ritual. Mozambican Refugees in Malawi', *Social Science & Medicine*, 46: 1165–74.

Fletcher, L.E. and Weinstein, H. (2002) 'Violence and Social Repair: Rethinking the Contribution of Justice to Reconciliation', *Human Rights Quarterly*, 24 (3): 573–639.

Fuchs, T. (2008a), 'Das Gedächtnis des Leibes', in Fuchs, T. (ed.) *Leib und Lebenswelt. Neue psychiatrische Essays*, Kusterdingen: Graue Edition.

——(2008b) *Leib und Lebenswelt. Neue psychiatrische Essays*, Kusterdingen: Graue Edition.

Glees, P. (1988) *The human brain*, Cambridge and New York, NY: Cambridge University Press.

Granjo, P. (2006) 'Back home. Post-War Cleansing Rituals in Mozambique', in Nicolini, B. (ed.) *Studies in Witchcraft, Magic, War and Peace in Africa*, Lewiston, NY: Edwin Mellen Press.

Hahn, A. (2010) *Körper und Gedächtnis*, Wiesbaden: VS Verlag.

Hume, D. (1962) *A Treatise of Human Nature*, ed. D.G.C. Macnabb, London: Collins/Fontana.

Igreja, V. (2012) 'Multiple temporalities in indigenous justice and healing practices in Mozambique', *International Journal of Transitional Justice*, 6: 404–22.

Igreja, V., Dias-Lambranca, B., Hershey, D. A. and Racin, L. (2010) 'The Epidemiology of Spirit Possession in the Aftermath of Mass Political Violence in Mozambique', *Social Science & Medicine*, 71: 592–99.

Halbwachs, M. (1980) *The Collective Memory*, New York, NY: Harper & Row.

Hamber, B. (2009) *Transforming Societies after Political Violence. Truth, Reconciliation, and Mental Health*, Dordrecht and New York, NY: Springer.

Husserl, E. (1970) *The Crisis of European Sciences and Transcendental Phenomenology. An Introduction to Phenomenological Philosophy*, trans. D. Carr, Evanston, IL: Northwestern University Press.

Kodalle, K.-M. (1994) *Verzeihung nach Wendezeiten. Über Unnachsichtigkeit und misslingende Selbstentschuldung. Antrittsvorlesung an der Friedrich-Schiller-Universität Jena am 2. Juni 1994*, Erlangen: Palm und Enke.

Koloma Beck, T. (2011) 'The Eye of the Beholder. Violence as a Social Process', *International Journal of Conflict and Violence*, 5: 346–56.

——(2012) *The Normality of Civil War. Armed Groups and Everyday Life in Angola*, Frankfurt/Main and New York, NY: Campus.

Lacan, J. (1966) *Ecrits*, Paris: Seuil.

Locke, J. (1975) *An Essay Concerning Human Understanding*, ed. P. H. Nidditch, Oxford: Clarendon Press.

MacGinty, R. (2008) 'Indigenous Peace-Making Versus the Liberal Peace', *Cooperation and Conflict*, 43: 139–63.

Meier, B. (2011), 'Mato Oput. Karriere eine Rituals zur sozialen Rekonstruktion in Norduganda', in Buckley-Zistel, S. and Carter, T. (eds) *Nach Krieg, Gewalt und Repression. Vom schwierigen Umgang mit der Vergangenheit*, Baden-Baden: Nomos.

Merleau-Ponty, M. (1962) *Phenomenology of Perception*, London: Routledge & Kegan Paul.

——(1976) *Phénoménologie de la Perception*, Paris: Gallimard.

——(2009) *La Structure du Comportement*, Paris: PUF.

Miller, Z. (2008) 'Effects of Invisibility: In Search of the "Economic" in Transitional Justice', *International Journal of Transitional Justice*, 2 (3): 266–91.

Myers, J.E.B. (2006) *Child Protection in America. Past, Present, and Future*, New York, NY, and Oxford: Oxford University Press.

Nordstrom, C. (1998) 'Terror Warfare and the Medicine of Peace', *Medical Anthropology Quarterly*, 12: 103–21.

Pasipanodya, T. (2008) 'A Deeper Justice. Economic and Social Justice as Transitional Justice in Nepal', *International Journal of Transitional Justice*, 2: 378–97.

Plato (1997) 'Theatetus', trans. M.J. Levett, rev. M. Burnyeat, in Cooper, J.M. (ed.) *Complete Works*, Indianapolis, IN: Hackett.

Powledge, T.M. (2009) 'Epigenetics and Development', *BioScience*, 59: 736–41.

Ricœur, P. (1965) *De l'interprétation. Essai sur Freud*, Paris: Seuil.

Roediger, H.L. (1980) 'Memory Metaphors in Cognitive Psychology', *Memory & Cognition*, 8: 231–46.

Steiner, G. (1975) *After Babel. Aspects of Language and Translation*, London and New York, NY: Oxford University Press.

Waldmann, P. (2007) 'Is There a Culture of Violence in Colombia?', *International Journal of Conflict and Violence*, 1: 61–75.

Zimmer, C. (2004) *Soul Made Flesh. The Discovery of the Brain, and How it Changed the World*, London: Heinemann.

Chapter 10

Understanding the political economy of transitional justice

A critical theory perspective

Hannah Franzki and Maria Carolina Olarte[1]

The term 'transitional justice' has come to denote not only a phenomenon to be studied, but also its dominant form of theorisation. In substance, it refers to a 'set of judicial and non-judicial measures that have been implemented by different countries in order to redress the legacies of massive human rights abuses' (ICTJ 2012; see also de Greiff 2010: 18) and to particular 'legal, moral and political dilemmas that arise in holding human rights abusers accountable at the end of conflict' (see Bell *et al* 2004: 305). Through the conflation of description and analysis, the concept of transitional justice has become the proper noun for truth commissions, trials, institutional reforms and reparation. What most transitional justice scholarship does not reflect on, is that the term does not constitute a neutral description of, but rather a particular *perspective* on, those institutions and processes and the contexts in which they are implemented. That is, it looks at truth commissions and trials as part of a global trend of political liberalisation and asks to what extent they bring about liberalising change. This policy-oriented research agenda of transitional justice has marginalised other perspectives on regime change. It begs the question of liberalisation where structural analyses would ask *which* political and socioeconomic projects will come to replace the authoritarian regime (so does Robinson 1996: 65). Additionally, it looks at trials and truth commissions as a problem of democratic norm construction rather than as one inscribed into the context of political struggle (as does, for instance, the 'politics of the past' perspective which has dominated the German-speaking debate on political measures that deal with the legacy of the Holocaust, see Bock and Wolfrum 1999; Herz and Schwab-Trapp 1997; Molden 2009).

It could be argued that within 20 years, the notion of transitional justice has accomplished what most advertising specialists can only dream of, namely, that most people identify a specific brand with an entire product group (such as the popular association of 'Googling' with performing an online search). What is considered a success in the marketing world should raise suspicion among scholars. This is because, as Robert W. Cox famously stated, '[t]heory is always *for* someone and *for* some purpose' (Cox 1981: 128).

Thus, in the moment in which a concept or a theory establishes itself as an ostensibly neutral description of a problem, it renders invisible its own conceptual limits and the political implications thereof. Social and political theory, Cox goes on to argue, is 'history-bound at its origin, since it is always traceable to a *historically-conditioned awareness* of certain problems and issues, a *problematic*' (Cox 1981: 128, our emphasis). There are different ways for a theory to reflect on this context of emergence. Problem-solving theory, as defined by Cox, 'takes the world as it finds it, with the prevailing social and power relationships and the institutions into which they are organized, as the given framework for action' (Cox 1981: 128). While problem-solving theory tends to present itself as ostensibly value free, it is in fact value bound 'by virtue of the fact that it implicitly accepts the prevailing order as its own framework' (Cox 1981: 130). Moreover, in contributing to the solution of problems generated by the prevailing order, problem-solving theory tends to legitimise and stabilise it (Cox 1981: 130). The central claim we make in this chapter is that transitional justice scholarship has developed as a problem-solving theory which is bound by its context of emergence, namely a presumed 'liberal consensus' and the disappearance of fundamental political agonisms after the end of the Cold War.

In contrast, 'critical theory', as defined by Cox (Cox 1981: 130), questions the prevailing order by analysing both its origins and possibilities for change. By showing the breadth of possible alternatives, it offers normative choices. It is such a perspective on transitional justice that we adopt in the present chapter. From this point of view, the ideas and norms that form the basis of transitional justice mechanisms and which are elaborated and justified in transitional justice research are conceptually reflective of the 'demo-liberal' context in which the field emerged in the 1990s. This notion designates the matrix of liberal, representative democracy and liberal market economy which has been championed in international politics and development cooperation since the 1980s. In this context, transitional justice seeks to establish liberal democratic orders, marginalising other, wider notions of democracy which put stronger emphasis on democratic control of the economy and/or social equality. In solving the 'problematic' of liberalising transitions, transitional justice scholarship is value-bound not only in that it militates for (an idealised) liberal democracy, but also in that it contributes to the legitimation of the economic counterpart of actually existing liberal democracies, that is, market economies, mostly in a neo-liberal variant. In so far as mainstream transitional justice scholarship does not reflect upon the context of emergence of its object of study but adopts the 'problematic' of transitions as it finds it, it can be considered part of this demo-liberal project.

Before outlining the argument in more detail, a few words on what we refer to by 'transitional justice' are in order. In contrast to comparative studies which subsume a wide array of historical instances of political change under this heading (see e.g. Teitel 2003, 2006; Elster 2004), we conceive of transitional justice as a distinctive field of knowledge and practice that emerged in response to the downfall of the communist regimes in the late 1980s (for a detailed analysis of the emergence of the notion, see Arthur 2009). It serves, as Bell highlights, as a 'cloak' which 'has been woven into a superficially coherent whole through processes of international diffusion, similarity in institutional provision and the common language of transitional justice fieldhood itself' (Bell 2009: 15; see also Nagy 2008). Even though the field unites many different approaches and research interests, its core consists of a relatively coherent set of assumptions. Principally, there are two: first, transitions to liberal democracy are desirable; and, second, truth commissions, trials, institutional reforms and reparations can contribute to the fostering of the democratic rule of law and societal reconciliation. Given that these assumptions inform most transitional justice practice and scholarship, it is possible to speak of a 'mainstream' in the field which is our main target of critique in this chapter (see e.g. United Nations Human Rights Council 2009, 2012; Van der Merwe *et al* 2009; de Greiff 2010; Muck and Wiebelhaus-Brahm 2011; ICTJ 2012).

In principle, by 'transitional justice' we mean both the political practice subsumed under this heading and its academic legitimation. In this chapter – in line with the overall aim of this volume – we focus attention on the latter, without losing sight of the former. In this sense, we hold the specific significance of transitional justice scholarship to lie in its efforts to provide legal, political, philosophical or moral concepts that back the practice of transitional justice and investigate strengths and weaknesses of different mechanisms in their capacity to support transitions to more liberal societies. In doing so, scholars contribute to the production and reproduction of transitional justice interventions (for a similar diagnosis for the field of democracy promotion in general, see Guilhot 2005: 170).

We begin our argument by distinguishing transitional justice as a field that begs the question of political liberalisation, which at the same time it seeks to bring about. In doing so, it takes the prevailing social and power relationships that characterise the period following the end of the Cold War as a given. Conceptually, this is reflected in its adoption of liberal democracy theory's idea of the political neutrality of this institutional order (first section of the chapter). Taking for granted the liberal separation of the political-institutional and the economic spheres, transitional justice as a field is seemingly reduced to the former; this means that scholarship turns a blind eye on the political economy of transitional justice processes. We illustrate the effects of this omission by discussing three examples. First, in focusing on the political-institutional change, transitional justice renders the continuity of socioeconomic dimensions of conflict irrelevant for the democratic legitimation of the new regime. Second, the focus on violations of civil and political rights generates a post-revolutionary victim-perpetrator dichotomy which does not take into account beneficiaries of past injustices.

Third, recent claims to consider economic dimensions of transitional justice frame social justice as a problem of best practice in peacebuilding and thereby de-politicise the question of the distribution of wealth in a demo-cratic society (second section of the chapter). In the remainder of the chapter, we seek to deepen such a critical understanding of transitional justice as part of actually existing liberalism. From this perspective, the exclusion of the economic from transitional justice is neither accidental nor in conflict with its aims. Rather it is central to transitional justice as a concept of political change. We substantiate this argument by going back to two crucial theoretical and conceptual 'informants' of transitional justice. First, we revisit the scholarly debates on 'transition to democracy' from the 1980s and 1990s, showing how their mode of conceptualising the relation between the economy and democratisation processes came to inscribe itself into the basic ontological assumptions of transitional justice scholarship. What this discussion shows is that the exclusion of economic justice from demo-cratisation processes was at one point a conscious decision, but one that has subsequently been rendered invisible in the transitional justice field (third section of the chapter). Subsequently, we situate transitional justice within the contemporary 'liberal peace' project. Thereby, we argue that transitional justice scholarship ignores how rule of law promotion in the context of this project – and of which transitional justice itself forms a crucial part – serves to legitimise the neo-liberal restructuring of states (fourth section of the chapter). We conclude the chapter by arguing that transitional justice is not a neutral method or theory; rather, it is a perspec-tive that sets bounds to the societal projects that can be envisioned through its discourse. It favours certain political assumptions and marginalises others. As such, it is itself part of the struggle for historical justice and societal reconstruction. To question the political neutrality of transitional justice discourse is in our view a first step towards opening the study of political change and the struggle for historical justice again for a critical-analytical perspective.

Begging the question of liberalisation

To claim that transitional justice is a liberal concept seems to be stating the obvious. Most of the project literature explicitly invokes liberal principles to justify transitional justice policies and recent efforts to provide a normative theory of transitional justice draw on genuine liberal constructs such as Rawls' 'political liberalism' or other contractual theories (see e.g. de Greiff 2010; Andrieu, Chapter 4 in this volume). However, what we mean by saying that transitional justice scholarship begs the question of liberalisation is not just that it is – explicitly or implicitly – normatively committed to liberalism or liberal democracy. Rather, what we seek to problematise is that it conceives of its *normative commitment* as *apolitical* and hence does not reflect on its *political implications*. In order to substantiate this argument, we engage in an exemplary fashion with the work of Ruti Teitel. Her texts epitomise a tendency in transitional justice literature to adopt a mode of circular reasoning which results in the mutual legitimisation of transitional justice measures, on the one hand, and the ideal of liberal democracy, on the other. Here, what is conceived as part of transitional justice and what is not is circumscribed by the aim of liberal democracy. However, the contributions do not provide any reason for why liberal democracy should be an objective in the first place, but merely presume its desirability. That is, they beg the question of political liberalisation.

Ruti Teitel's seminal work on transitional justice (in particular 2000, but also 2002, 2003) illustrates the tendency in transitional justice scholarship to conflate description and analysis of regime changes. Her writings have become a central point of reference in the academic debate and have served as an academic foundation of transitional justice policies (see e.g. United Nations Human Rights Council 2012). In the introduction to her volume *Transitional Justice*, she writes:

> The constructivist approach proposed by this book suggests a move away from defining transitions purely in terms of democratic procedures, such as electoral processes, toward a broader inquiry into other practices signifying acceptance of liberal democracy and the rule-of-law. The inquiry undertaken examines the normative understandings, beyond majority rule, associated with liberalizing rule-of-law systems in political flux.
>
> (Teitel 2000: 5)

The qualities of transitional law, according to Teitel, are that it enables transition through combining a 'process of established, measured legitimation and gradual political change' (Teitel 2000: 223). Transitional justice is imperfect and partial but, Teitel holds, this is precisely why it is valuable in constructing liberalising change and hence should not be easily dismissed (Teitel 2000: 225, 227). She characterises transitional justice measures as re-definitional ('performative', see Teitel 2000: 9, 221) in that they seek to contribute to the legitimisation of the new regime by condemning past injustices and expelling them from the present. What is considered the target of transitional justice measures, she argues, depends on the injustices committed by the past regime.

In contrast to this claim, we suggest that it is the very liberal democracy ideal which circumscribes the scope of transitional justice and informs the interpretation of past 'injustices' in the first place. Thus, transitional justice and liberal democracy enter into a relation of mutual legitimation: scholars, NGOs and international donors justify transitional justice measures with their alleged contribution to the democratisation and reconciliation of post-authoritarian and post-conflict societies (see e.g. de Greiff 2010). According to this logic, transitional justice precedes democracy. At the same time, the scope of transitional justice measures is already circumscribed by the envisioned democratic project and by the ideal of transition (cf. Miller 2008). The implications of transitional justice's commitment to liberal democracy are the subject of the next section. For now, we conclude our present line of argument, fleshing out how this commitment is rendered politically neutral in the literature.

While transitional justice presumes a consensus on liberal democracy as the aim of transition, it does not provide a justification for this normative stance. It appears that being a 'democrat' does not require any further justification. What goes undetected is that the meaning of democracy which dominates transitional justice scholarship – liberal or constitutional democracy – is by no means the only possible meaning of the term. In this vein, Wendy Brown reminds us that 'no compelling argument can be made that democracy inherently entails representation, constitutions, deliberation, participation, free markets, rights, universality, or even equality' (Brown 2011: 45; see also the other contributions in Agamben *et al* 2011). Transitional justice's uncritical embracing of the aim of liberal democracy speaks of the success of political liberalism to present itself as post-political, that is, as a political order that is acceptable to everyone. Certainly, recent liberal democracy theory – such as Habermas' account of deliberation or Rawls' political liberalism – has, by and large, successfully presented its normative framework as *neutral* with regards to cultural, social and economic values and hence as potentially universal. In this spirit, John Rawls holds that the 'problem of political liberalism is to work out a political conception of political justice for a (liberal) constitutional democratic regime that a plurality of reasonable doctrines, both religious and nonreligious, liberal and nonliberal, may endorse for the right reasons' (Rawls 1996: xxxix; for a critical discussion of this claim, see Brown 2008: 23).

In the following section we develop our counter-argument, particularly that the very notion of liberal democracy is political in that it reduces the problem of democratic legitimation to the realm of politics, thereby barring questions concerning democratic control of the economy from political debate and marginalising claims for social equality. If we accept that political liberalism is not *only* political (as opposed to cultural, economic) but *already* political, 'transitional justice' has to be considered part of this politics in so far as it seeks to legitimise liberal democratic institutions. Before we proceed, however, one clarification should be made; to say that transitional justice is a genuinely liberal concept is not to say that some of the assumptions it is based on cannot also be at odds with its ideal of liberal democracy. Andrieu, for example, points to a number of disconnects and contradictions between liberal thought and transitional justice, such as the construction of a foundational narrative in transitional justice, which goes against the principle of plurality upheld by liberalism (Andrieu, Chapter 4 in this volume).

Teitel, referring to the idea of 'posthistory', has asked whether it '[m]ight it not be a normative imperative of the liberal state that it allow for ongoing historical change?' (Teitel 2000: 108). Ismael Muvingi warns us that if transitional justice does not embrace claims for redistributive justice to counter the effects of neo-liberal policies implemented in the course of transition to democracy, it undermines its aim of democracy (Muvingi 2009: 182). We suggest that these 'contradictions' should *not* be conceived as a incoherency of transitional justice which needs to be 'solved', but that they are proper of liberalism in its always historical form. In this regard Wendy Brown has noted: 'Even in the texts of its most abstract analytic theorists, [liberalism] is impure, hybridized, and fused to values, assumptions, and practices unaccounted by it and unaccountable within it' (Brown 2008: 23).

The politics of transitional justice

As we argue in the previous section, political liberalism has managed to equate a cultural form (liberalism) with a political practice (democracy) (Rancière 1999: 97; Brown 2008: 23). The post-political conception of democracy as a consensus on basic equal rights and institutions clouds the fact that this consensus reduces the idea of democracy to a certain state of social relationships, namely constitutional government and market economy.

Liberalism as a political ideology evaluates institutions according to their ability to protect individual liberty. While in classical liberalism this included the inalienable right to private property, new liberalism recognises that property rights can constitute impediments for the realisation of political liberty. This is probably best exemplified by Rawls' egalitarian liberalism which seeks to secure by its second justice principle that social and economic inequalities do not infringe on the exercise of equal basic rights (Rawls 2001: 44). Still, new liberalism reduces democracy to a problem of political justice which only concerns itself with the distribution of economic wealth insofar it affects political equality (cf. Marks 2000: 71–72). For liberals, neither social equality nor the democratic control of the means of production constitutes a problem *of democracy*. Even though some commentators have argued that, taking his own principles of justice seriously, Rawls should be considered a socialist, his theory of justice has mostly been read as a philosophical justification for welfare capitalism (Schweickart 1979: 23; O'Neill 2009: 379).[2] Moreover, regardless of what kind of economic arrangement could possibly be legitimised by political liberalism, actually existing liberal democracies have invariably been accompanied by capitalist market economies (Brown 2003: 21). In this context, the notion of 'democracy' is reduced to a kind of 'democratic rule of law' which merely consists of the institutional guaranteeing of civil and political rights (Humphreys 2010: 6).

Justified as a tool to foster democratic norms, transitional justice thus engages with a specific kind of justice centred around liberal democratic values. The emphasis on violations of civil and political rights, institutional change and legal reform in transitional justice is the very result of assumptions made in liberal democracy theory about what constitutes a properly political matter, and what belongs to an allegedly non-political economic realm (see also Miller 2008: 267–68). Analysing transition in South Africa, Christodoulidis and Veitch conclude that it is *the line* between 'what is political and what is economic' that has been relevant for 'the demarcation of responsibility' in transitional justice processes:

> What conditions are assumed as negotiable and what not, and how are the boundaries drawn between what is taken as political contestable, and what is deemed beyond the reach of politics? These are of course deeply political questions. But when the boundary between politics and economics is drawn in a particular way, they quickly become de-politicised. De-politicization, that is, is a political choice but one that easily fails to get seen as such.
>
> (Christodoulidis and Veitch 2009: 18)

The political economy of transitional justice, then, is rooted in the implied reproduction of the separation of the economic and the political inherited from liberal political rationality. In the following, we point out three inter-related consequences of this separation.

First, if the notion of democracy is separated from socioeconomic conditions of the people the symbolic break which transitional justice seeks to perform can be restricted to the political/institutional level, without that socioeconomic continuities posit a threat to the idea of rupture itself, or to the perceived democratic quality of the emerging society. The way the economy enters and escapes transitional justice in its attempt to legitimise liberal democracy and market economy can be exemplified by the readings it offers of the 'evil' character of the socialist regimes in CEE and the military dictatorships in Latin America. In the case of the former communist countries, the merger of politics and economics was deemed part of the problem, which needed to be overcome in the transition to democratic market economies (see e.g. Teitel 2000: 129–31). The term 'transition', in the political and academic discourse on political change in CEE, established a link 'between a liberalized, de-regulated and privatized market economy, and a form of regulation and governance in which the State withdraws from strong forms of economic and social regulation' (Fairclough 2005: 3). In transitional justice literature on CEE this tendency is epitomised by the discussion on why new constitutions should not embrace socioeconomic rights that were entrenched in the communist constitutions (see e.g. Teitel 1994: 172).

In contrast, transitional justice scholarship focussed on Latin America does not consider the neo-liberal economic rationale behind the authoritarian regimes of the 1970s and 1980s as something to be targeted. Even though

Teitel remarks that in the Americas 'the attempt to adhere to a Western-style economy went hand in hand with oppression' and that transition from authoritarianism 'meant a struggle over subjecting the military to civilian rule', this exclusion of the economic realm from the transition process does not seem to constitute a contradiction to her position (Teitel 2000: 173; see also Barahona Brito 2001; Elster 2004). It is only through this exclusion that the new democratic regimes in South America could legitimise themselves as representatives of a consequent break with the authoritarian past. Regarding the emblematic case of Chile, Levinson argues: 'the imposition of the free market was the reason for Pinochet's installation; the forgetting of this fact renders easier the adoption of free market values as those of democracy' (Levinson 2003: 98).

Second, the focus on fostering liberal democratic values has had implications for how transitional justice conceives of those who have suffered injustices in the past. Most importantly, the focus on civil and political human rights violations has led to a rigid distinction between 'victims' and 'perpetrators' which does not include 'beneficiaries' in the justice equation. In this vein, Meister points out that transitional justice is characterised not only by the assumption that a 'moral consensus on evil is ... necessary' but also 'sufficient to put it in the past' (Meister 2011: 14). Victims are thereby conceded a moral victory at the expense of further claims for historical (social) justice. Meister summarises the consequences of this arrangement as follows: 'Those who benefited passively from social injustice can now comfortably bear witness to the innocence of idealized victims whose ability to transcend their suffering reveals that they were never really a threat' (Meister 2011: 24). In contrast, revolutionary ideologies, mainly present in Marxist thought, have pictured beneficiaries of injustice as 'would-be perpetrators'. Their claims for historical justice consequently include all those who profited from the past regime. In this context, initial victory over the perpetrators of oppression 'would be merely a first stage in a longer struggle against the passive beneficiaries of the old regime'. Insofar as it replaces this concept of revolutionary justice, transitional justice is to be characterised, according to Meister, as a counter-revolutionary project (Meister 2011: 21f).

Such revolutionary concepts of historical justice, in turn, challenge the clear break with the past and the moral antagonism between the 'old' and the 'new' or re-defined State that is performed by transitional justice. By framing historical justice as a claim to be negotiated only once, the exclusion of material justice occurs not only in the very moment of transition. It is also made more difficult to raise that issue in the future, as doing so would shed light on the fraught foundations of the newly established 'democracy' and is thus resisted by the political elites. Thus, the logical fallacy of transitional justice as a kind of historical justice is that it restricts claims for justice to the moment of transition and assumes that 'democracy can be conceived as an originary act or foundational moment', not a political practice (Marks

2000: 74). Any further claims for justice thus question the quality of the foundational moment – and are treated as a danger to the new societal project. It is in this context that Madlingozi argues for the South African case that '[b]ad victims are a thorn in the side of the new government because, by continuing to campaign for social justice, they expose the poverty of this elite compromise, which involves maintaining the ill-gotten gains provided that a section of the new elite is placed in positions of economic power and privilege' (Madlingozi 2007: 112).

The third consequence concerns the way in which recent transitional justice scholarship has attempted to broaden the scope of transitional justice by including a stronger focus on social and economic justice. In one of the first critiques of the 'absence of the economic' in transitional justice practice and theory, Zinaida Miller draws attention to the coincidence of (in terms of 'correspondence in time of occurrence') transitional justice and neo-liberal economic reforms. She argues that current transitional justice practices neglect economic root causes of conflict and structural socioeconomic violence to the effect that emerging democracies come to be marked by high social inequality, which in turn is often further aggravated by neo-liberal reforms approved in the contexts of transitions (Miller 2008: 267). By now, various publications have engaged with this absence (see e.g. the contributions in the *International Journal of Transitional Justice*, (2008) 2 (3), and in Arbour 2006; Laplante 2007, 2008; de Greiff and Duthie 2009; for a recent overview on socioeconomic dimensions of transitional justice, see Hecht and Michalowski 2012). What is common to most of these contributions, however, is that they present their demands to address socioeconomic dimensions of past conflict again as a post-political claim to inform a consensus among a peace-willing community. Louise Arbour, for instance, holds that: 'Transitional justice having as an objective to contribute to the building, in societies in transition, of a solid foundation for the future based on the rule of law, it is imperative to see *how best to equip a country* to redress often deep-seated social and economic inequalities' (Arbour 2006: 22, our emphasis). In a similar vein, Muvingi argues that the unequal distribution of resources and poverty is at the root of many conflicts which makes socioeconomic justice in processes of transition a *conditio sine qua no* for reconciliation and societal peace (see e.g. Addison 2009: 111; Muvingi 2009).

As such, the question of the role of social justice in the institutional design of society is not posited as a question to be subjected to public debate nor a matter of conflicting interests. Rather, it is re-injected at the technical level. Social justice, and the means to achieve it, enter the transitional discourse in an already-colonised form where questions of, for instance, economic self-determination are not part of what is debatable. What is at stake here, borrowing Christodoulidis' expression, is the 'denial of economic democracy' in an understanding of democratic politics that removes 'need' from what is conceived of as the 'properly political' (Christodoulidis 2007:

199). What is not substantiated in these analyses, however, is *why* the societal actors that supported physical violence to secure economic interests would now subscribe to a societal consensus that puts their profits in danger.

Thus, while this strand of transitional justice literature has rendered visible the selective character of transitional justice, from its proponents' suggestions to 'include' socioeconomic matters into transitional justice, it seems as though the former had merely been forgotten. In what follows, we question this assumption, suggesting that the exclusion of the economic is indeed at the very heart of transitional justice as a concept of political change and reflects the social and power relationships that characterise the post-Cold War period. We do so by relating transitional justice to two of its main conceptual 'informants'. First, we revisit the scholarly debates on 'transition to democracy' from the 1980s and 1990s, showing how their mode of conceptualising the relation between the economy and democratisation processes inscribed itself into the basic ontological assumptions of transitional justice scholarship. What this discussion shows is that the exclusion of economic justice from democratisation processes was at one point a conscious decision, not merely the product of negligence, but one that has subsequently been rendered invisible in the transitional justice field. Subsequently, we situate transitional justice within the contemporary 'liberal peace' project. We argue that transitional justice scholarship ignores how rule of law promotion in the context of this project – and of which transitional justice itself forms a crucial part – serves to legitimise the neo-liberal restructuring of States. Both studies show how transitional justice scholarship has failed to engage with the context of emergence of its object of study.

The conceptual legacies of 'transition to democracy' literature

In mainstream political science, scholars started studying the political changes of the 1980s and 1990s – the end of military dictatorships in various regions of the world, especially in Latin America, and the subsequent decomposition of the Soviet bloc and its satellites – under the heading of 'transition to democracy'. The three volumes that document results from a project on 'Transitions from authoritarian rule', co-ordinated by Guillermo O'Donnell and Philippe Schmitter (1986), set the foundation for this new line of scholarship. This literature shares, despite some internal differences, various commonalities which distinguish it from earlier comparative studies on democracy and democratisation. Indeed, the emergence of the transition paradigm marks a turning point, for it fundamentally altered the concept of and the view on social change underpinning democratisation studies. Early comparative research concerned with the conditions for transitions from authoritarian to democratic regimes – and vice versa – were interested in factors *explaining* transitions. Against the backdrop of regime collapses in the Southern Cone and Eastern Europe, however, the academic interest in the field shifted towards a '*programming* of transition' (Guilhot 2002: 234, our italics).

In his book, Nicolas Guilhot (2005) provides a detailed analysis of this change and its implications for the study of democracy. For our purpose, two interrelated observations are important. First, the shift from *explaining* to *programming* transitions parallels a shift in the theoretical framework of regime change. The early works of comparative political researchers such as Guillermo O'Donnell, Philippe Schmitter, Laurence Whitehead and Adam Przworski were led by structural analyses (often inspired by Marxist theory) of the relationship between economic development and democratisation. With the prospects of the fall of communist regimes, the 'transitologists' increasingly prioritised theories that emphasise the role of individual agency in political change (Guilhot 2005: 146). In this vein, Guilhot concludes, that '[f]rom a science having as its object the evolution of societal structures, the study of democratization had successfully become a science of political conflicts within the state apparatus' (Guilhot 2005: 161). He summarises the findings of 'transition to democracy' literature as being the safest coalition for democratic reforms, 'one that controls its supporters and channels mobilization toward moderate goals that do not threaten the benefits that the dominant classes derived from the authoritarian arrangement' (Guilhot 2005: 147, with reference to Kaufman 1986: 100; O'Donnell and Schmitter 1986: 12–14).[3]

The second relevant observation is how this shift of focus came accompanied by an explicit normative commitment to electoral democracy. Thus, O'Donnell argued that 'even after recognising the significant tradeoffs that its installation and eventual consolidation can entail in terms of more effective, and more rapid, opportunities for reducing social and economic inequities' it was the preferable option (O'Donnell and Schmitter 1986: 10, cited in Guilhot 2005: 143). In this vein, O'Donnell and Schmitter define democracy in strictly procedural terms: secret and universal vote, regular elections, free competition of political parties, and the right to create associations and join them (O'Donnell and Schmitter 1986: 22; see also Linz 1996: 17). In contrast, Gills, Rocamora and Williams challenge the straightforward equation of 'democracy' with this minimalist institutionalist design, which instead they characterise as 'low-intensity democracy'. In an alternative reading of the transitologists' preferred case studies, they argue that '[a]lthough they may have formally instituted some of the trappings of Western liberal democracies (e.g. periodic elections), in a real sense these new democracies have preserved ossified political and economic structures from an authoritarian past' (Gills *et al* 1993: 3). Low intensity democracy rests on the premise that in order to preserve stability, institutional opening has to occur gradually. Its effectiveness, the authors hold, 'is its ability to implement limited and carefully selected agendas of change' (Gills *et al* 1993: 28). In practice, these 'agendas of change' consisted mostly of neo-liberal-inspired legal reforms for the promotion of market economies (see the next section). The conscious postponement of social democracy by transition to democracy literature, then, 'generated a formula for democratisation' which enabled precisely the implementation of neo-liberal economic policies that, as a general tendency, led to increasing social inequality in targeted countries (Kiely 2004; Wade 2004; Guilhot 2005: 142).

Transition to democracy scholars participated in a series of international conferences and encounters with 'human rights activists, lawyers and legal scholars, policymakers, journalists, donors, and comparative politics experts' concerned with the dynamics of a transition to democracy which lead to the proliferation of the term 'transitional justice' (Arthur 2009: 324). Furthermore, they contributed to the conceptual background for Neil Kritz's three-volume study on transitional justice (see Kritz 1995: Vol. 1, especially sections two and three). Revisiting transition to democracy literature and its critiques thus produces two interconnected insights that have so far been neglected by transitional justice scholarship. The first one concerns the above-mentioned move away from *structural* analysis to a focus on *agency* and *institutions* as main factors for social change. This ontological shift constitutes the foundation of the constructivist potential attributed to transitional justice. It is only on its basis that the assumptions that transitions can be modeled or guided according to what is considered *best-practice* works. Vice versa, acknowledging this theoretical inheritance shows that transitional justice's long-standing neglect of economic dimensions of conflict is not a coincidence, but consequence of the disavowal of structural analysis which it took from transition to democracy scholarship. Second, transitional justice literature also adopts the normative preference for liberal democracy from this literature, but with one important difference: other than the authors of the *Transitions from Authoritarian Rule* volumes (O'Donnell and Schmitter 1986), it adopts the original compromise for the sake of transition as its desirable *goal*. While in terms of political consequences this might not make a difference, it is relevant for how transitional justice scholarship has come to engage with the socioeconomic dimensions of transition. In embracing the notion of liberal democracy as the only possible meaning of democracy, it fails to reflect on the fact that transitologists, concerned above all with political stability, favoured this constitutional arrangement precisely because it would *not* put in danger the economic interests of pre-transition elites. Hereby, the ontological assumption that a rational consensus on the basic institutions of liberal democracy is possible and desirable has trumped analyses that focus on conflicting interests in the moment of transition. Nevertheless, we suggest that rather than merely making normative arguments for the inclusion of social and economic rights into existing transitional justice mechanisms and research, critical studies should provide analyses of why those dimensions have been excluded so far, and to what extent this exclusion is due to the very normative preference for 'transitions' (i.e. gradual and stable change).

Liberal peacebuilding and the rule-of-law

We now move on to make a similar claim for the way transitional justice scholarship has failed to account for the economic dimensions of the wider liberal peacebuilding and development project in the context of which transitional justice measures are implemented in post-conflict societies. Both liberal peacebuilding and development cooperation promote the implementation of free market and trade policies based on their respective beliefs – either that an economy integrated globally according to liberal principles fosters international peace, or that it boosts economic development. As transitional justice conceives of itself as a tool for political liberalisation, it fails to take account of the fact that in most post-conflict societies the reconstruction of the liberal rule-of-law it seeks to support consists of a transformation of states in accordance with neo-liberal ideas about its appropriate role in economy and society.

The promotion of the 'democratic rule-of-law' in post-conflict societies draws its legitimation from the 'democratic norm' thesis developed in different strands of scholarship, especially in international law and international relations (see e.g. Slaughter 1990, 1995). As Susan Marks observes in her discussion of the work of Fukuyama and international law scholars, this thesis is based on two assumptions: first, that a liberal revolution is under way; and, second, that this opens the way for a 'democratic peace', which needs to be actively promoted by the international community (Marks 2000: 33). The scholarly work on the 'democratic norm' has served as legitimating background for 'democratic peacebuilding' practice which seeks to promote low-intensity democracy through the strengthening of State institutions, the rule-of-law, privatisation and the integration of local economies in the world market (for a detailed analysis of the different strands within the democratic peacebuilding paradigm, see Heathershaw 2008; Richmond 2010).

Under the 'liberal peace' label, critics have started to question this international peacebuilding practice and its theoretical underpinnings. In addition to the fundamental challenge that the assumption that democracies actually wage less war does not stand the reality test, critics address internal contradictions of the framework. According to Richmond, liberal peace critique challenges cultural imperialism and top-down approach within contemporary peacebuilding practice from different angles (Richmond 2010: 26–33; see also Sriram 2007: 588f). These criticisms can be (and have been) applied to transitional justice practice as well (see e.g. McEvoy and McGregor 2008).

In the following, we particularly engage with a further strand of critique that connects the corner stones of liberal peacebuilding, political and economic liberalisation. We hold that these do not constitute separate agendas but are linked to each other via the concept of the rule-of-law which has also become central to transitional justice in the context of its growing attention for post-conflict scenarios. In his latest report, UN Special Rapporteur on the promotion of truth, justice, reparation and guarantees of non-recurrence Pablo de Greiff points out that the shift in context requires a change in transitional justice practice because 'weak institutions' and 'economic scarcity' complicate a successful implementation of transitional justice measures as we know them from post-authoritarian settings (see United Nations Human Rights Council 2012: §§ 16–18). Against this background, transitional justice processes and mechanisms are to be considered a 'critical component of the United Nations framework for strengthening the rule-of-law' in societies emerging from conflict (United Nations 2010; United Nations Human Rights Council 2012: § 40). In a similar vein, the Transitional Justice Plan commissioned by the United States Department of State for 'post-Saddam' Iraq 'is aimed at transforming an unstable and chaotic state, caused by a dictatorship with a legacy of human rights abuses, to a democratic pluralistic system which respects the rule of law' (United States Department of State 2003: 5). And also the *World Development Report 2011* holds that transitional justice initiatives in post-conflict societies 'send powerful signals about the commitment of the new government to the rule of law' (World Bank 2011: 125).

Transitional Justice research, however, has so far failed to reflect on the contested nature of the concept of 'rule-of-law' which has been infused with different meanings implying very different political, social and economic structures. In international rule-of-law promotion, as opposed to its theoretical elaborations, rule-of-law serves as an empty signifier to legitimise all sorts of development cooperation, especially the exportation of laws to secure property rights and institutional models (Humphreys 2010: 5–6). While project literature (the one on transitional justice included) writes about 'rule-of-law' as though it was an economically and politically neutral concept, several recent academic publications have suggested that its promotion is actually connected to the wider neo-liberal economic project of the last two decades (Tamanaha 2008, Humphreys 2010; Rittich 2010: 469). As part of the liberal peace paradigm, post-conflict societies have been subject to economic reforms that emphasise 'macro-economic stability, reduction of the role of the state, the squeezing of collective and public space, a quest for private affluence, and a reliance on privatization and on exports and foreign investment to stimulate economic growth' (Pugh 2005: 25). Brian Tamanaha notes how rule-of-law has been 'put forth as the "front man" in the liberal package international development organizations provide for developing countries' (Tamanaha 2008; see also Newton 2006; Trubek and

Santos 2006). This package generally includes 'training judges and police, and drafting and implementing legal codes that protect property and foreign investment' (Tamanaha 2008: 36; also Newton 2006: 191). As such, the rule-of-law 'constrains, overrides, and dictates to domestic law-making in connection with liberal economic matters (affecting property rights, tariffs, subsidies, efforts to protect jobs)' (Tamanaha 2008: 35). The World Bank's work as a development agency illustrates this economic shaping of the rule-of-law. Under the Bank's new strategic focus on poverty reduction, its alleviation is seen as dependent upon the strengthening of a kind of rule-of-law which enables private sector confidence, foreign investment and, as a result, economic growth. The notion of rule-of-law advocated in the project literature and manifested for instance in the Bank's World Governance and Doing Business Indicators is depoliticising in that it '[naturalises] a certain view of economy and the role of law within', while its homogenising character presents 'the political in the guise of the technical' (Humphreys 2010: 148). Instead of serving as a framework to channel the definition of fundamental economic decisions, the rule-of-law turns into a precondition for a particular economic form of organising society. That is, the market is designated as the 'dominant organizing position within capitalist societies' (Tamanaha 2008: 35).

The prominent role of the rule-of-law in liberal peacebuilding and development assistance is a prime example for how liberal ideas are invoked to legitimise neo-liberal policies (cf. Brown 2003: 27; see also Humphreys 2010). The distinction between political liberalism and neo-liberalism is important here. Political liberalism treats the political and the economic as two distinct spheres operating according to their own logic; in contrast, neo-liberal rationality, as Wendy Brown summarises, 'while foregrounding the market, is not only or even primarily focused on the economy; rather it involves extending and disseminating market values to all institutions and social action, even as the market itself remains a distinctive player' (Brown 2003: 7). Transitional justice's 'innocent' championing of the liberal rule-of-law thereby provides legitimacy for a general rule-of-law promotion which models states according to the needs of the market. For our purposes, the specific relevance of the liberal peace critique for transitional justice lies in the connection they draw between both pillars of liberal peacebuilding, namely the promotion of free markets and liberal rule-of-law. The critique emphasises that since the end of the Cold War, actually occurring political and economic liberalisation have been two sides of the same coin (rule-of-law). In making this link explicit, it also sheds light on how transitional justice scholarship places beyond consideration 'the ways in which the free market constrains democratic processes by generating and sustaining systematic inequalities of wealth that serve to entrench systematic inequalities of power' (Marks 2000: 72). To understand transitional justice merely as a problem of political liberalisation renders invisible the fact that it is part of a wider socioeconomic project.

Regaining a critical distance

In this chapter, we have advanced a critical theory perspective on transitional justice as a field of practice and knowledge. In particular, we have argued that mainstream transitional justice scholarship adopts a problem-solving stance in that it does not reflect on social and power relationships that brought about its object of study. By this, we refer to the breakdown of actually existing communism, which gave way, among other things, to the proclaimed success of liberal democracy and market economy as a way to organise society which is superior to possible alternatives and thus desirable beyond political differences. In summary, the problem with transitional justice's commitment to political liberalism is twofold. First, it presents itself as a presumably neutral project when in fact it legitimises a particular institutional arrangement. Second, with its focus on political institutions, transitional justice has turned a blind eye to the economic counterpart of the spread of actually existing liberal democracies, namely the advancement of 'globalisation' largely following neo-liberal parameters. Rather than providing a language for an emancipatory project of justice, it is confined within the limits of institutional democracy and marginalises questions of social equality. Thus, transitional justice, even in its most progressive forms, those that advocate the inclusion of social and economic justice, bears witness to what Nancy Fraser has called the 'postsocialist' condition, namely 'an absence of any credible overarching emancipatory project despite the proliferation of fronts of struggle; a general decoupling of the cultural politics of recognition from the social politics of redistribution; and a decentering of claims for equality in the face of aggressive marketization and sharply rising material inequality' (Fraser 1997: 3).

To be clear, the problem with transitional justice scholarship is not that it is normative, but that it presents transitional justice's normativity as *unpolitical*. It presumes a (fictitious) consensus on both transitional justice mechanisms and the aim of liberal democracy. As a consequence, transitional justice as a concept of political change and the propagated aims of this change are placed in a sphere presumed to be beyond political contestation. Thus, they stabilise the prevailing power relationships on a global scale. Following the earlier transitologists, it posits 'transition' as a superior way of political change, delegitimising claims that might threaten these processes, and it does so by adopting a notion of justice which substitutes intra-societal claims for justice with the binary opposition between the evil past of the perpetrators and the democratic present of the victims. In consonance with the wider 'liberal peace' project, transitional justice then prescribes and seeks to render 'natural' political decisions that could have been very distinct. It exerts a judgment on what can be conceived of as contestable political matters, and what should be understood as part of an undisputable liberal juridical project established in a pre-political realm. In sum, the promotion of liberal democracy in the context of transitional justice means at the same time 'to constrain democracy, against the efforts of those seeking to transform relations of domination by insisting on the link between democratization and change in the structures of power and wealth' (Marks 2000: 61).

To gain a critical distance from transitional justice and highlight its political and economic implications is a first step to offering perspectives on diverse normative choices in the moment of political change. We have suggested that its underlying concepts do not only reflect transitional justice's historical embeddedness in post-Cold War politics, but also set structural boundaries to possible societal projects that can be pursued through and legitimised in the context of this field. As such, transitional justice must be seen as part of, rather than a frame for, the societal struggle surrounding the organisation of society and distribution of wealth.

Notes

1 The authors would like to thank Matthias Ebenau and Peter Fitzpatrick for helpful comments on a previous version of this chapter.
2 It was only in his last book, *Justice as Fairness*, that Rawls explicitly rejected welfare capitalism as an institutional regime that could fulfill political democracy's principles of justice, and argued instead for a property owning democracy (Rawls 2001: 135ff). See also contributions in O'Neill, M. and Williamson, T. (2012) *Property-owning Democracy: Rawls and Beyond*, Oxford: Wiley-Blackwell.
3 O'Donnell and Schmitter, for example, conclude that 'It seems crucial that … a compromise among class interests somehow be forged to reassure the bourgeoisie that its property rights will not be jeopardized for the foreseeable future' (O'Donnell and Schmitter 1986: 46–47).

Bibliography

Addison, T. (2009) 'The Political Economy of the Transition from Authoritarianism', in de Greiff, P. and Duthie, R. (eds) *Transitional Justice and Development. Making Connections*, New York, NY: Social Science Research Council.

Agamben, G. *et al* (eds) (2011) *Democracy, in What State?*, New York, NY, and Chichester: Columbia University Press.

Arbour, L. (2006) *Economic and Social Justice for Societies in Transition*, Centre for Human Rights and Global Justice Working Paper Nr. 10, New York, NY: Center for Human Rights and Global Justice.

Arthur, P. (2009) 'How "Transitions" Reshaped Human Rights: A Conceptual History of Transitional Justice', *Human Rights Quarterly*, 31 (2): 321–67.

Barahona Brito, A. de (2001) 'Truth, Justice, Memory, and Democratization in the Southern Cone', in González Enríquez, C., de Barahona Brito, A. and Aguilar Fernández, P. (eds) *The Politics of Memory. Transitional Justice in Democratizing Societies*, Oxford: Oxford University Press.

Bell, C. (2009) 'Transitional Justice, Interdisciplinarity and the State of the "Field" or "Non-Field"', *International Journal of Transitional Justice*, 3 (1): 5–27.

Bell, C., Campbell, C. and Ní Aoláin, F. (2004) 'Justice Discourses in Transition', *Social & Legal Studies*, 13 (3): 305–28.

Bock, P. and Wolfrum, E. (1999) *Umkämpfte Vergangenheit*, Göttingen: Vandenhoeck & Ruprecht.

Brown, W. (2003) 'Neo-Liberalism and the End of Liberal Democracy', *Theory & Event*, 7 (1).

——(2008) *Regulating Aversion. Tolerance in the Age of Identity and Empire*, Princeton, NJ: Princeton University Press.

——(2011) 'We Are All Democrats Now', in Agamben, G. *et al* (eds) *Democracy, in What State?* New York, NY, and Chichester: Columbia University Press, pp. 44–57.

Christodoulidis, E. (2007) 'Against Substitution, The Constitutional Thinking of Dissensus', in Loughlin, M. and Walker, N. (eds) *The Paradox of Constitutionalism*, Oxford: Oxford University Press.

Christodoulidis, E. and Veitch, S. (2009) 'Reconciliation as Surrender: Configurations of Responsibility and Memory', in Du Bois, F. and du Bois-Pedain, A. (eds) *Justice and Reconciliation in Post-Apartheid South Africa*, Cambridge: Cambridge University Press, pp. 9–36.

Cox, R.W. (1981) 'Social Forces, States and World Orders: Beyond International Relations Theory', *Millennium – Journal of International Studies*, 10: 126–55.

de Greiff, P. (2010) 'A Normative Conception of Transitional Justice', *Politorbis*, 50: 17–29.

de Greiff, P. and Duthie, R. (eds) (2009) *Transitional Justice and Development. Making Connections*, New York, NY: Social Science Research Council.

Elster, J. (2004) *Closing the Books: Transitional Justice in Historical Perspective*, Cambridge: Cambridge University Press.

Fairclough, N. (2005) 'Critical Discourse Analysis in Trans-disciplinary Research on Social Change: Transition, Re-scaling, Poverty and Social Inclusion', *British and American Studies*, 11: 9–34.

Fraser, N. (1997) *Justice Interruptus, Critical Reflections on the 'Postsocialist' Condition*, New York, NY: Routledge.

Gills, B.K., Rocamora, J. and Wilson, R.A. (1993) 'Low Intensity Democracy', in Gills, B.K., Rocamora, J. and Wilson, R. (eds) *Low Intensity Democracy. Political Power in the New World Order*, London and Boulder, CO: Pluto Press.

Guilhot, N. (2002) 'The Transition to the Human World of Democracy. Notes for a History of the Concept of Transition', *European Journal of Social Theory*, 5: 219–42.

——(2005) *The Democracy Makers. Human Rights & International Order*, New York, NY, and Chichester: Columbia University Press.

Heathershaw, J. (2008) 'Unpacking the Liberal Peace: The Dividing and Merging of Peace-building Discourses', *Millennium – Journal of International Studies*, 36 (3): 597–622.

Hecht, L. and Michalowski, S. (2012): *The Economic and Social Dimensions of Transitional Justice* (Essex Transitional Justice Network). Available at: <http://www.essex.ac.uk/tjn/documents/TheeconomicandsocialdimensionsofTJ.pdf> (accessed 18 November 2012).

Herz, T. and Schwab-Trapp, M. (1997) *Umkämpfte Vergangenheit: Diskurse über den National-sozialismus seit 1945*, Opladen: Westdeutscher Verlag.

Humphreys, S. (2010) *Theatre of the Rule of Law. Transnational Legal Intervention in Theory and Practice*, Cambridge: Cambridge University Press.

ICTJ (2012) *What is Transitional Justice?* Available at: <http://ictj.org/about/transitional-justice> (accessed 6 December 2012).

Kiely, R. (2004) 'The World Bank and "Global Poverty Reduction": Good Policies or Bad Data?', *Journal of Contemporary Asia*, 34 (1): 3–20.

Kritz, N.J. (1995) *Transitional Justice. How Emerging Democracies Reckon with Former Regimes*, Vol. 1, General Considerations, Washington, DC: United States Institute of Peace Press.

Laplante, L.J. (2007) 'On the Indivisibility of Rights: Truth Commissions, Reparations, and the Right to Development', *Yale Human Rights and Development Law Journal*, 10: 141–77.

——(2008) 'Transitional Justice and Peace Building: Diagnosing and Addressing the Socio-economic Roots of Violence through a Human Rights Framework', *International Journal of Transitional Justice*, 2 (3): 331–55.

Levinson, B. (2003) 'Dictatorship and Overexposure: Does Latin America Testify to More than One Market?', *Discourse*, 25 (1 and 2): 98–118.

Linz, J. (1996) *La Quiebra de las Democracias*, Madrid: Alianza Editorial.

McEvoy, K. and McGregor, L. (2008) 'Transitional Justice from Below: An Agenda for Research, Policy and Praxis', in McEvoy, K. and McGregor, L. (eds) *Transitional Justice from Below. Grassroots Activism and the Struggle for Change* (Human Rights Law in Perspective, Vol. 14), Oxford: Hart Publishing.

Madlingozi, T. (2007) 'Good Victim, Bad Victim: Apartheid's Beneficiaries, Victims and the Struggle for Social Justice', in Le Roux, W. and van Marle, K. (eds) *Law, Memory, and the Legacy of Apartheid: Ten Years After Azapo V. President of South Africa*, Pretoria: University Law Press.

Marks, S. (2000) *The Riddle of All Constitutions. International Law, Democracy and the Critique of Ideology*, Oxford: Oxford University Press.

Meister, R. (2011) *After Evil. A Politics of Human Rights*, New York, NY: Columbia University Press.

Miller, Z. (2008) 'Effects of Invisibility: In Search of the "Economic" in Transitional Justice', *International Journal of Transitional Justice*, 2 (3): 266–91.

Molden, B. (2009) 'Mnemohegemonics. Geschichtspolitik und Erinnerungskultur im Ringen um Hegemonie', in Mayer, D. and Molden, B. (eds) *Vielstimmige Vergangenheiten – Geschichtspolitik in Lateinamerika*, Münster: LIT-Verlag.

Muck, W. and Wiebelhaus-Brahm, E. (2011) *Patterns of Transitional Justice Assistance Among the International Community*, paper presented at the Sixth ECPR General Conference, 24–27 August 2011, Reykjavik, Iceland (copy on file with the authors).

Muvingi, I. (2009) 'Sitting on Powder Kegs: Socioeconomic Rights in Transitional Societies', *International Journal of Transitional Justice*, 3: 163–82.

Nagy, R. (2008) 'Transitional Justice as Global Project: Critical Reflections', *Third World Quarterly*, 29 (2): 275–89.

Newton, S. (2006) 'The Dialectics of Law and Development', in Trubek, D. and Santos, A. (eds) *The New Law and Economic Development: A Critical Appraisal*, Cambridge: Cambridge University Press.

O'Donnell, G.A. and Schmitter, P.C. (eds) (1986) *Transitions from Authoritarian Rule*, London: Johns Hopkins University Press.

O'Neill, M. (2009) 'Liberty, Equality and Property-Owning Democracy', *Journal of Social Philosophy*, 40 (3): 379–96.

O'Neill, M. and Williamson, T. (eds) (2012) *Property-owning democracy. Rawls and beyond*. Malden, MA: Wiley-Blackwell.

Pugh, M. (2005) 'The Political Economy of Peace Studies: A Critical Theory Perspective', *International Journal of Peace Studies*, 10 (2): 23–42.

Rancière, J. (1999) *Disagreement. Politics and Philosophy*, Minneapolis, MN: University of Minnesota Press.

Rawls, J. (1996) *Political Liberalism*, New York, NY: Columbia University Press.

——(2001) *Justice as Fairness: A Restatement*, London: Belknap Press.

Richmond, O.P. (2010) 'A Genealogy of Peace and Conflict Theory', in Richmond, O.P. (ed.) *Palgrave Advances in Peacebuilding: Critical Developments and Approaches*, New York, NY: Palgrave McMillan.

Rittich, K. (2010) 'Governing by Measuring: The Millenium Development Goals in Global Governance', in Ruiz, H., Wolfrum, R. and Gogolin, J. (eds) *Select Proceedings of the European Society of International Law*, Vol. II, London: Hart Publishing.

Robinson, W.I. (1996) *Promoting Polyarchy. Globalization, US Intervention, and Hegemony*, Cambridge: Cambridge University Press.

Schweickart, D. (1979) 'Should Rawls be a Socialist? A Comparison of His Ideal Capitalism With Worker-Controlled Socialism', *Social Theory and Practice*, 5 (1): 1–27.

Slaughter, A.M. (1990) 'Revolution of the Spirit', *Harvard Human Rights Journal*, 3 (1): 1–11.

——(1995) 'International Law in a World of Liberal States', *European Journal of International Law*, 6: 503–38.

Sriram, C. (2007) 'Justice as Peace? Liberal Peacebuilding and Strategies of Transitional Justice', *Global Society*, 21 (4): 579–91.

Tamanaha, B. (2008) 'The Dark Side of the Relationship Between the Rule of Law and Liberalism', *NYU Journal of Law and Liberty*, 33: 516–47.

Teitel, R.G. (1994) 'Post-Communist Constitutionalism: a Transitional Perspective', *Columbian Human Rights Law Review*, 26: 167–90.

——(2000) *Transitional Justice*, Oxford and New York, NY: Oxford University Press.

——(2002) 'Transitional Justice in a New Era', *Fordham International Law Journal*, 26: 893–906.

——(2003) 'Transitional Justice Genealogy', *Harvard Human Rights Journal*, 16: 69–94.

——(2006) 'Transitional Justice: Postwar Legacies', *Cardozo Law Review*, 27: 1615–31.

Trubek, D. and Santos, A. (eds) (2006) *The New Law and Economic Development: A Critical Appraisal*, Cambridge: Cambridge University Press.

United Nations (2010) *Guidance Note of the Secretary-General. United Nations Approach to Transitional Justice*. Available at: <http://www.unrol.org/files/TJ_Guidance_Note_March_2010 FINAL.pdf> (accessed 26 October 2012).

United Nations Human Rights Council (2009) *Analytical Study on Human Rights and Transitional Justice*. Available at: <http://www.unrol.org/files/96696_A-HRC-12-18_E.pdf> (accessed 15 November 2012).

——(2012) *Report of the Special Rapporteur on the Promotion of Truth, Justice, Reparation and Guarantees of Non-Recurrence*, A/HRC/21/4. Available at: <http://www.ohchr.org/Documents/HRBodies/HRCouncil/RegularSession/Session21/A-HRC-21-46_en.pdf> (accessed 25 November 2012).

United States Department of State (2003) *Transitional Justice in Post-Saddam Iraq. The Road to Re-establishing the Rule of Law and Restoring Civil Society*, Report of the Working Group on Transitional Justice in Iraq. Available at: <http://www.gwu.edu/~nsarchiv/NSAEBB/NSAEBB198/FOI%20Transitional%20Justice.pdf> (accessed 6 December 2012).

Van der Merwe, H., Baxter, V. and Chapman, A.R. (eds) (2009) *Assessing the Impact of Transitional Justice: Challenges for Empirical Research*, Washington, DC: United States Institute of Peace Press.

Wade, R. H. (2004) 'Is Globalization Reducing Poverty and Inequality?', *World Development*, 32 (4): 567–89.

World Bank (2011) *The World Development Report 2011. Conflict, Security, and Development*, Washington, DC: World Bank.

Index